American
SPEAK
OUT

Upper-Intermediate
Student Book

with DVD/ROM and MP3 Audio CD

Frances Eales • Steve Oakes

)) CONTENTS

DVD-ROM: ▶ DVD CLIPS AND SCRIPTS   ▶ INTERVIEWS AND SCRIPTS

LISTENING/DVD	SPEAKING	WRITING
understand informal conversations	have interesting conversations	write an advice forum message; edit for accuracy
	talk about new experiences	
handle phone inquiries	make phone inquiries	
▶ **50 Things To Do Before You Die**: watch a documentary about adventures	recommend an experience	write a forum entry
	talk about different issues	
listen to opinions about surveillance	discuss surveillance	write a letter of complaint; use formal written language
listen to people discuss issues	give and respond to opinions; support your viewpoint	
▶ **A Quiet Revolution**: watch a program about changes in working patterns	give a presentation about traditional gender roles	write notes for a presentation
	tell anecdotes	write a narrative; use adverbs
listen to a radio program about very short stories	talk about life stories	
listen to people recommending books	talk about your reading; summarize a plot	
▶ **Tess of the D'Urbervilles**: watch a drama	describe a TV/movie scene	describe a TV/movie scene
	discuss how you use your time	write an opinion essay; use linkers
listen to people talk about vacations	plan an alternative vacation	
listen to people describing TV game shows	describe procedures; use mirror questions	
▶ **The Happiness Formula**: watch a program about happiness	do a class survey	write your top tips for how to be happy
	talk about inventions	
listen to a program about advertising	describe ads	write a report; make writtten comparisons
listen to a brainstorming session	take part in a brainstorming session	
▶ **Genius**: watch a program about presenting ideas	present a novel idea	write a product review

▶ CLASS AUDIO AND SCRIPTS

�))) CONTENTS

LISTENING/DVD	SPEAKING	WRITING
	discuss different ages and generations	
listen to a program about letters to your future self	talk about your future	write an informal email; focus on informal style
listen to a call-in radio show about life's milestones	discuss the right age for different things	
▶ **Horizon: How to Live to 101**: watch a program about living longer	hold a debate	write a forum comment
	talk about TV programs	
listen to an expert talking about hoax photographs	talk about celebrity and media	write a discursive essay; use linkers of contrast
listen to people talking about recent news stories	express strong reactions	
▶ **The Funny Side of the News**: watch a program about live news	retell a news story	write a short news article
	talk about a difficult decision you've made	
listen to an experiment about fairness	talk about values and behavior	write an informal article; use linkers of purpose
	deal with awkward situations	
▶ **The Human Animal**: watch a documentary about body language	give advice on how to behave in your culture	write about behavior in your culture
	discuss how good a witness you are	
listen to people talk about getting tricked	speculate about scams	write a "how to" leaflet; learn to avoid repetition
listen to someone report an incident	talk about emergency situations	
▶ **Horizon: How to Survive a Sea Disaster**: watch a program about a sea rescue	agree on priorities	write a story about a lucky escape
listen to people talk about movies	talk about a movie you never get bored with	write a movie review
	talk about popular culture and art experiences	
listen to tours of two very different places	show a visitor around part of your town	
▶ **The Culture Show: The People's Palace**: watch a program about an innovative building	discuss an artistic project for your town	write a competition entry

COMMUNICATION BANK page 158   AUDIO SCRIPTS page 164

PARTS OF SPEECH

1 A Work in pairs and complete the questionnaire.

HOW I LEARN

1 It's useful to know grammatical terminology ...
  a) because it's ¹**much** easier to talk about grammar rules.
  b) to read and understand grammar books ²**better**.
  c) ... actually, I don't think it's ³**useful**.

2 When I meet a new word, I ...
  a) ⁴**look it up**, then write it in my notebook with a translation.
  b) write ⁵**a** phrase or sentence with ⁶**the** word in it.
  c) think about it, but don't write anything down.

3 I enjoy using English outside the class ...
  a) to communicate on social networking sites.
  b) when I'm ⁷**watching** movies and listening ⁸**to** music in English.
  c) ... I ⁹**don't** use English outside class.

4 In addition to ¹⁰**doing** homework, I study English ...
  a) ¹¹**every day**.
  b) two or three times a week.
  c) not at all—I don't have time!

5 I think it's important ¹²**to speak** English during the lesson ...
  a) 100% of the time.
  b) whenever we ¹³**can**.
  c) only when we're ¹⁴**told** to.

B Match the grammatical terms a)–n) with words 1–14 in bold above.

a) dependent preposition
b) past participle
c) present participle
d) gerund
e) infinitive with to
f) adverb in comparative form
g) gradable adjective
h) adverbial phrase
i) quantifier   *1*
j) auxiliary verb
k) definite article
l) indefinite article
m) modal verb
n) multi-word verb

VERB PATTERNS

2 A Correct the sentences.

working

1 I can't stand ~~to work~~ with music on.
2 I learned driving last year.
3 I want that the teacher corrects everything I say.
4 I'd rather to eat out than at home.
5 I'd like traveling abroad this year.
6 I enjoy be alone.
7 I like it when the teacher tells to repeat words.
8 I'd better to spend more time studying, or I'll never make progress in English.

B Find two examples above for each pattern:

1 verb + gerund   *1*
2 verb + infinitive
3 verb + infinitive with to
4 verb + object + infinitive with to

C Work in pairs. Which sentences are true for you? How would you change the other sentences to make them true?

PRONUNCIATION

3 A Work in pairs. Complete the table with words from the box.

completely	extremely	guarantee	future
minutes	push	public	system	reach
thorough	took	absolutely	

1	/ɪ/	this	women
2	/i/	these	leave
3	/ə/	again	pronunciation
4	/æ/	actually	angry
5	/ʌ/	fun	money
6	/ʊ/	book	pull

B Listen and check. Then listen and repeat.

C Work in pairs. How can phonemic symbols help you learn new words?

COLLOCATIONS

4 A Cross out the noun or noun phrase that does not collocate with the verb in the word web.

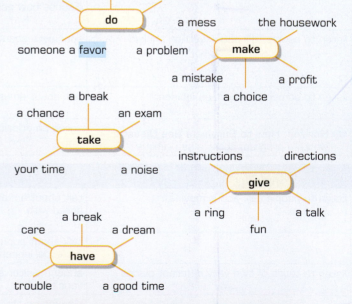

nothing
your best   your homework
do
someone a favor   a problem   a mess   the housework
make
a mistake   a profit
a break   a choice
a chance   an exam
take
your time   a noise
instructions   directions
give
a break   a ring   a talk
care   a dream   fun
have
trouble   a good time

B Work in pairs and take turns. Student A: say a noun or noun phrase. Student B: say the verb that collocates with it.

movies / learned / traveling / favor   films / learnt / travelling / favour

1 new things

TIME FOR A CHAT   p8

TRY SOMETHING NEW   p11

I'D LIKE TO INQUIRE   p14

GREAT EXPERIENCES   p16

What makes a good roommate?

INTERVIEWS

Inquire / inquiries   Enquire / enquiries
program / ads   programme / adverts
roommate   flatmate

G direct and indirect questions
P sentence stress
V personality

Eat, Chat, and make friends

Come to a sociable and stimulating evening of conversation that goes beyond the normal "What do you do?" or "Did you see last night's TV?" You'll have a number of different conversation partners during the evening and have a menu of interesting topics to get you started. There will be Turkish mezé dishes on the tables, and coffee or other drinks are available. Some of our most recent conversation topics include:

* When do you feel most alive?
* Which three adjectives might people use to describe you?
* What was the last picture you took on your phone?
* Where do you feel most "at home"?
* What three ingredients would you look for in an ideal job?
* Would you prefer to live with a view of the ocean or of a city?
* What three questions would you ask a potential roommate?
* What do you always have in your wallet or purse?
* What music do you have on your phone or MP3 player?

SPEAKING

1 A Work in pairs. Write three things that people talk about when they meet for the first time.

B Read the text above about a conversation evening and discuss the questions.

1 What is special about the conversations?
2 Which four conversation topics mentioned would you be the most interested in discussing?
3 Are there any conversation topics which you would avoid asking in your culture/country?

LISTENING

2 A Listen to people at the conversation evening. Which two topics from the text above do the speakers discuss? What can you remember from each conversation?

B Listen again. Are the sentences true (T) or false (F)? Correct the false sentences.

1 The woman would like someone very sociable.
2 She is at her best in the mornings.
3 She is really neat.
4 She would ask a roommate about their salary.
5 The man has a lot of original ideas.
6 He thinks carefully before making a decision.
7 He works for an outdoor adventure school.
8 He agrees with the three adjectives.

C Work in pairs and discuss the questions.

1 What examples do the speakers give about being: antisocial, tidy, reliable with money, creative, adventurous and nonjudgmental?
2 Which of the two topics would you prefer to talk about? What would your answers be for these topics?

VOCABULARY

PERSONALITY

3 A Complete the extracts from the conversations with words and phrases from the box.

> a people person   a computer geek   keep to yourself
> witty   down-to-earth   a good laugh
> spontaneous   a morning person

1 For me, an important question is "Do you _____, or do you tend to be around a lot?"
2 I like having friends around. I suppose I'm _____.
3 I'm not _____—I can't stand people who are all bright and cheerful first thing.
4 Well, at least you're _____. You're quick, and you make me laugh.
5 I get an idea, and I do it, no hesitation. So I'm _____.
6 Well, people say I'm fun to be with, _____, if you know what I mean.
7 I'm very practical and _____.
8 I'm not _____. I don't sit in front of my computer for hours.

B Work in pairs and discuss. Which words or phrases would you use to describe yourself or someone you know?

▶ page 148 VOCABULARYBANK

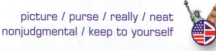

picture / purse / really / neat
nonjudgmental / keep to yourself

photo / handbag / quite / tidy
non-judgemental / keep yourself to yourself

GRAMMAR

DIRECT AND INDIRECT QUESTIONS

4 A Look at the conversation extracts. Complete B's questions and then check in the audio script on page 164.

1 **A:** Another question is about housework and cleaning.

   B: Yes, something like "_Who_ _cleans_ the place where you live now?"

2 **A:** You need to know they can afford the rent.

   B: But I wouldn't ask, "Could you tell me _____ _____ _____ earn?"

3 **A:** ... I like doing new things, things that are out of the ordinary.

   B: Such _____?

4 **A:** That's useful in my job, too.

   B: Can I ask _____ _____ _____?

   A: I work for a web design company.

5 **A:** My friends would say "creative, spontaneous and disorganized".

   B: I'd be interested to know _____ _____ agree with them.

6 **B:** What _____ _____ _____ by "nonjudgmental"?

   A: Well, I try not to make up my mind about people until I get to know them, ...

B Check what you know. Look at the questions in Exercise 4A and find:

a) a direct question with an auxiliary verb.

b) three indirect questions.

c) a question with a question word as the subject.

d) a short question with a preposition at the end.

C Circle the correct word in bold to complete the rules for indirect questions.

> **RULES**
>
> 1 Indirect questions are often used when a question is **pretty** personal/impersonal or to make a question sound more **polite/interesting**.
>
> 2 Word order in indirect questions is **the same as/different from** positive statements.
>
> 3 Indirect questions **use/don't use** the auxiliaries *do* or *did*.
>
> 4 When there **is/isn't** a question word in the direct question, add *if* or *whether* in the indirect question.

5 A Make sentences with the opening phrases.

1 Why are you studying English?
   Can you tell me *why you are studying English?*

2 How long do you plan to study?
   Do you have any idea ... ?

3 What do you do in the evenings?
   Can I ask ... ?

4 Do you have a full-time job?
   Do you mind me asking ... ?

5 Which countries have you visited?
   I'd be interested to know ... .

6 Where did you get that watch?
   Could you tell me ... ?

7 Is there a good café anywhere near here?
   Do you know ... ?

8 Would you like to go for a coffee?
   I was wondering ... .

B Listen and check your answers. Which opening phrase is best for asking a very personal question?

6 A SENTENCE STRESS Listen again and underline the main stressed syllables in each sentence.

B Say the sentences at the same time as the recording and copy the stress.

7 A Choose three questions from Exercise 5A to ask other students and write two more indirect questions of your own.

B Work in pairs and practice saying your five questions.

C Work with other students and ask your questions.

D Work with a new partner. What did you find out about the other students?

▶ page 128 **LANGUAGE**BANK

SPEAKING

8 A Work in pairs. Choose a conversation topic from the text on page 8 and discuss it with your partner.

B Work with a new partner. Choose a new conversation topic.

C Discuss. What do you think of the idea of a conversation evening? Where would you hold it? What other food or drink could you have?

pretty / practice   rather / practise

WRITING

AN ADVICE FORUM MESSAGE; LEARN TO EDIT FOR ACCURACY

9 A Work in pairs and answer the questions.

1 How important is speaking English for you?

2 Which aspects of speaking do you find difficult?

3 What problems are there in practicing speaking outside class if you are studying in a) your own country b) an English-speaking country?

B Read the messages from a discussion forum and answer the questions.

1 What do you think of the suggestion in the reply?

2 What types of video would you choose?

Rafael

Hi everyone, I live in Spain, and I don't use English at work, so I don't have any chance to practice speaking English. Does anyone have any good ideas how I could improve my speaking?

Galya

Hi Rafael,

I know exactly how you feel because I'm in a similar situation. I live in Bulgaria and also struggle to find opportunities to practice my spoken English. I know a really great idea that has really helped me. It's called "shadowing."

You find a short video that has the words on the screen at the same time. I really like sitcoms, so I often use these, or you can find some good English video podcasts with the script under them. You listen to the speaker, and you say the words at the same time. It's really good because you have to listen very carefully to the "music" of English. You notice the stress and the intonation, how the person phrases things and where the pauses are. It's really helped me to become more confident and fluent and has improved my pronunciation.

Hope that helps. Good luck!

The Internet has changed the way learners improve their language skills. English language learners can improve their pronunciation, expand their vocabulary, and practice English online for free!

C Read the list of features which appear in this type of advice. Which ones are in the message above?

1 Show you identify with the problem.

2 Give advice referring to personal experience.

3 Say where to get more information.

4 Sign off and wish the person luck.

10 A Read the advice. Which of the features in Exercise 9C does the writer include?

Radu

Hi Rafael,

I think it's easy to solve your problem. You just have to make some research.[1][ww]

There are a lot of opportunities to practice speaking on Internet.[2][gr] You can found them by searching for "practice speaking English online free."[3][v] Be careful, some arent really free![4][p] On some sites, you can find a speaking partner in another country and talk to them on Skype. Often they are at the same level as you, but it's good for practise and for getting more confidence. [5][sp] It helped me become more fluent, and I also liked very much meeting new people. [6][wo]

I hope you try this out and enjoy it as much as I did. I wish you the best success in your future endeavors! [7][st]

B Read the advice again and correct the mistakes. Use the teacher's correction code at the end of each sentence.

Correction Code:	
v = verb form	sp = spelling
gr = grammar	p = punctuation
ww = wrong word	wo = word order
	st = style

11 A Read the forum question below and write a reply either to Miki or Rafael (120–180 words).

B Swap replies with another student. Read their text and tell them one thing you like about their advice. Then read it again and mark a maximum of three mistakes with correction codes.

C Look at your own text again. Check it carefully and make corrections.

D Read other students' advice. Whose advice is the most useful?

American Speak TIP We often miss our own mistakes, so it's a good idea to give your text "a rest" and come back after several minutes or hours to take a fresh look. Also try reading your text aloud. You will probably spot more mistakes.

A B

C

1.2)) TRY SOMETHING NEW

G present perfect
P word stress; connected speech
V feelings; word building: nouns

VOCABULARY

FEELINGS

1 A How do you feel about trying new things, such as a challenging sport, a new dish or a new skill? Check (✓) the statements that best fit you. Then work in pairs and compare your answers.

☐ Fine if no one's watching.
☐ Food, yes; sports, no.
☐ I love it!
☐ Why should I?
☐ Not very positive, but I know it's good for me.

B Match the comments below with pictures A–D. What activities are the people talking about?

 1 All my friends put pressure on me to do it. Looking down, I felt scared out of my wits—who wouldn't be? Then I jumped, and I don't remember much, but I was relieved when it was all over.

2 The very thought of eating them made my stomach turn. I thought I'd throw up, and I knew that would be awkward, with everyone in the restaurant watching! So I simply ate them as fast as I could. When I finished, everyone clapped. They were really impressed.

3 The really interesting thing was how quickly we learned the steps; I was fascinated by the way the teacher taught us. At the end of the lesson, the teacher gave us a prize for best beginners—we were on top of the world.

4 I was shaking like a leaf as I stood up. Everyone was staring at me, and I just ran out of the room. I'd wanted so much to do it, and it was over before it began; I've never felt so frustrated in my life. All my co-workers were watching, and I wished the ground would swallow me up.

C Work in pairs and circle ten adjectives or verb phrases in the comments which describe feelings. How many have a positive meaning?

D

D Match the adjectives or verb phrases you circled to words with a similar meaning 1–10.

1 disappointed and angry	6 very interested
2 felt embarrassed	7 felt nervous
3 thrilled	8 petrified
4 disgusted me	9 admiring
5 glad it was finished	10 embarrassing

E WORD STRESS Underline the stressed syllables in the adjectives and phrases from Exercise 1C. Listen and check. Then listen and repeat.

2 A Check what you know. Work in pairs and cross out the incorrect alternative in each sentence. Explain the reason for your choices.

1 A: I felt really *frustrating/frustrated* because I tried so hard, but I still failed the driving test.
B: And it's your fifth time! How *embarrassing/embarrassed!*

2 A: I was *very/really/totally* interested in the book.
B: Yes, it was *very/really/totally* fascinating.

3 A: I was *very/really/absolutely* relieved at the end.
B: Yes, and we won! I was *very/really/absolutely* on top of the world.

B What other modifiers could be used instead of *absolutely* or *totally*?

3 A Choose three adjectives or phrases from Exercise 1C and write notes about times you felt those emotions.

B Work in pairs. Tell your partner about the experiences. Are any of your experiences similar?

Check / on top of the world / co-workers the ground would swallow me up Tick / over the moon / colleagues the earth would swallow me up

30 Days to a New Life

It's a simple idea: Choose something you've never done before, and spend the next 30 days doing it. It can be something ordinary, like walking more, or changing your diet—or something that really takes you outside your comfort zone, such as mountain climbing, writing a story or getting up before sunrise every day.

It's all about changing old habits into new ones, overcoming your fears and moving your life in a healthier and more interesting direction. So go ahead, pick one of the ideas from my list or one of your own, and get started. Today. Let me know how you get along.

Easy
- Take a 30-minute walk each day.
- Keep a daily journal.
- Take a new route to work/school every day.
- Meditate for 30 minutes each day.

Intermediate
- Try a new recipe each day.
- Learn how to draw a human face.
- Stop using the Internet for 30 days.
- Take a daily cold shower.

Hard
- Talk to a stranger every day.
- Take one picture a day.
- Write a 10,000-word short story in a month.
- Get up before sunrise every day.

Comments

Jasmine21: I've just finished my first challenge: no Internet for 30 days. At first, I thought it would be impossible, but I noticed after five or six days that I felt much more relaxed. For one thing, I had more time on my hands ... but, more importantly, I began to pay attention to things around me more, especially the people. I realized that I often used things like social networking to avoid the outside world.

TallThinGuy: Talking to strangers is relatively easy for me because I do it all the time in my job. So I tried something a bit different—talking to a friend every day, a different friend every day. I wasn't sure I had 30 friends altogether, so, after going through the obvious people—the ones I'm in touch with and socialize with now—I started digging into my past, going back to friends I'd lost touch with from college, then high school, then elementary school. Since then, I've made much more of an effort to stay in touch with a few really precious friends.

Chiek: I started doing this half a year ago, and, in the last six months, I've learned how to sail, taken art lessons and become a member of an online book club. For me, the best experience has been meditation. I've done yoga for years, but I've never really tried meditation before. It's not just that I feel calmer and don't get so stressed, I also find I can focus on tasks more clearly, and I sleep better. So that one's something I'm going to keep on doing.

READING

4 A Work in pairs and look at the title of the article above. What do you think it is about?

B Read the first two paragraphs and check your predictions.

C Work in pairs and look at the writer's list of suggested activities. Do you agree with the level of difficulty (easy, intermediate, hard) that the writer gives for each?

5 A Read the comments, then work in pairs. Cover the texts and discuss. What did each person do and how successful were they?

B Find phrases in the texts which mean:

1 new and difficult for you (paragraph 1)
2 what happens to you (paragraph 2)
3 had spare time (Jasmine21)
4 searching carefully (TallThinGuy)
5 tried hard to (TallThin Guy)
6 continue (Chiek)

C Work in pairs and discuss. What would you like to try for 30 days?

GRAMMAR

PRESENT PERFECT

6 A Complete these sentences using the words in parentheses. Then check in the texts.

1 Choose something you _____ before. (never/do)

2 I _____ my first challenge. (just/finish)

3 In the last six months, I _____ how to sail. (learn)

4 I _____ yoga for years. (do)

B Check what you know. Match 1–4 above with rules 1–3.

get along / realized / socialize / college
elementary school / keep on / parentheses

get on / realised / socialise / university
primary school / carry on / brackets

7 A Look at the time phrases in the box. Which are usually used with the present perfect (PP), the past simple (PS) or both (B)?

> up to now *PP*   so far   this time last week
> recently   this morning   over the last two weeks
> not + yet   still + not   for several years

B CONNECTED SPEECH Listen and write sentences 1–6.

C In each sentence:

1 Underline two stressed words.

2 Circle *have/has* where *a* is weakened to /ə/.

3 Draw a line to show linking between a final consonant and an initial vowel.

(Have) you tried it before?

▶ page 128 LANGUAGEBANK

8 A Complete the sentences with the present perfect or past simple of the verbs in the box. Include the adverbs in parentheses.

> do   give   be   go   live   play   try   learn   buy   get

What would you like to try for one month?

- I [1]_____ (always) afraid of water, but I finally [2]_____ to swim in the summer. Now I'd like to try diving.

- I [3]_____ (just) a high-quality video camera; my sister [4]_____ it to me for my birthday. So I'd like to learn how to edit a film.

- I love music, and I [5]_____ the piano for many years now, but there's one instrument I [6]_____ (not so far): the guitar.

- I [7]_____ (never) anything online—I'm paranoid about giving my credit card details, but I know it's cheaper, so that would be my choice.

- Hiking in the Alps. I [8]_____ in Austria since I was born, and everyone in my family [9]_____ to the Alps hiking lots of times. But, somehow, I [10]_____ (still not) a real hike.

B Work in pairs. Which activities in Exercise 8A would you both like to try?

SPEAKING

9 A Work alone and make notes on:

- two activities you started more than a month ago and still do.
- two activities you used to do, but don't do now.
- two activities you haven't done, but would like to do.

B Work in groups. Tell each other about three of the activities that are/were important to you.

VOCABULARY *PLUS*
WORD BUILDING: NOUNS

10 A How would you feel if you were asked to give up the Internet for 30 days or speak in public? Choose adjectives from the box or your own ideas.

> frustrated   awkward   embarrassed   creative
> disappointed   anxious   angry   fascinated
> worried   spontaneous   nervous   amused

B Work in pairs and complete the groups with the noun form of the adjectives in the box. Then listen and check.

1 -ion: *frustration*   3 -ity/-ety: 5 other:

2 -ment: 4 -ness:

C Underline the stressed syllable in each noun. Use a dictionary to help. Then listen again and check.

D Match the nouns with the rules below.

1 The stress is always on the syllable before the suffix.

2 The stress is on the same syllable as in the adjective.

11 A Complete the sentences in the personality quiz with the correct noun or adjective form.

Personality quiz

1 People often comment on my spon_____.

2 My greatest fru_____ are related to my relationships rather than money.

3 When I was younger, I was awk_____ in social situations, but not anymore.

4 I get a lot of amu_____ from being with children.

5 I often feel quite dis_____ in my friends, for example, when they don't have time for me.

6 For me, ang_____ is a complete waste of energy.

7 I suffer from ner_____ in large groups.

8 I often feel intense anx_____ in elevators.

B Check your answers. Add two more sentences to the quiz using a noun and an adjective from Exercises 10A and 10B.

C Read the quiz again. For each sentence decide if you strongly agree (✓✓), agree (✓), disagree (✗) or strongly disagree (✗✗).

D Work with a new partner. Compare your answers. In what ways are you most similar or different?

▶ page 148 VOCABULARYBANK

two weeks / lots of
real / elevators

fortnight / loads of
proper / lifts

1.3)) I'D LIKE TO INQUIRE

- **F** polite inquiries
- **P** polite intonation
- **V** ads

VOCABULARY
ADS

1 A Work in pairs and discuss.

1 How do you usually find out about local news, events and courses?

2 Do you ever make phone calls about these in English? What is difficult about doing this?

B Look at the ads A–D. Which ones would interest you the most?

A

Roommate Wanted

Spare room available in 3-bedroom apartment, ideal for full-time student or working professional. Shared bathroom, kitchen, living room. Rent $480/month. Pets **negotiable**.

B

EXCEL
School of English

Advanced Course in Business English

Real business scenarios including telephoning, presentations, meetings and negotiations.

Limited enrollment – guarantee your place with a $56 **non-refundable deposit**.

Phone 1-251-649-1859 to enroll.

C

FREE
Introductory Offer

OLYMPIA
SPORTS CENTER

Print the flyer on the right, **fill out your personal information** and present it at the gym to **sign up for** a FREE training session with a certified trainer, worth $34.

Offer ends January 30th.

D

Walk&TalkEnglish

Join us for our weekly walk, and practice your English along the way. Group walks $6/walk—**two-for-one deal** if you bring a friend (that's $6 for both of you!). Or schedule your own one-on-one walk with an English teacher, $11/hour. **Free trial** for first-timers!

C Work in pairs and match meanings 1–7 with the words/phrases in bold from the ads.

1 You pay for one and get two.

2 You can try it out at no cost.

3 You need to pay part of the cost now, and you can't get the money back.

4 It's possible—we can talk about it.

5 Put your name on a list for a course.

6 There's a maximum number for this course.

7 Write your name, address, etc. on a form.

D Which words/phrases can be used to talk about a restaurant, a cooking class, buying a used car or a hotel reservation?

FUNCTION
POLITE INQUIRIES

2 A Listen to the phone conversation and answer the questions.

1 Who is the caller phoning?

2 What does she want?

3 Is the receptionist able to help her?

4 Does the caller sound polite to you?

B Complete the sentences. Then listen again and check.

1 I _____ like to _____ about a course.

2 I _____ wondering _____ it _____ be _____ for _____ to change to that group.

3 Can _____ tell _____ why I have to do it in person?

4 Would _____ be any _____ of doing the level test on the phone?

5 Do you _____ me _____ what it involves?

6 I'd be really _____ if you _____ hold a place for me till Saturday morning.

7 Would you mind _____ that in an email for me?

8 _____ you tell me _____ the school opens?

C POLITE INTONATION Listen and say the inquiries at the same time as the speaker. Copy the polite intonation.

I'd like to inquire about a course.
Can you tell me why I have to do it in person?

D Work in pairs and discuss. How do you sound polite in your language? What is more important, the words or the intonation?

▶ page 128 LANGUAGEBANK

3 A Make the inquiries more polite using the words in parentheses.

1 Where are you located? (Could/tell)

2 Can I use your two-for-one deal more than once? (wondering)

3 Can my dog come with me? (like/know)

4 Tell me about the other people living there. (Would/mind)

5 How many other people have inquired? (mind/asking)

6 Could you explain how the free trial works? (I/grateful)

B Work in pairs. In which situations from Exercise 1B could you make the inquiries 1–6 above?

---

apartment / enrollment / center
fill out your personal information
one-on-one / cooking class / reservation

flat / enrolment / centre
fill in your details
one-to-one / cookery course / booking

LEARN TO
MANAGE INQUIRIES

4 A Work in pairs. Read phrases 1–6 from the phone conversation. Who do you think is speaking, the receptionist (R) or the caller (C)?

1 Bear with me a minute.
2 Sorry to keep you.
3 Sorry to be difficult, it's just that …
4 I'd really appreciate your help.
5 Can you hold on a minute? I'll just see.
6 I have one more question, if I'm not keeping you.

B Look at the audio script on page **164** and check your answers.

C Work in pairs and find:

1 two phrases showing the caller thinks she's causing a problem.
2 one polite phrase from the receptionist meaning *please be patient.*

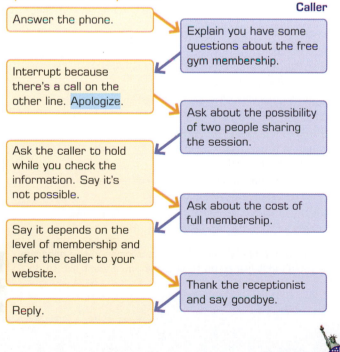

5 Work in pairs and role-play a phone call to a sports center. Use the flow chart to help. Remember to use polite intonation.

Sports Center Receptionist

Caller

Answer the phone.

→ Explain you have some questions about the free gym membership.

Interrupt because there's a call on the other line. Apologize.

→ Ask about the possibility of two people sharing the session.

Ask the caller to hold while you check the information. Say it's not possible.

→ Ask about the cost of full membership.

Say it depends on the level of membership and refer the caller to your website.

→ Thank the receptionist and say goodbye.

Reply.

Apologize   Apologise

SPEAKING

6 A Work in pairs. Student A: look at Situation **1** below. Student B: turn to page **158**.

Situation 1: Student A (Customer)
You've just received your flight confirmation below. You entered the wrong flight date by mistake; you want to fly one day later. Phone customer service to change the reservation. When you finish the call, you should know a) when you will fly and b) how much extra you have to pay.

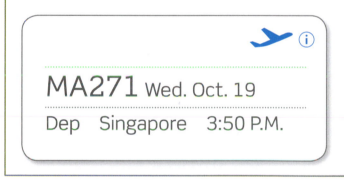

MA271 Wed. Oct. 19

Dep   Singapore   3:50 P.M.

B Student A: turn to page **160**.
Student B: turn to page **158**.

American Speak TIP
Before making a phone inquiry, note what you want to say and what the other person might ask you. This can help your confidence, especially in formal situations.

7 Work with a new partner. Choose EITHER: the other two situations in Exercise 1B OR situations you have been in. Decide who is the caller in each situation and make notes on what you want to ask. Role-play the situations.

DVD PREVIEW

1 Work in pairs and discuss the questions.

1 What's one thing you've always wanted to try and one place you've always wanted to visit?

2 What's stopped you from doing both of these things?

2 A Work in pairs. Read the program information. Who decided what the top fifty things to do are?

B Match the activities mentioned in the text to pictures A–E.

▶ 50 Things to Do Before You Die

When the program asked its viewers what one thing they'd like to do in their lifetime, the response was overwhelming, with some 20,000 members of the public sending in their ideas. *50 Things to Do Before You Die* takes the viewers on a tour through the top 50 viewer choices. These range from observing rare and exotic animals in their natural habitat; to traveling a historic route by train, car or jet plane; to some more extreme activities not for the faint-hearted, among them bungee jumping, husky dog sledding and wing-walking. Whether you're a hard-core traveler or an armchair tourist, you're sure to find inspiration for your next journey.

DVD VIEW

3 A Work in pairs. Write down two words you think someone will mention for each of the activities in pictures A–F.

B Watch the DVD. Which of your adjectives are used? Which activity is not in the DVD?

C Mark the sentences true (T) or false (F). Then watch again and check.

1 The main thing people say they love about sledding is the scenery.

2 The host preferred driving the sled to sitting in it.

3 Pilots used to strap themselves to the wings at airshows.

4 Rebecca found it surprisingly easy to wave and look elegant.

5 The legendary Route 66 runs from Chicago to San Francisco.

6 One of the bungee jumpers likes the feeling of being stretched and bounced.

7 People have always been fascinated by dolphins' playfulness and intelligence.

8 The speakers like dolphins because they are helpful to humans.

D Work in pairs. Which activities in the program do these sentences refer to? Complete the phrases in bold so that they mean the same as the words in parentheses. Then watch the DVD again and check.

1 … and you can really _____ **it in** because the dogs are doing all the hard work. (absorb)

2 … and feeling like you're in or out of control is definitely _____ **it's at**. (the key experience)

3 … wanted nothing more than to be strapped to the outside of a plane and _____ **part in** your very own wingwalking display. (be involved in)

4 Once upon a time it was, the kind of **the _____ to do**. (the fashionable experience)

5 The feeling you get when you jump off, fall off, dive off **or** _____, is just awesome. (anything like that)

6 … they're so huge and powerful **and** _____ so playful and, I'm really, really lucky to be here with them. (but)

E Work with a new partner. Order the five activities in the program from the one you'd most like to do to the one you'd least like to do.

American Speakout a recommendation

4 A Think about something you have tried that you would recommend to someone else, for example, a journey, an experience with animals/nature, a sport. Make notes on questions 1–3.

1 What was the activity?

2 How did you feel before/while/after you did it?

3 Why do you think it's worth trying?

B Listen to someone describing an activity, and answer questions 1 and 2 above.

C Listen again and check (✓) the key phrases you hear.

> ### KEYPHRASES
>
> I'm (not) the kind of person who likes …
>
> The activity I'd like to recommend may seem …
>
> It's one of the [best/most challenging] experiences I've ever had.
>
> The thing I'll remember most is [the feeling of …/ the moment when …].
>
> I'd recommend this experience because it helps you understand [something about fear/how wonderful X is].
>
> It's an activity I'd like to recommend to all my friends.

D Work in small groups. Use your notes from Exercise 4A and the key phrases to tell each other about your activity.

writeback a forum entry

5 A Read the introduction to this web forum and an extract from one writer's contribution. What activity is she writing about?

> We're looking for true stories that will inspire others to try something they've never done before. Whether it's a place you've been, a food you've tried, a sport or an activity you've done, tell us about it in 200 words or less. Remember, your goal is to get others to try it, so tell us what's so extraordinary about it and why it's one thing we should do in our lifetime.
>
> **Stacey:** … Each day we walked slowly through the section of the jungle where they live.
>
> The first two days, we didn't see any, but I was determined to stay as long as it took, and, on the third day, we saw an adult female and her baby on a branch, eating leaves, with their auburn fur glinting in the sunlight.
>
> The thing I'll remember most is the moment our eyes met.

- Newsfeed
- Sharing
- Timezone

B Write an entry (120–200 words) for the forum.

C Swap entries with your partner. Make suggestions on how he/she could make the experience sound more exciting.

D Read other students' entries. Which experience would you most like to try?

F

V PERSONALITY

1 A Complete the sentences with an adjective phrase.

1 She has a quick mind and is good with words. She's wi_____.

2 He's quite reserved and ke_____ t_____ hi_____.

3 She does things without planning. She's spo_____.

4 He doesn't like working alone. He's a pe_____ pe_____.

5 She's very do_____-t_____-e_____, uncomplicated and practical.

6 He's fun to be with, a go_____ l_____.

7 She's definitely a mo_____ pe_____, not at her best late at night.

8 He's a real computer ge_____— he's always talking about gigabytes and new software.

B Work in pairs and discuss. What combination of personal qualities above would make a good friend, a good **TV** talk show host and a good accountant?

G DIRECT AND INDIRECT QUESTIONS

2 A Choose a topic from the box and complete the questions.

> transportation   family   travel
> shopping   study   fashion

1 Do you like ... ?

2 What's ... like?

3 How often do you ... ?

4 Have you ever ... ?

5 Would you like to ... ?

6 Why do you ... ?

B Make your questions indirect using the phrases below.

Can I ask ...

Could you tell me ...

Do you mind me asking ...

I was wondering ...

I'd be interested to know ...

C Work in pairs and take turns asking and answering your questions.

V FEELINGS

3 A Complete the conversations with words and phrases from the box. Not all items are needed.

> on top of the world   fascinated
> awkward   relieved   impressed
> shaking like a leaf   frustrated
> wished the ground would swallow
> me up   made my stomach turn

A: Hey, I got the job!

B: Congratulations! You must be
   ¹_____.

A: Yes, I'm ²_____ because I thought I'd done badly at the interview. I was so nervous that I was ³_____.

B: Did the interviewer notice?

A: Well, I spilled my coffee on her.

B: Oh, that's ⁴_____!

A: Very embarrassing. At that moment I ⁵_____.

B: You got the job, so I guess they were ⁶_____ with you.

B Work in pairs and add *very*, *really*, *absolutely*, *totally* or *completely* before the adjectives and adjective phrases (but not the verb phrases) in Exercise 3A. Then practice the conversation.

G PRESENT PERFECT

4 A Complete the sentences with the present perfect or past simple of the verbs in parentheses.

1 Since I _____ this course, I _____ my speaking. (start / improve)

2 I _____ to Canada twice, but I _____ to the USA yet. (go / not go)

3 I _____ a real celebrity, but once someone _____ I was one. (never meet / think)

4 When I was young, I _____ in a band, and recently I _____ again. (play / start)

5 I _____ breakfast at home this morning, and I also _____ any coffee yet today. (not eat / not have)

B Work in pairs and discuss. Are any of the sentences in Exercise 4A true for you?

F POLITE INQUIRIES

5 A Rewrite the sentences to make them more polite. Use the phrases in parentheses.

1 I need some information about train times to Vienna. (I'd like to inquire)

2 Which train do I need to take to get to Vienna by 3 p.m.? (Can you tell me)

3 How far is it from the western to the southern train station? (Can I ask)

4 Where can I get information on local transport in Vienna? (Do you mind me asking)

5 Do I need to reserve a seat on the train? (I was wondering)

6 Can I reserve on the phone? (Could you tell me)

7 Could you reserve it for me? (I was wondering if)

8 Could you send me an email confirmation? (I'd be grateful if)

B Work in pairs and take turns. Role-play a phone conversation between a travel agent and a customer. Use the sentences in Exercise 5A to help you.

A: *I'd like to inquire about train times to Glasgow.*

B: *Certainly. What would you like to know?*

A: *Can you tell me what train I need to take to get to Glasgow by 6:00 p.m., please?*

B: *Let me just check.*

2 issues

MAKING A DIFFERENCE p20

YOU'RE BEING WATCHED p23

GOOD POINT! p26

Does money make you happy?

INTERVIEWS

A QUIET REVOLUTION p28

19

2.1)) MAKING A DIFFERENCE

G present perfect simple & continuous
P word stress; weak forms: auxiliaries
V issues; verbs/nouns with the same form

VOCABULARY

ISSUES

1 A What are the major news stories in your country now?

B Listen and match the news headlines to the topics below.

pollution   disease   unemployment   hunger
poverty   street crime

2 A Match the beginnings 1–8 with the endings a)–h).

1 This is a purely **domestic** issue   *c*

2 It's not about money. It's an **ethical** question,

3 It's a **rural** problem that involves people in the countryside,

4 The decision on the election date is a **political** question

5 The country has serious **economic** problems,

6 The typhoid epidemic started here in the city as an **urban** problem

7 It's a **global** issue and affects the whole world,

8 These are typical **industrial** questions and affect most factories,

a) so taxes will double next year.

b) not people living in cities.

c) and has nothing to do with any other country.

d) not just one or two countries.

e) but has spread to the countryside.

f) and depends on the government.

g) from food to car production.

h) a question of right or wrong.

B WORD STRESS Match the syllable patterns to the adjectives in bold. Then listen and repeat.

1 Oo   2 Ooo   3 oOo   4 oOoo   5 ooOo

neighbor's / yard   neighbour's / garden

C Work in pairs. Read the sentences in Exercise 2A again. Which three nouns often follow the adjectives in bold?

D Which adjectives relate to your news stories in Exercise 1A?

▶ page 149 VOCABULARYBANK

READING

3 A Work in pairs and look at the pictures. How are they connected to the problems in Exercise 1B?

B Read the article below and check your ideas.

Local Heroes

Big help can start out as small-scale. With simple acts of generosity, like offering a morning's work in an elderly neighbor's yard or buying a coffee for a homeless person, individuals are making a big difference. And the creativity underlying some of these acts of generosity is remarkable.

Making a Good Impression: A dry cleaner is offering its services free of charge to unemployed people to help them look their best for job interviews. Ken Thind, who owns Thind Cleaners in Vancouver, got the idea from an article he read on the Internet. "It was about a dry cleaner in the States who put an ad in its window: 'Need a job, we'll clean your suit for you for FREE,'" explained Indian-born Ken, "And I thought that was a great way to give something back to the local community. We've been doing this for three years now, and, since we started, the company has cleaned over a hundred outfits. I don't vet people to see if they really are unemployed, but it's a one-time deal. The money comes out of my profits, but, to me, it's worth it. I always say to them, 'Go out and get that job!' and a lot of people do. That makes it all worthwhile."

4 A Choose the correct option to complete the statements, then read the text again to check.

1 Ken Thind's business helps unemployed people by offering _____.

　　a) jobs　b) clothes　c) services

2 The thing that makes Ken happiest is when someone _____.

　　a) says thank you　b) gets a job　c) offers to pay from their profits

3 Ryan Sinclair _____ the charity.

　　a) works full-time for　b) set up　c) is a volunteer for

4 The couple in Zambia was able to _____.

　　a) learn to read and write　b) send their children to school　c) get a job in the market

5 Sarah was inspired by the twelve-year-old kid because he needed _____.

　　a) a caregiver　b) support　c) help with his schoolwork

6 The author visited the dance marathon at _____.

　　a) 5 o'clock　b) 12 o'clock　c) the end of the event

B Underline words/phrases in the text that match meanings 1–6.

1 check someone's background information (paragraph 1)

2 a special arrangement that you can do only once (paragraph 1)

3 gives for free (paragraph 2)

4 astonishing (paragraph 2)

5 promise to give money (paragraph 3)

6 do something at the same speed as others (paragraph 3)

Re-cycling Bicycles: Twenty-six-year-old Ryan Sinclair has always loved bikes. "I can't remember a time when I wasn't either on a bike or fixing one," he says. "And it was when I was cycling in Holland that I heard about a charity that fixes old bikes and sends them to people who are living in extreme poverty." Ryan now donates all his spare time on weekends to fixing bikes for the charity. "People often have old bikes in their garages and don't realize what a huge difference a bike can make. I recently went out to Zambia to see where our bikes end up. It was an eye-opening experience. In one family, the man and woman had to walk for over an hour to get to their fields and the trip to the market took the whole day. The bike has turned their lives around. Their income has tripled, and the parents now have time to go to classes to learn to read and write. I get an enormous sense of satisfaction from it, and I've made some lifelong friends."

Would you like to dance? That was the suggestion made by students at one Oxford college to raise money for young caregivers in the local area. They've organized a 24-hour dance marathon, where locals pledge $7-14 for every hour a couple dances. Sarah Lupien and Tom Wang took a break from dancing to explain. "I met this kid, he was only twelve years old and was the full-time caregiver for his mother who had multiple sclerosis," Sarah said. "He never got to play with other kids, and he couldn't keep up with his schoolwork." Tom joins in, "So we decided to raise money for a center that gives children like this time off, where they can meet each other and just have some fun. We've already raised $5,800." Sarah signals the end of their break as they head back to the dance floor. "We've been dancing since 5 o'clock, and I'm exhausted! Only 12 more hours to go!" And their next project? "A sponsored silence at a local school. No talking for the kids all day. The teachers are looking forward to it!"

C Work in pairs and discuss. Would you be willing to do any of the activities in the article? Why/Why not?

GRAMMAR
PRESENT PERFECT SIMPLE AND CONTINUOUS

5 A Work in pairs and check what you know. Underline the correct alternative. Then check in the article. In which sentence are both forms possible?

1 We've done this/'ve been doing this for three years now.

2 Since we started, the company has cleaned/has been cleaning over a hundred outfits.

3 Twenty-six-year-old Ryan Sinclair has always loved/ has always been loving bikes.

4 The bike has turned/has been turning their lives around.

5 We've already raised/'ve been raising $5,800.

6 We've danced/'ve been dancing since 5 o'clock, and I'm exhausted!

B All the present perfect examples in Exercise 5A link the past to the present in some way. Work in pairs and discuss how.

C Work in pairs and complete the rules for choosing between the present perfect simple and the present perfect continuous. Give examples from the sentences in Exercise 5A.

RULES

1 Use the present perfect _____ when we want to emphasize that an action is repeated or has lasted for a long time and continues up to now, e.g., _____

2 Use the present perfect _____ when an action is shorter and completed before now. It has present relevance or a present effect, e.g., _____

3 Use the present perfect _____ when we say how many times someone did something or say how much they did, e.g., _____

4 Use the present perfect _____ OR the present perfect _____ with verbs such as work, live, wait, study, do with little or no difference in meaning, e.g., _____

5 Use the present perfect _____ with state verbs such as know, have, be, love, e.g., _____

6 A WEAK FORMS: auxiliaries Listen and write the sentences.

B Underline the main stresses and mark any weak forms (/ə/ or /ɪ/) in the auxiliary verbs. Listen and check. Then listen again and repeat.

How long have you been working here?

　　　　　　/ə/　　　/ɪ/

▶ page 130 LANGUAGEBANK

caregiver / fixes
on weekends / tripled
Would you like to dance?

carer / mends
at weekends / trebled
Shall we dance?

21

7 A Read the text below about an organization which helps people at a local level. Who is Kufuo?

> [1]*I've been working/I've worked* with Fairtrade organizations to help developing markets get fair prices for goods since I finished college, and I [2]_____ over thirty countries in connection with my work. This year I [3]_____ in a village in one of my favorite countries, Ghana.
> I [4]_____ so many wonderful people here. One of my closest friends is Kufuo, whom I [5]_____ since I started coming here.
> He [6]_____ cocoa all his life and [7]_____ Fairtrade guidelines for producing cocoa for several years now. Recently he [8]_____ more than thirty other farmers in the local area into our group, and they [9]_____ the volume of cocoa exported. As a result, Fairtrade [10]_____ one of the most important movements in this region.

B Complete the text with the present perfect simple or continuous form of the verbs in the box. Where are both forms possible?

> ~~work~~ follow become visit meet live
> recruit know double grow

C Discuss. How does the organization make a difference at a local level?

SPEAKING

8 A Work in groups and read about the Longitude Prize. Which issue do you think should win?

> The Longitude Prize 2014 was a $14.5 million prize fund to help solve one of the greatest issues of our time. People were invited to vote for one of the six challenges.
>
> **FLIGHT**—How can we fly without damaging the environment?
>
> **ANTIBIOTICS**—How can we prevent the rise of resistance to antibiotics?
>
> **DEMENTIA**—How can we help people with dementia live independently for longer?
>
> **WATER**—How can we ensure everyone can have access to safe water?
>
> **PARALYSIS**—How can we restore movement to those with paralysis?
>
> **FOOD**—How can we ensure everyone has nutritious, sustainable food?

B Vote on the top three ideas in your group. Which ones should get the most support?

9 A Work in pairs and choose two other issues/questions to add to the list above.

B Work in groups and present your ideas. Listen to other students' ideas and take notes. Then vote on the top idea.

C Look on page 158 to find out which issue won the Longitude Prize.

VOCABULARY *PLUS*
VERBS/NOUNS WITH THE SAME FORM

10 A Complete the sentences with the correct form of one of the words in the box.

> ~~project~~ record permit decrease appeal

1 The environmental group Ocean __*Project*__ has __*projected*__ that sea levels will rise three feet in …
2 Fortunately, malaria has _____ in recent years, and the _____ is due to the use of …
3 When a major charity _____ for donations to help the deaf, their _____ was broadcast mainly …
4 Bonnie Tyler _____ her song "Total Eclipse of the Heart" in 1983, and in 2008 it set a _____ for …
5 Tourists at a well-known site were given _____ to take pictures, but they were not _____ to …

B Work in pairs and discuss. How do you think each sentence ends? Listen and check.

C Which words in Exercise 10A are nouns (N) and which are verbs (V)?

D Listen again and mark the stress on the words. Which have the same stress in the noun and verb?

11 A Work in pairs. Student A: look at the quiz below. Underline the stress in the words in bold. Student B: turn to page 158.

QUIZ

1 Which country **imports** more Japanese used cars than any other? Canada, Brazil or Russia?

2 In India, which colors are unlucky to wrap a birthday **present** in? Black and white, red and green or purple and yellow?

3 Which fruit do some plant experts **suspect** was the earth's first? The apple, the banana or the pear?

4 Which is the largest subtropical **desert**? The Arabian, the Kalahari or the Sahara?

5 **Research** shows what percentage of homemade dinners in the USA include vegetables? 43%, 63% or 93%?

B Work in pairs and take turns. Student A: read out your questions. Student B: guess the correct answer.

C Check the answers on page 162.

▶ page 149 VOCABULARY BANK

three feet / colors   one metre / colours

2.2)) YOU'RE BEING WATCHED

G the passive
P sentence stress: passives
V surveillance

1) A CCTV camera helps **crime prevention**; potential criminals know their actions might be filmed, and this acts as a **deterrent to crime**.

4) User-data monitoring on TVs and other appliances sends data to manufacturers and businesses.

5) Cell phone tracking can **keep track of** any individual's location.

2) License plate recognition enables **the authorities** to follow our movements wherever we drive and **store the information** indefinitely.

3) Microchips on credit cards make it easy **to monitor** and record information about our habits and movements.

6) Facial recognition technology can **identify** any individual. Software then **accesses data** about the person via social networking websites.

Surveillance Technology: Keeping us safe or **an invasion of privacy**?

VOCABULARY
SURVEILLANCE

1 A Work in pairs. Look at the picture and discuss.

1 How many of these surveillance techniques are you aware of?

2 How many are common where you live or where you are now?

3 How does surveillance make you feel? Why?

B Match meanings 1–8 with the phrases in bold in the picture.

1 an offcial group, e.g., the government or the police

2 to watch or follow (two phrases)

3 to keep data (on a computer) for future use

4 getting information about someone's private life in a way they don't like

5 to say/find out who someone is

6 stopping people from doing something illegal (two phrases)

7 to obtain information

8 a situation in which there is a lot of observation, filming or recording of people

C Work in pairs and discuss. How might each surveillance technique be used in a good or a bad way? How would you answer the question at the bottom of the picture.

LISTENING

2 A Listen to two people discussing types of surveillance technology and complete the table. Put ✓ if they like it or ✗ if they don't like it.

B Work in pairs and listen again. Student A: make notes on the woman's opinion. Student B: make notes on the man's opinion.

	Technology	Woman	Man
1	CCTV		
2	facial recognition technology		
3	microchips in products		
4	license plate recognition		

C Work in pairs and complete both columns of the table.

D Which speaker do you agree with more? Which one gave more convincing arguments?

Surveillance has become an important issue all over the world with CCTV cameras in most businesses and public areas, and some law enforcement have even begun to use drones to monitor downtown areas.

Cell phone / license plate   Mobile phone / number plate

GRAMMAR

THE PASSIVE

3 A Check what you know. Look at the sentences from the conversation and underline the passive forms.

1 Not long ago, a friend of mine was robbed at a bus stop.

2 I think, statistically, more crimes are solved because of CCTV than not.

3 I don't want to be sent ads from companies that I don't know.

4 But we're being sent stuff all the time anyway.

5 I've been given quite a few tickets over the years.

6 Money should be spent somewhere else to be honest.

B Underline the correct alternative to complete the rules. Use the sentences above to help.

> **RULES**
>
> **1** Use the passive to put the focus on the person or thing *doing the action/affected by the action*.
>
> **2** Use the passive when one or more of these is true:
>
> The person or thing that did the action:
>
> **a)** *is/isn't* obvious.
> **b)** *is known/is unknown*.
> **c)** *is/isn't* important.
> **d)** *is/isn't* the main focus.
>
> **3** Use the passive to bring the object of the verb to the *beginning/the end* of the sentence.
>
> **4** Use the passive to make certain written texts (e.g., academic) more *personal/impersonal* or *formal/informal*.

4 SENTENCE STRESS: passives Mark the stress in phrases 1–6. Listen and check. Then listen again and repeat.

1 A friend of mine was robbed.

2 More crimes are solved.

3 I don't want to be sent ads.

4 We're being sent stuff all the time.

5 I've been given quite a few tickets.

6 Money should be spent somewhere else.

▶ page 130 LANGUAGEBANK

5 A Read the text about microchips. How many different uses for microchips are described?

Microchips are everywhere ...

... and their uses range from the ordinary to the more worrying. For example, ¹*companies can place them/they can be placed* in food packaging. Then your fridge monitors your food so that ²*they can remind you/you can be reminded* when it's time for ³*you to buy something/a product to be bought*.

The medical world has suggested that ⁴*doctors could implant microchips/microchips could be implanted* in newborn babies. Then the person's movements and habits can be tracked throughout their lives. ⁵*Scientists could also implant/Microchips could also be implanted* in criminals so that police can ⁶*keep/be kept* track of them and possibly identify the whereabouts of known criminals at the time ⁷*someone commits a crime/a crime is committed*.

And, if you're the kind of person who loses things easily, ⁸*you can buy a set of clip-on microchips/a set of clip-on microchips can be bought* that ⁹*you can attach/can be attached* to any object you want to keep track of–for example, your purse. If the object gets lost, ¹⁰*you can use your phone/your phone can be used* to find it.

B Underline the best form, active or passive, so that it a) keeps the focus on the main ideas and b) is correct.

C Work in pairs and discuss. Which ideas in Exercise 5A do you find disturbing and which don't bother you?

SPEAKING

6 A Work in pairs. Read the article and answer the questions.

1 Which plans would be the most useful for reducing crime?

2 Would you like to have these things in your local area?

3 How do you think the following groups of people would feel about the plans: the police, parents, teenagers?

POLICE TO INSTALL TOWN-WIDE SURVEILLANCE

In response to the recent surge in crime, police have announced plans to install the following security systems:

» CCTV cameras to cover the whole town.
» police checkpoints for identity checks.
» monitoring of phone calls.
» monitoring of social networking websites.
» all teenagers' cell phones to be registered on police GPS systems.
» license plate recognition cameras on all main roads.

B Work in pairs. You belong to one of the three groups in Exercise 6A, question 3. Make a list of your reasons for or against the plans.

C Role-play a meeting with the three groups of people. Take turns and discuss your opinions.

D Vote for one of the other two groups. Which one gave better reasons for their opinion?

WRITING

A LETTER OF COMPLAINT; LEARN TO USE FORMAL WRITTEN LANGUAGE

7 A Work in pairs and discuss. In what circumstances would you write a letter of complaint or make an official complaint? Have you ever done this? What happened?

B Read the letter and answer the questions.

1 Who is the letter to?
2 Why is the writer complaining?
3 What does she want to achieve?

LaGrande Travel Agency
1422 La Grande Avenue
Hartwood, 03735

To Whom It May Concern:

I am writing with regard to the misuse of a personal photograph of myself and two of my friends on your website.

The photograph in question is one I posted on my personal blog several months ago, and it involves my friends and I celebrating the end of final exams at college. Several days ago, I was shocked to discover that my picture had been used in an online advertisement for your study abroad program. This is both unfair and illegal because you have been using the photograph without my permission, and, because you are advertising a product with it, you are in fact using it for personal gain.

I have taken up this matter with a lawyer, who has advised me to contact you in writing. She has also indicated what further steps might be taken should you fail to respond promptly and appropriately.

To resolve this matter, I request that you remove the photograph without delay. In addition, I ask that you issue a statement of your policy regarding use of images that are not your property.

Please contact me within one week of the date of this letter to confirm that these steps have been taken. If you need to reach me by telephone, my number is (141) 985-001.

Thank you for your prompt attention to this matter.

Yours faithfully,

Charlene Jones

Charlene Jones (Ms.)

C Put the parts of a letter of complaint a)—f) into a possible order. Then check your ideas with the order in the letter above.

a) explain what you have done so far
b) give a time frame for action and a way of contacting you
c) state the overall reason for writing, in one sentence 1
d) write a polite closing comment
e) ask for specific action from the person/company you are writing to
f) give additional detail about the reason for writing

8 A Find the formal phrases in the letter that match the informal phrases below.

1 Get in touch soon to let me know that you've done something.
2 To make things right, I want you to …
3 I'm writing about
4 With best wishes
5 Thanks for dealing with this problem quickly.
6 I've already discussed the problem

B In the last four paragraphs of the letter, circle the passive verbs and underline the active ones. Why does the writer choose each?

> **American Speak TIP**
> A letter of complaint should follow "The Four Cs." It should be: concise, clear, constructive and considerate. Reread the letter. Does it follow the rules of "The Four Cs"?

9 A Plan a letter of complaint.

1 Read the notes below and choose one of the situations.
2 Decide what you want to achieve with the letter.
3 Make notes on the content of each paragraph.

> **Situation 1**
> Your neighbors / new burglar alarm / alarm gone off three times / neighbors away / tried to talk to them / too busy
> Write a letter of complaint to your neighbors.

> **Situation 2**
> Recently you parked car / thought it was legal / returned / parking fine / no-parking sign behind tree
> Write a letter of complaint to city hall.

B Write the letter (120—180 words).

C Check the grammar, spelling and punctuation of your letter.

D Exchange your letter with another student. Check that he/she has:

- followed "The Four Cs."
- used paragraphs well.
- used a formal style.

2.3)) GOOD POINT!

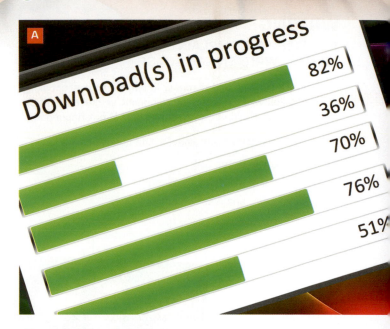

F opinions
P intonation for partially agreeing
V opinion adjectives

SPEAKING

1 Work in pairs. Match the newspaper extracts 1–3 with the pictures A–C. Then discuss the questions.

1 Research done at a high school in Italy showed that teenagers who played violent video games were not only more aggressive than those who didn't, but also cheated eight times more and ate three times as much chocolate.

2 One study showed that nearly 100 percent of those who get cosmetic surgery reported an increase in self-esteem, and there was a 30 percent decrease in the use of anti-depressants.

3 This is theft and thieves can be punished. In 2012, an American man was fined $1.5 million for downloading and sharing movies, and several people have been fined large amounts for downloading and sharing music.

1 Which extracts are for and which are against the topics?

2 Can you think of any other reasons for and against each idea?

3 What is your opinion about each idea?

FUNCTION
OPINIONS

2 A Listen to three conversations. Which person agrees with the statements above, the man or the woman?

B Listen again and make notes. Write one reason each person gives for their opinion.

C Work in pairs and compare your notes. Which reasons are the best?

D Work in pairs and complete the phrases.

Giving Opinions	Agreeing
I'm really ¹ _____ it.	That ³ _____ sense.
I'm in ² _____ of …	I ⁴ _____ what you mean.

Partially Agreeing	Disagreeing
I see your ⁵ _____, but …	Actually I ⁷ _____ …
I agree to a ⁶ _____ extent, but …	I'm still not ⁸ _____.

E Check your answers in the audio script on page 165.

A

Download(s) in progress
82%
36%
70%
76%
51%

3 A Add the phrases in the box to the correct groups in Exercise 2D.

Exactly!   Personally, I think …   I totally disagree.
I suppose so.   Good point.   Fair enough, but …
Basically, I think …   I'm not so sure.   I do think …

B INTONATION FOR PARTIALLY AGREEING
Listen to the phrases for partially agreeing and copy the intonation.

▶ page 130 **LANGUAGEBANK**

4 A Work in pairs and practice the conversations using the prompts.

Conversation 1
A: I / favor / banning smoking / all public places.
B: Actually, / think / people / be free to choose.
A: Fair enough, but what about / rights / other people?
B: Personally, / think / freedom / choose / more important.
A: see / point / but passive smoking / can / very bad / you.
B: I suppose / but banning / all places / too much!

Conversation 2
A: What / think / banning cars / downtown?
B: against. / Basically, / think / bad for business. / you?
A: not / sure. / agree / certain extent / but / do think / better / the environment.
B: Good point. / And / people could / public transportation / more. / makes sense.
A: Exactly!

B Which person do you agree with in each conversation? Close your book and discuss the two topics with your partner. Use phrases for agreeing and disagreeing.

downtown / transportation   city centre / transport

B

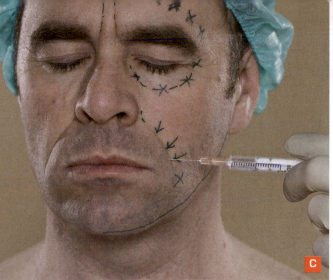

C

LEARN TO
SUPPORT YOUR VIEWPOINT

5 Look at the phrases in bold in 1–6 below. Which phrases are used:

a) to give an example?

b) for facts which you have read, heard or believe to be true?

1 **According to** one article I read, kids are less aggressive …

2 **Apparently**, the games give them a chance to use up some of their energy.

3 **As far as I know**, musicians these days get very little money …

4 **For instance**, what about that man in America?

5 **Like** Mike's girlfriend—she actually had some Botox injections …

6 … serious health problems. **Such as** maybe they're extremely overweight.

6 **A** Cover Exercise 5 and put the underlined phrases in the correct order.

A: [1]article to this according, teachers shouldn't give kids homework because kids learn better without it.

B: Yes, but homework is beneficial in a lot of ways, [2]for for content memorizing instance.

A: It says here that homework robs kids of the time to do other important things, [3]spending such time as with their families.

B: Well, [4]is homework essential apparently for developing discipline and time-management skills.

A: Well, this article says the exact opposite.

B: You shouldn't believe everything you read [5]that in magazines like.

A: I suppose not. [6]far I as know as, teachers are giving less homework these days, and I like that.

B Work in pairs and discuss. Do you agree with any of the points about giving homework in the conversation in Exercise 6A? Give examples and reasons.

VOCABULARY
OPINION ADJECTIVES

7 **A** Read sentences 1–6 and match the adjectives in bold with items a)–f) which are similar in meaning.

1 I find it deeply **disturbing** that children are forced to work in factories.

2 It's completely **unethical** for a company to profit by paying workers less than a living wage.

3 It seems **reasonable** to steal food if you're poor and hungry. Otherwise you would die.

4 It is **irresponsible** when people leave newspapers on the train. It's just trash that someone else has to pick up.

5 College education has become too expensive—I think it should be free for all. It's totally **outrageous**.

6 Eating and drinking on public transportation is **illegal**, and people who get caught have to pay a fine.

a) having good reasons

b) against the law

c) morally wrong

d) shocking and unacceptable

e) very worrying

f) not thinking about the results of your actions

> **American Speak out TIP** When stating your opinion, it's important to use specific adjectives to get your exact point across. Vague adjectives like *good, bad* or *nice* are unlikely to be persuasive enough.

B Work in pairs. Student A: rephrase a sentence in Exercise 7A beginning *It's terrible/bad/OK*. Student B: close your book and reply with one of the adjectives.

A: It's terrible that children have to work in factories.

B: Yes, it's deeply disturbing.

SPEAKING

8 **A** Work in pairs and choose three topics from Exercise 7A to discuss. Make notes on why you agree or disagree with each statement.

B Work in groups and discuss the statements. Give reasons for your opinion.

memorizing / trash   memorising / rubbish

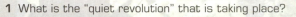

2.4 A QUIET REVOLUTION

DVD PREVIEW

1 A Work in pairs and discuss. Are there traditional gender roles in your country? What are they?

B Look at the statements and check (✓) the ones you agree with. Then compare in pairs.

1 A husband and wife should have clearly defined roles in terms of who does what.

2 I would say I have traditional values regarding these roles.

3 I would prefer my partner to take care of the children so that I can develop my career.

4 If I were the opposite gender, I would still answer question 3 in the same way.

2 Read the program information and answer the questions.

1 What is the "quiet revolution" that is taking place?

2 What reasons can you think of for this change? List at least three ideas.

▶ BBC News: A Quiet Revolution

Traditionally, it has always been women who do part-time jobs when a family needs one parent at home, while the man's career has always come first. But, more recently, it's men, not women, who are scaling down their work time, and, with over a million British men now working part-time, a quiet revolution is taking place. BBC reporter Emma Simpson meets three of these men to find out more about this trend.

DVD VIEW

3 A Watch the DVD. How many of your ideas from Exercise 2 are mentioned?

B Watch the DVD again. Who mentions each reason for working part-time? Write 1 (Rob), 2 (Richard) or 3 (Bernard).

• to make money
• to get back lost energy
• to help his partner's career
• to have more time for himself
• to avoid getting bored
• to spend more time with his family

C Work in pairs and choose the correct alternative to complete the phrases in bold from the DVD. Then watch again to check.

1 With two young boys, he and his wife realized **something had to** *give/go*.

2 It seemed to make sense for me to **take the** *lead/load* in moving down to working part-time …

3 He has to **make** *up/do* **with less** money, but, for Rob, life's now **on a more even** *keel/cool*.

4 He could have retired two years ago and **put his feet** *down/up*. Instead he's choosing to stay busy.

5 It's never easy, but these men are **breaking the** *mold/roles*.

D Match the phrases in 1–5 above with meanings a)–f).

a) less troubled and more balanced
b) live on not so much
c) end a restrictive practice
d) have a relaxed life
e) have to change to remove the pressure
f) act first

E Work in pairs and discuss. Is your country seeing similar trends to those described in the DVD clip? Which reasons for men going part-time in Exercise 3B would be a "revolution" in your country?

mold mould

American Speakout a joint presentation

4 **A** Work in pairs and discuss. What are the pros and cons of traditional gender roles? Look at the two ideas below and add two more of your own.

pro: women have more time with children—closeness with mother is important
con: family depends primarily on man for financial support

B Listen to two people giving a presentation about the pros and cons of traditional gender roles. Which of your ideas do they mention?

C Listen again and check (✓) the key phrases you hear.

> **KEYPHRASES**
>
> Our presentation is about ...
>
> We'd like to talk to you about ...
>
> First, to make it clear what we mean by [traditional roles] ...
>
> What tends to happen is that ...
>
> Generally speaking, [the woman does the housework]
>
> On the [positive/negative] side ...
>
> That's bound to be [good/bad] for ...
>
> Finally, and perhaps most importantly, ...
>
> It also can be [risky/problematic], in that, if [the man can't work/the woman hates housework] ...

5 **A** Work in pairs and prepare a presentation on the pros and cons of one of the topics below. Make a list of three pros and three cons.

- Women and men competing on the same teams and in the same leagues in sports.
- Laws that say companies should have 50 percent men and 50 percent women as directors.
- Husbands and wives sharing household chores equally (housework and home repairs).

B Practice your presentation together. Agree on who will:

—introduce the presentation.
—give more information about your topic.
—state the pros.
—state the cons.
—make a summary statement.

C Make your presentation to other students. Ask them to vote on the stronger argument.

writeback notes for a presentation

6 **A** Read the notes for the presentation. Which topic below is it about? Which side of the argument appears stronger to you?

- Full salary for whichever parent stays at home with children
- Gender-blind hiring—your name, gender and picture do not appear on job applications
- Compulsory school uniforms, identical for boys and girls

> **PROS:**
> – best person chosen for job
> – no problems re sex discrimination
> – may change how society regards men/women
>
> **CONS:**
> – impractical: how to conduct interviews?
> – resistance from traditionally minded people/cultures
> – problem with gender-specific positions, e.g., casting female role in movie

B Look at the notes again. How does the writer make the notes as short as possible?

C Choose a new topic from Exercise 5A or 6A and write notes for a presentation.

D Work in pairs. Read your partner's notes and:

- say which argument appears stronger.
- identify where they can make their notes shorter by using the techniques you noticed in Exercise 6B.

V ISSUES

1 A Add letters to complete the adjectives.

1 Why is gang violence more of an ur_ _ _ problem than a ru_ _ _ problem?

2 Do politicians focus more on do_ _ _ _ _ _ issues or gl_ _ _ _ issues before an election?

3 Here's a typical eth_ _ _ _ question: You see a co-worker steal money from your boss. What do you do?

4 The rich are less affected by inflation and unemployment than poorer people, but when there are ec_ _ _ _ _ _ problems, they spend less than usual. Why is this?

5 Which type of problems do you think affect you less: pol_ _ _ _ _ _ or indu_ _ _ _ _ _?

B Work in pairs and discuss the questions in Exercise 1A.

G PRESENT PERFECT SIMPLE AND CONTINUOUS

2 A Make questions with the prompts. Use the most suitable verb form: the present perfect simple or continuous or the past simple.

1 How long / you / learn / English?

2 Your English / improve / a lot recently. What / you / do?

3 How many teachers / you / have?

4 How far / you / travel / on public transportation today?

5 you / do / your homework for today?

6 How long / take / you / do it?

7 you / study / a lot this week?

8 you / ever / forget / to bring anything to class?

B Work in pairs and take turns. Ask and answer the questions.

V SURVEILLANCE

3 A Put the jumbled letters in order.

1 The best form of mcrie niovpenter at home is to get a big dog. It will act as a real treednret to crime.

2 I would like to have facial recognition technology on my phone so I could etdfniiy people on the street.

3 If I could csscea the personal data of my friends, I would. Maybe it's an nonsiiva of cvarpiy, but so what?

4 It wouldn't bother me if the uahisrtoeit were triminogon my phone calls.

5 Technology to epek arctk of things would be useful, particularly for keys and wallets.

6 I don't know where to srtoe taoiirnmfon like my passwords.

B Work in pairs and discuss. Which statements in Exercise 3A do you agree with? Say why.

G THE PASSIVE

4 A Change the sentences into the passive.

1 I don't like people calling me by my nickname.
   I don't like being called by my nickname.

2 My parents brought me up in a house full of pets.

3 No one has ever robbed me.

4 I hate it when people give me clothes as a present.

5 People often tell me I look like my father.

6 I've always wanted people to admire me for my intelligence.

B Check (✓) the sentences in Exercise 4A which are true for you. Then make the other sentences true by adding or changing no more than three words.

C Work in pairs and compare your sentences.

5 A Put the words in the correct order to make passive questions.

1 an / by / bitten / been /ever /you / Have / animal?

2 you / by / invited / a / like / to / celebrity / to / Would / dinner / be?

3 being / you / Do / enjoy / photographed?

4 the / want / told / if / you / always / to / truth / Do / even / it / hurts / be?

5 die / remembered / What / for / will / after / you / you / be?

B Work in pairs and take turns. Ask and answer the questions.

F OPINIONS

6 A Correct the mistakes in the phrases for agreeing/disagreeing.

A: [1]I'm in favorite of banning people from eating food on public transportation.

B: [2]I real against it. What about long journeys? For instance, with kids?

A: [3]I see and point, but I meant on shorter journeys.

B: [4]Actual, I think I think it'd be impossible to check.

A: [5]I'm agree to a certain extent, but maybe the guards could check.

B: [6]I'm still not convincing. Some people would keep on doing it anyway.

A: [7]Hmm … I see when you mean.

B Choose one of the topics below and have a conversation. Use the phrases in Exercise 6A to help you.

• banning homework

• making it more difficult to get married, e.g., having a pre-marriage exam

• lowering the voting age

A: Personally, I think lowering the voting age is a great idea!

B: Really? I'm not so sure. I think …

3))) stories

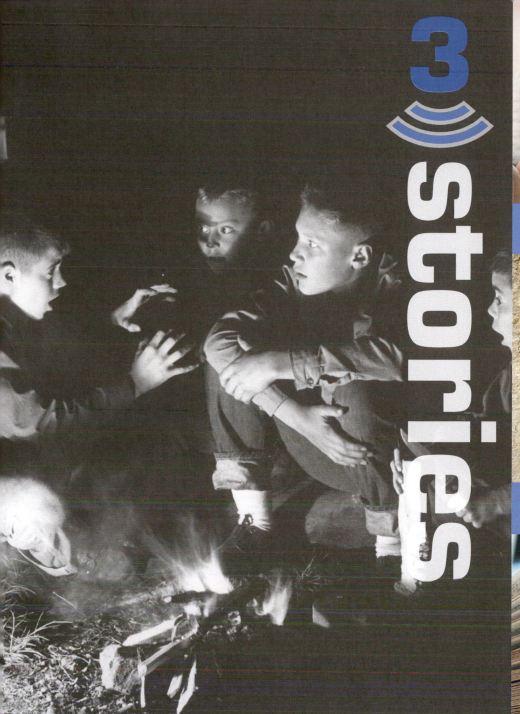

**AND THE
MORAL IS ...**   p32

6

**A LIFE IN
SIX WORDS**   p35

**IT'S A
GREAT READ**   p38

TESS   p40

What was the last book you read?

INTERVIEWS

3.1)) AND THE MORAL IS ...

G narrative tenses
P weak forms: auxiliaries
V sayings

Performance of a lifetime?

Many years ago, a crowd gathered outside the Paris Opera House to see a performance by one of the most famous opera singers of the time. Tickets had sold out weeks before, and opera fans had been looking forward to this epic moment ever since the performance was announced. It was a gorgeous spring evening, and everyone was wearing their finest clothes in celebration of the event.

In the moments before the curtain went up, the house lights **dimmed** slightly, and a hush fell over the audience as they saw something every theatergoer **dreads**. A man in a suit was slowly walking out onto the stage. It was the house manager, and he announced to the audience that, unfortunately, the famous singer had fallen ill and that her understudy, an unknown opera singer, would be performing in her place. A sense of disappointment **pervaded** the theater. Some people got up and left.

Moments later, the curtain went up, and the performance ¹began. Throughout the nearly three-hour opera, the understudy, who ²had never appeared in a major opera before, **gave the performance of her life**. At the end of each major scene, when people usually applaud, there was literally no sound at all from the audience. Finally at the end of the opera, as the understudy sang her final notes and the orchestra played the last bars and stopped, there was only very faint applause. Suddenly, on one of the upper balconies, a little boy stood up.

READING

1 A Work in pairs. Look at the pictures and the titles of the stories above. What do you think the stories are about?

B Read the stories and check your ideas. Work in pairs and think of an ending for each one.

C Turn to page 158 and read the two possible endings for each story. Which one do you prefer?

2 A Work in pairs. Guess the meanings of the words in bold in the stories in Exercise 1B.

B Check your ideas. Match meanings 1–8 with the words in bold in the stories.

1 did something better than ever
2 didn't give up
3 expected to arrive
4 fears
5 got darker
6 shaking, usually from cold
7 spread through
8 in a way that can be seen

C Work in pairs and discuss. Which versions of the stories have a point or moral? Which story is more effective?

GRAMMAR
NARRATIVE TENSES

3 A Read the first paragraph of "Performance of a lifetime?" again and underline examples of the past simple, the past perfect simple, the past continuous and the past perfect continuous.

B Underline the correct verb form in the rules. Use the first paragraph of "Performance of a lifetime?" to help.

> **RULES**
>
> **1** Use the *past simple/past continuous* for completed actions which give the main events in a story.
>
> **2** Use the *past simple/past continuous* for actions in progress at a particular time or when another (shorter) action happened. Also use it to set the scene of a story.
>
> **3** Use the *past perfect simple/past perfect continuous* for completed actions that happened before the main events.
>
> **4** Use the *past perfect simple/past perfect continuous* for longer actions that started before other events and often continued up to them.

C Work in pairs and look at the numbered verbs in both stories. Discuss how each example fits one of the rules above.

4 A WEAK FORMS: auxiliaries Work in pairs. Mark the stress on the phrases in bold. Circle any weak forms (/ə/ or /ɪ/).

1 The woman (had) been **standing** there for a long time and **was shivering** badly.

2 When she **was paying** for her meal, the old lady remembered what Steve Hunt **had said**.

B Listen and check. Then listen and say the sentences at the same time as the audio.

▶ page 132 LANGUAGEBANK

theatergoer   theatregoer
theater   theatre

It Pays to be Honest

One day, a man [3]was driving down a small country road in Tennessee on a cold winter evening when he saw an elderly woman standing by her car, apparently in some kind of trouble, so he stopped. The woman [4]had been standing there for a long time and [5]was **shivering** badly. She looked anxious as he got out of his car, so he introduced himself. "I'm Steve Hunt. You look like you need some help." The woman had a flat tire, so Steve sat her in his car to stay warm while he changed it.

After [6]he'd finished the job, the old lady tried to give him money, but Steve refused. She **persisted**, so Steve said, "Listen, the next time you see someone in need, do something to help them. That's the best way to pay me back."

They said goodbye, and the woman [7]drove into the next town and stopped at a busy diner. There was only one waitress, and she was moving a bit awkwardly because she was **visibly** very pregnant. "When's it **due**, honey?" the old lady asked. "Any day now," answered the waitress. "You don't look too happy." "To be honest, I don't know how we're going to manage on just my husband's pay."

When she [8]was paying for her meal, the old lady [9]remembered what Steve Hunt [10]had said and left five one-hundred dollar bills on the table, then left quickly. The waitress was astonished and grateful. She went home and found her husband watching TV.

"Paying it forward", or helping strangers and then encouraging them to help others, has become a global phenomenon. Nowadays, stories about chains of random acts of kindness are found in nearly every country.

5 A Complete the story below with the correct form of the verbs in parentheses.

Once there was a king who received a gift of two magnificent falcons. He [1]_____ (never see) such beautiful birds before. He gave them to a man who [2]_____ (train) falcons for him for many years.

A month later, the king [3]_____ (sit) on his balcony when he [4]_____ (notice) one of the falcons in the sky, but he [5]_____ (not see) the other one. Deeply disappointed, he discovered that the falcon [6]_____ (sit) on the same branch since its arrival.

The king [7]_____ (call) healers and magicians from all over the land to find out what the problem was, but no one could make the bird fly. After he [8]_____ (try) everything, eventually the king [9]_____ (realize) that he needed someone who understood the countryside, so he called for a farmer.

The very next morning, the king was thrilled to see that the second falcon [10]_____ (fly) high in the sky alongside the first. He called the farmer and asked, "How did you make the falcon fly?" The farmer answered, "It was very easy, Your Majesty. I simply [11]_____ (cut) the branch where the bird [12]_____ (sit)."

B Work in pairs. What is the moral of this story? How could you apply the moral in your life?

VOCABULARY

SAYINGS

6 A Work in pairs and read the sayings. What do you think they mean?

1 Every cloud has a silver lining.
2 What goes around comes around.
3 Once bitten, twice shy.
4 Nothing ventured, nothing gained.
5 When in Rome, do as the Romans do.

B Match the sayings 1–5 to their meanings a–e. Which one could go well with one of the stories in Exercise 1B?

a) Follow the local customs wherever you go.
b) Get hurt once, never try again.
c) A bad situation always has something good in it.
d) Take risks or you'll never achieve anything.
e) If you do something good/bad, the same will happen to you.

C Complete the conversations with one of the sayings in Exercise 6A.

1 **A:** Did you eat snake in China?
  B: Yes, you know what they say: _____.

2 **A:** You should buy your new phone online.
  B: No, last time I shopped online my credit card information was stolen. _____

3 **A:** Since my accident, Pam's been so helpful.
  B: You were always there for her. _____

4 **A:** Should I enter the talent show?
  B: Oh, go on! After all, _____.

5 **A:** Joe was fired, but now he's found an even better job!
  B: Really? Well, _____.

American Speak TIP People often use the beginning of a saying and expect the listener to understand the full idea, e.g., *You know what they say, "When in Rome ..."* Look at B's sentences in Exercise 6C. Which part could you leave out?

tire / credit card information / Should   tyre / card details / Shall

SPEAKING

7 A Choose an experience in your life that illustrates one of the sayings in Exercise 6A.

B Prepare to tell your story. Write down eight to ten key words to help you. Think about the verb forms you want to use.

C Work in groups and take turns. One student: tell your story. The other students: guess the saying it illustrates.

WRITING

A STORY

8 A Read the story below. Did the ending surprise you? Why/Why not?

B Read the story again and answer the questions.

1 How does the writer link the introduction (under the title) and end of the story?

2 Which paragraph sets the scene? Which verb forms are used to do this?

3 Which paragraphs develop the story? Which verb forms are used to do this?

4 Where does the writer include his feelings?

5 Where does he describe what he learned from the incident?

9 A Work in pairs and circle eight adverbs ending in *-ly* in the story.

B Match meanings 1–7 with the adverbs.

1 not a very clever way to do something *stupidly*

2 normally and as expected

3 unluckily

4 might be true but not completely certain

5 in a clumsy and uncoordinated way

6 after a long time (two adverbs)

7 showing good manners

C Write the adverbs in the correct category in the table.

Adverbs of Manner (describing how an action happened)	*stupidly*
Attitude Markers (expressing the writer's attitude toward something in the story)	
Time Markers (referring to time)	

American Speak out TIP

To make a story more interesting, use a range of different adverbs. When you write the story in Exercise 10A, try to include at least two of each type of adverb.

10 A Choose one of the following tasks and write a story (120–200 words) for a magazine. Use a saying as a title.

• an experience that illustrates a saying

• an experience that disproves a saying

• your story from Exercise 7A

B Check your story for accuracy of verb forms and spelling and for use of adverbs of manner, attitude and time.

C Read other students' stories. Which is the most interesting?

▶ page 150 VOCABULARYBANK

Nothing ventured ...

I used to love the saying "Nothing ventured, nothing gained," but now I'm not so sure.

I started work as a computer programmer just after college, but it had always been my ambition to be a stand-up comedian. I'd been thinking about it for some time, and my friends were always telling me I was funny, but I was nervous about the idea of going on stage.

Anyway, stupidly, I listened to my friends. I worked on some material and put together a twenty-minute show. I practiced it for my girlfriend, which wasn't easy since naturally it was difficult for her to laugh at the same joke twenty-five times.

Finally, after I'd waited a couple of months, I was given time at a local comedy club. It was late at night when I went on, and the audience had already been sitting there for three hours. My friends were there—they'd reserved seats in the front row.

I started, and, on the first joke, I tripped over my words awkwardly. Apparently, the surest way to kill a joke is to hesitate. But I pushed on and realized that my mouth was so dry I couldn't speak. Unfortunately, a couple of people in the audience started to giggle, but I knew they were laughing at me, not my jokes. My friends smiled politely.

Well, twenty minutes isn't such a long time, and eventually I finished. As I collapsed into a chair backstage, in my mind I rewrote my favorite saying to: "Nothing ventured, nothing lost." And I ventured nothing after that for a very long time.

G *I wish, If only*

P sentence stress

V adjectives for stories; multi-word verbs

For Sale: baby shoes, never worn.

A life in six words

In the 1920s, the American author Ernest Hemingway bet ten dollars that he could write a complete story in just six words. He wrote: "For Sale: baby shoes, never worn." He won the bet.

An American online magazine has used the Hemingway story to inspire its readers to write their life stories in just six words, and they've been overwhelmed by the thousands who took up the challenge. They have published the best in a book, which they have given the title of one of the submissions: *Not Quite What I Was Planning*. The online magazine editor, Larry Smith, appeared on *Today*, Radio 4's early morning current events program.

Today then invited its listeners to send their own six-word life stories to their website.

VOCABULARY

ADJECTIVES FOR STORIES

1 A Work in pairs and discuss. Which sentences probably come from a conversation and which from a written text?

1 I've never seen such a dramatic change! Her hair went white overnight!

2 A collection of jokes and hilarious anecdotes. Guaranteed to make you laugh.

3 She told us some really moving stories about her life during the war.

4 It was incredible—the car hit her, but she was OK.

5 This teacher was so inspiring that he changed each of his students' lives.

6 A poignant tale of heartbreak and loss. Don't miss it!

7 She was just too intense for me. I never felt I could relax.

8 This woman's remarkable story of success at the age of eighty-five will amaze you.

B Underline the adjective in each sentence in Exercise 1A. Then match the adjectives with the meanings below.

1 not believable

2 making you want to achieve things

3 very amusing

4 sudden and extraordinary

5 impressive, e.g., … achievement

6 making you feel sadness (two adjectives)

7 concentrated/strong, e.g., … heat

C Work in pairs. Choose three of the adjectives and outline a news or movie story that fits each.

Poignant: a movie about two teenagers in love, but they know one of them is going to move to the other side of the world.

D Read out your descriptions to other students. They guess the adjectives.

LISTENING

2 A Work in pairs. Read the text above and discuss the questions.

1 What do you think Hemingway's story is about?

2 Who is Larry Smith, and why is he on Today?

3 Where does the title of the book come from?

B Work in pairs. Predict the correct alternative in sentences 1—5. Then listen to the interview with Larry Smith and check your answers.

1 Larry expected/didn't expect a large number of entries.

2 People were very intense about the challenge/didn't take the challenge seriously.

3 People wrote about their own lives/someone else's life.

4 Many stories had a sense of excitement and drama/regret and disappointment.

5 A lot of people had had a satisfying/tough life.

C Listen again and complete the six-word stories.

1 Not quite   *what I was planning*   .

2 Wasn't born _____.

3 Found _____.

4 Never _____.

D Work in pairs and discuss.

1 Which adjectives in Exercise 1A could be used to describe the stories in Exercise 2C? Why?

2 Which story sounds most interesting? What do you think happened in this person's life?

current events program   current affairs programme

GRAMMAR
I WISH, IF ONLY

3 A Work in pairs. Look at these six-word stories. What does each person want to change about their life?

1 Wrong era, wrong class, wrong gender.
2 Really should have been a lawyer.
3 Born London, lived elsewhere, died inside.
4 Any chance I could start again?
5 Worry about tomorrow, rarely enjoy today!
6 Married, TV, computer, never any flowers.

B Match sentences a)—f) with stories 1—6 above.

a) I wish I could do it all again.
b) I wish I weren't so anxious.
c) I wish I'd stayed where I was happy.
d) I wish he'd pay more attention to me.
e) If only I hadn't become a doctor.
f) If only I'd been born twenty years later.

C Match sentences a)—f) with the rules below.

> **RULES**
>
> **1** Use *wish/if only* + past subjunctive or *wish/if only* + *could* when you would like something to change, but it's impossible or not likely.
> _____, _____
>
> **2** Use *wish/if only* + past perfect subjunctive to talk about regrets about the past.
> _____, _____, _____
>
> **3** Use *wish/if only* + would to talk about things you want to happen or stop happening because they annoy you. _____

D SENTENCE STRESS Listen to the sentences from Exercise 3B and underline the stressed words. Then listen and repeat.

▶ page 132 LANGUAGEBANK

4 A For each pair of sentences, complete the second sentence so that it means the same as the first.

1 I'd really like to have a new laptop.
   I wish _I had a new laptop_.
2 I regret growing up in a small family.
   I wish _____.
3 I'm not very sociable.
   If only _____.
4 I have a friend who speaks too quietly. It's very annoying.
   I wish _____.
5 I can't get to sleep before about 2 a.m.
   If only _____.
6 I often lose my temper with people.
   I wish _____.
7 I'm sorry I don't have my camera with me.
   I wish _____.
8 I can't cook very well.
   I wish _____.
9 I'm frustrated because it's raining.
   I wish _____.
10 I regret not spending more time with my grandfather.
   If only _____.

B Check (✓) the sentences in Exercise 4A which are true for you. Change the others so that they are true.

I wish I had a new laptop.

C Work in pairs and choose three sentences you changed. Student A: say your sentences from Exercise 4B. Student B: ask follow-up questions.

A: I wish I could cook better.
B: Do you? Why's that?

SPEAKING

5 A Work in pairs and look at these "short" stories. Which do you think is the most powerful?

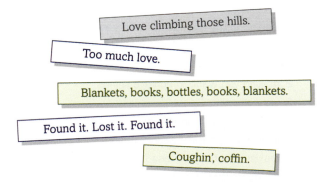

Love climbing those hills.

Too much love.

Blankets, books, bottles, books, blankets.

Found it. Lost it. Found it.

Coughin', coffin.

B How have the writers above shortened their stories? What kinds of words have they left out or included?

C Write your own six-word story about an aspect of your life, the life of someone famous or someone you know.

D Work with other students. Ask and answer questions about the stories.

VOCABULARY *PLUS*
MULTI-WORD VERBS

6 A Underline the multi-word verbs in stories 1—4 below. Then match each verb with meanings a)—f).

1 Alas, Mr. Right never turned up.

2 Gave up chocolate, took up running.

3 Loved Sonia. Settled down with Elena.

4 Set up company. Money ran out.

a) start (a hobby or habit)

b) be completely used up

c) arrive

d) start (a business)

e) start living a quiet life—get married and have children

f) stop (a hobby or habit)

B Work in pairs. Look at the extracts from a dictionary. Which verb:

1 can sometimes be used without an object?

2 must be used with an object?

3 can be separated with an object?

4 can be followed by a preposition?

> **S** **set up** *phr v* **1** to start a company or organization [=**establish**]: **set sth ↔ up**. *She left the company to set up her own business.*

> **R** **run out** *phr v* **1 a)** to use all of something, so that there is none left; **+of** *We've run out of sugar.* | *I'm running out of ideas.* **b)** If something is running out, there will soon be none left: *We'll have to make a decision soon —time is running out.*

From Longman Active Study Dictionary.

American Speak TIP

A dictionary gives useful information about multi-word verbs, including: the meaning, an example, whether the verb takes an object, whether the verb and its particle can be separated. How are these features shown in the extracts above? How does your dictionary show them?

7 A Look at the photo in the article on the right. What do you think this woman's life has been like?

B Read the text and answer the questions.

1 Did she have an easy life?

2 What jobs did she have in her life?

3 What were her major interests?

4 Why is she a role model?

Maya Angelou

Celebrated African–American writer and actress Maya Angelou was born in St Louis, Missouri (USA), in 1928 and **grew up** in St Louis and in Stamp, Arkansas. She **was brought up** first by her grandmother and then her mother. As a child, she suffered violence and racism and, at one point, even decided to stop speaking for five years.

Because of her love for the arts, she won a scholarship to study dance and drama in San Francisco, but, at fourteen, she **dropped out** and was the first African–American woman to become a cable car conductor. After going back and finishing high school, she gave birth to a son, then **took on** a number of different jobs, mainly as a waitress and a cook, to support her family.

Her great passion, however, was the arts. She studied modern dance and, in the 1950s, performed regularly in clubs around San Francisco, singing and dancing to calypso music, as well as touring around Europe.

In the 1950s, she traveled extensively, living abroad in Cairo and Ghana, and **picked up** several languages along the way. In the 1960s, after she'd become increasingly active politically, she was devastated when two of her heroes and associates, Malcolm X and Martin Luther King Jr., were assassinated. It was then that she published her first memoir, *I Know Why the Caged Bird Sings.*

She **went on** to write seven other memoirs as well as poetry, drama and even cookbooks. As the years **went by**, Maya remained active as an inspiring lecturer and she received many awards and recognition from world leaders. Millions of women **looked up to** her as a role model. To many people, her name **stands for** great courage and a huge appetite for life and expression.

Maya Angelou **passed away** on May 28th, 2014.

C Read the article again and match meanings 1—10 with the multi-word verbs in bold. Write the multi-word verbs in the infinitive.

1 spend your childhood *grow up*

2 learn by experience not study

3 respect

4 die

5 continue to do something

6 pass (about time)

7 agree to do some work

8 represent

9 stop doing (a course)

10 be raised

SPEAKING

8 A Work in pairs and write notes about your life story, the life story of someone you know or of a famous person. Use at least five of the multi-word verbs from Exercise 6A or 7C.

B Work with other students and use your notes to tell them about the life story. If the person is famous, do not say their name. Other students: guess who it is. If the person is not famous, other students listen and ask two follow-up questions each.

▶ page 150 VOCABULARYBANK

F expressing likes and dislikes

P sentence stress

V reading genres

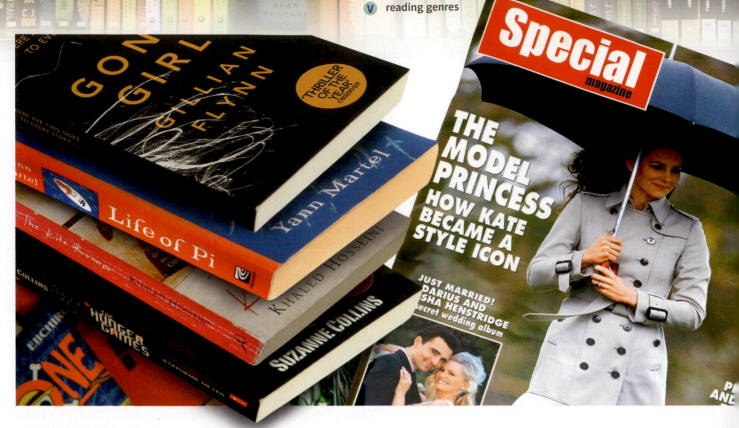

VOCABULARY
READING GENRES

1 A Work in pairs. Look at the words in the box and answer the questions. Use a dictionary if necessary.

> novel   blog   lyrics   tweet   gossip magazine
> biography   social media update   manga
> autobiography   poetry   manual   Wikipedia
> website forum   online article   blockbuster

Which things:

1 can only be read on a screen?

2 often include rhymes?

3 are about real people's lives?

4 aim to give factual information?

5 usually have pictures, photos or diagrams?

6 are fictional stories?

B Work in pairs. Student A: tell Student B the kinds of things you read the most and which you like reading and give examples. Student B: ask questions.

A: I enjoy gossip magazines. My favorite is "¡Hola!"
B: Why do you like it?
A: It's a really easy read after a long day …

2 Work with other students and discuss the questions.

1 What type of book would you take on a long flight?

2 Which book might you say you have read in order to impress someone?

3 What books would you recommend for someone who enjoys biographies or other factual books?

4 Do you know a movie that is better than the book it is based on?

FUNCTION
EXPRESSING LIKES AND DISLIKES

3 A Work in pairs. What do you know about the four books in the photo?

B Listen to the conversation and complete the second column of the table. Write ✓ (they liked it), ✗ (they didn't like it) or − (they haven't read it). Which book does Amy decide to take?

	1 *The Hunger Games*
Amy	−
Beth	
	2 *The Kite Runner*
Amy	
Carl	
	3 *Life of Pi*
Amy	
Beth	
Carl	

C Listen again and make notes about their feelings about each book.

D Discuss. Which of these books would you choose to read? Why?

5

A Rewrite the sentences using the words in parentheses. Make sure the meaning is the same.

1 I liked the characters in *Atonement* (What / liked)
 What I liked about Atonement were the characters.

2 Reading on my tablet hurts my eyes. (I / stand)
_____

3 Detective stories bore me. (I / that much)
_____

4 Blockbusters such as the *Bourne* series really don't appeal to me. (I / into) _____

5 I like the way *Twelve Years a Slave* teaches you about history. (thing / is) _____

6 The best thing about Agatha Christie books are the plots. (What / like) _____

7 I enjoy anything by Stieg Larsson. (I / big fan) _____

B Think of one type of reading that you really like and one that you don't like. Write two sentences about each using phrases from Exercise 5A.

C Work with other students. Find one type of reading you all like and one that none of you likes.

▶ page 132 LANGUAGEBANK

LEARN TO
SUMMARIZE A PLOT

6

A Read the summary of *Gone Girl*. Would you like to read the book?

> On the morning of his fifth wedding anniversary, Nick Dunne [1]_____ home and [2]_____ that his wife Amy [3]_____. During the next few days, the police and media [4]_____ Nick's life. Unfortunately for him, they [5]_____ that Nick is the number one suspect in Amy's murder. Through her diary entries, we find out that Amy [6]_____ happy in the marriage. However, as the story [7]_____, we [8]_____ to change our opinions of Nick and Amy as more information [9]_____ about the true state of their relationship.

B Listen and complete the summary of *Gone Girl*.

C Work in pairs and answer the questions.

1 Which verb forms are used in the summary?

2 Why do you think these verb forms are used?

3 Do you use the same verb forms when you summarize the plot of a book or movie in your language?

SPEAKING

7

A Choose a book or a movie adapted from a book. Make notes about: the main events in the story, why you like it, why the other students should read or watch it.

B Work in groups. Persuade the other students to read your book.

Has anyone read "Cien Años de Soledad" by Gabriel García Márquez? I think it's called "A Hundred Years of Solitude" in English. It's about ...

4

A Put the words in the correct order to make sentences. Then check in audio script S3.4 on page 166.

1 of sci-fi / big fan / novels anyway / I'm a

2 really liked / What I / main character / was the / about it

3 I don't / that much / sci-fi / to be honest / really like

4 whole story / about it / builds the / I love / The thing / is the / way it

5 into it / couldn't get / I just

6 that sort / stand books / I can't / at you / of preach

B Work in pairs and answer the questions.

1 Which phrases mean *I don't/didn't like*?

2 Look at sentence 2. How is it different in form from *I really liked the main character*? Which word/idea is emphasized?

3 Look at sentence 4. How is it different in form from *I love the way it builds the whole story*? Which word/idea is emphasized?

4 How could you change each sentence to the opposite meaning?

C SENTENCE STRESS Underline the main stresses in sentences 1–6 in Exercise 4A. Listen and check. Then listen and repeat.

DVD PREVIEW

1 Read the program information and answer the questions.

1 Where is the story set?
2 What two things do the female characters have in common?
3 How do you think they react when Angel arrives?
4 How do you think he "saves" them?
5 Do you think the story has a happy ending?

▶ Tess of the d'Urbervilles

This movie of Thomas Hardy's 19th-century novel tells the tragic story of Tess, the daughter of uneducated peasants in rural Wessex, the semi-fictional setting for many of Hardy's novels. In this episode, Tess and three other dairymaids* are all in love with Angel Clare, the son of a local clergyman. On their way to church one Sunday, the four dairymaids find their way blocked by a flood, but fortunately Angel arrives to save them.

*dairymaid—traditional female farm worker involved with the production of milk

DVD VIEW

2 A Watch the DVD. How did each woman feel when she was crossing the water? Check (✓) two adjectives for each person.

1 1st woman (Marian): eager / anxious / pleased
2 2nd woman (Retty): nervous / thrilled / awkward
3 3rd woman (Izzy): excited / disappointed / pleased
4 4th woman (Tess): anxious / happy / amused

B Watch again. Who says each sentence? What do they mean by it?

1 There's nothing in it, Retty.
2 A nice easy one this time.
3 You wouldn't mind, would you, if I tried?
4 I've undergone three-quarters of the labor just for this moment.
5 That's not what I meant at all.

C Work in pairs and discuss the questions.

1 Why do you think this type of period drama is popular?
2 Is it a kind of drama you like to watch? Why/Why not?

labor / labour

American Speakout a favorite scene

3 A Listen to a description of a favorite scene in a TV program called *Fawlty Towers*, and answer the questions.

1 One of the characters is Basil Fawlty, who runs a hotel. Who is the other one?

2 What happens?

B Listen again and check (✓) the key phrases you hear.

> **KEYPHRASES**
>
> I've seen this (X) times, and it's my absolute favorite.
>
> The thing I like best about it is …
>
> It always [makes me laugh/cry/sends shivers up my spine].
>
> It's like a lesson in [comic acting/timing/directing].
>
> My favorite scene is [the one where/the scene with …]
>
> It's very cleverly done.
>
> If you've never seen it, you really should.

C Think of a favorite scene in a TV program or movie. Write notes on:

• the point in which it appears in the program/movie (what has happened to set the scene?).

• the moment itself (what happens exactly?).

• why you like it.

D Work in pairs. Tell your partner about your favorite TV/movie scene.

writeback a description of a scene

4 A Read the magazine article. What type of movie is it? Have you seen it? Can you complete the missing words?

My Favorite Movie Moment

My favorite scene is the one in _____. It doesn't happen until a long way into the movie. You have been getting glimpses of the monster for a long time, so the tension has been building up for over an hour. You've mainly seen shots of people trying to get away and heard the disturbing music several times. It's very cleverly done with a very slow build-up and lots of tension.

So there are now three of them on a boat, the police chief, a biologist and a World War II veteran, and it's all very quiet, and one of them is just throwing meat into the water. There's no music, just the sound of the water and the people talking. Then _____ suddenly appears when you least expect it. And Roy Scheider is so cool. He goes quiet for a minute, then he walks back into the cabin and says, "You're gonna need a bigger boat." He doesn't even drop his cigarette. It's a lesson in perfect timing, and it always sends shivers up my spine. If you've never seen it, you really should.

B Write a description of a favorite TV/movie scene for a magazine. Use phrases from the description above and the key phrases in Exercise 3B to help your writing. Don't include the name of the program/movie.

C Read other students' descriptions and write the type of program/movie and, if you know it, the name.

3.5)) LOOKBACK

G NARRATIVE TENSES

1 A Complete the first part of the story with the verbs in parentheses in a correct narrative tense.

He ¹_____ (be) an old man who kept himself to himself, and he ²_____ (live) in the same house all of his life. The house ³_____ (fall) apart, and he ⁴_____ (not paint) it for years, so it ⁵_____ (look) as if it would collapse at any moment. We ⁶_____ (walk) past his house every day, and he ⁷_____ (always work) in his yard, and he ⁸_____ (always say) hello. One day, I ⁹_____ (come) home alone. I ¹⁰_____ (never walk) home alone before. I ¹¹_____ (look) up and ¹²_____ (see) the man at his window. He ¹³_____ (watch) me, and I felt as if he ¹⁴_____ (watch) for a long time. Then he ¹⁵_____ (come) out of the house …

B Work in pairs and write an ending to the story.

V SAYINGS

2 A Work in pairs. Look at the prompts. What are the sayings?

1 ventured—gained
2 Rome—Romans
3 bitten—shy
4 goes—comes
5 cloud—silver

B Choose three sayings and paraphrase them. Don't use any of the words in the original saying.

5 In all bad experiences there's something good.

C Work in pairs and take turns. Student A: read your paraphrased saying. Student B: guess the "real" saying.

V ADJECTIVES FOR STORIES

3 A Complete the adjectives in the stories.

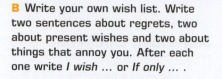 STORYTELLER PODCASTS

This Week's Recommendations

1 A young person who starts up her own business and succeeds despite dr_____ changes of fortune. This is an int_____ story about a re_____ woman. It makes you think anything is possible if you want it enough.

2 A hi_____ description of a trip across India, full of laugh-out-loud situations; Jerry manages to lose his passport five times and meets up with a series of inc_____ fellow-travelers whose stories you just can't believe!

3 A depressing picture of the difficulties facing a poor family in 1930s America. The story of their search for work is poi_____ and very mo_____, but their strength is truly ins_____.

B Work in pairs and discuss. Which story would you most/least like to listen to?

G I WISH, IF ONLY

4 A Look at the list and complete the sentences.

My wish list

1 I didn't travel very much when I was younger. I wish …
2 My friends don't really listen to me, and it's annoying. I wish …
3 My partner doesn't like the same kinds of music as me. I wish …
4 I didn't finish college. If only …
5 My roommate never thanks me for anything. It really makes me mad. I wish she …
6 It's impossible for me to afford a new car. If only …

mad cross

B Write your own wish list. Write two sentences about regrets, two about present wishes and two about things that annoy you. After each one write *I wish …* or *If only … .*

C Work in pairs and take turns. Student A: read out one of the sentences on your list. Student B: try and complete the sentence.

A: I didn't study English when I was younger. I wish …
B: You wish you'd studied English?

F EXPRESSING LIKES AND DISLIKES

5 A Complete the phrases with words from the box.

get	that	stand	what
	fan	thing	

1 _____ I really like about it is …
2 I don't like X _____ much.
3 The _____ I love about it is …
4 I just can't _____ into …
5 I'm a big _____ of …
6 I can't _____ …

B Work in groups. Make a list of 8—10 books, movies and bands that you all know.

C Take turns. Student A: say how you feel about one of the things on the list using the expressions in Exercise 5A, but don't say the name. Other students: guess what Student A is talking about.

6 A Work in pairs. Take turns saying the past form of each phrase from Exercise 5A.

A: What I really liked about …

B Choose a TV program that you watched when you were younger. Make notes about what you liked and disliked using the phrases in Exercise 5A.

C Work in pairs and take turns. Tell each other about your programs.

When I was about ten, I was really into cartoons, and I was a big fan of a cartoon from the U.S.A. called …

4 ((•)) downtime

What's the perfect way to switch off?

INTERVIEWS

G present and past habits
P connected speech: contractions
V free time

VOCABULARY

FREE TIME

1 Work in pairs and discuss. Do you have enough free time? What do you do with it?

2 A Work in pairs and check what you know. What's the literal (or basic) meaning of the words in the box? Which can be used with *a drink*, *a phone*, *an old clock* or *someone's face*?

> burn up   switch off   focus on   recharge   chill

B Complete the sentences with the correct form of one of the verbs in the box above.

1 My phone's dead. I need to _____ it.
2 I need to _____ _____ my ancient watch.
3 Please _____ the air conditioning; it's not that hot.
4 _____ the lemonade before you serve it—it tastes better cold.
5 If you _____ your camera _____ that tree over there, you'll get a better picture.

C Work in pairs. All the verbs above have another informal or idiomatic meaning. Which verbs do you think mean:

1 relax completely? _____ out
2 think about, listen or watch something or someone carefully? _____
3 get your energy back _____
4 say or do something to annoy someone? _____
5 stop listening or thinking? _____

D Complete the sentences with the correct form of one of the verbs in Exercise 2C.

1 I completely _____ when people talk about work at parties. It's so boring!
2 It really _____ me _____ when a friend checks his email when we're out together.
3 A summer vacation is a time to _____ so you have all your energy when you go back to school or work.
4 By Saturday I need some downtime, so I stay home and _____—you know, relax, do nothing.
5 I find the easiest way to unwind in the evenings is to _____ something different like cooking.

E Work in pairs. Which sentences in Exercise 2D do you agree with/are true for you?

More free time than ever?
I don't think so!

Do you have more or less free time than you used to? In our survey, an overwhelming majority (96%) said they have far less than they used to. And they were shocked to discover that according to recent research, we actually have far more than we had a decade ago. So where does the time go?

One would be quick and perhaps right to blame the Internet. Eight out of ten adults say they now go online in any location, not just at home or at work.

But contrary to current opinion, television still rules. Looking at adults of all ages, over 90% reported watching TV as their main free-time activity. Spending time with friends and family came in a close second (87%), followed by listening to music (79%). Spending time on the Internet ranked 4th in the 16–44 age range, but much lower among the 45-plus group. Shopping seems to have greater appeal for senior citizens—it's their third-favorite way to spend free time.

Perhaps it is most revealing then to look at what people actually enjoy. Unsurprisingly, spending time with family and friends ranked near the top, and doing household chores near the bottom. But what was most surprising is that watching television—an activity we seem to devote most of our leisure time to – also ranks very low in terms of pleasure.

READING

3 A Look at the headline of the article above and check (✓) the topics you think will be in the article.

shopping   working hours   the Internet
exercise   housework   sleep   television

B Read the article and circle the topics in Exercise 3A that it mentions. Were your predictions correct?

C Which of the following statements can be supported by the article?

Most people ...

1 have less free time than they used to.
2 use the Internet wherever they are.
3 prefer watching TV to listening to music.
4 over 65 spend less time on the Internet than younger adults.
5 have a negative attitude toward their job.
6 enjoy the Internet more than watching TV.

senior citizens   pensioners

4 A Read the opening sentences from two experts responding to the article. Work in pairs and list two things you think each expert will say.

THE EXPERTS HAVE THEIR SAY:
....

Sandra McCullough, Psychologist and Parent

"What's changed isn't the amount of free time, it's people's ability to do nothing."

Gerald van Halen, Sociologist and Parent

"Nothing has changed except what we mean by 'free-time activities.'"

B Student A: turn to page 159. Student B: turn to page 160.

C Students A and B: work in pairs and discuss.

1 What were your expert's main points?

2 Who identifies a more serious problem?

3 How could either problem be solved?

GRAMMAR
PRESENT AND PAST HABITS

5 A Look at sentences 1–5 and underline the phrases that express habits.

1 We used to have more free time …

2 People would sit around and watch TV or read.

3 Why are they always talking on their cells?

4 … or they'll often play a computer game together.

5 They usually watch YouTube clips together …

B Work in pairs and check what you know. Look at the rules and underline the correct alternative. Use the sentences above to help.

RULES

a) Use *used to* + infinitive for activities and states that *happen regularly now/happened regularly in the past but not now*.

b) Use *would* + infinitive for regular *activities/ states* in the past which no longer happen now.

c) Use frequency adverbs (*always, usually, generally, normally, typically*, etc.) + present *simple/continuous* for present habits or + past *simple/continuous* for past habits.

d) Use *always* + present continuous to talk about *long/repeated* activities that are often *annoying/surprising*.

e) Use *will* + infinitive to talk about *activities/ states* which are *present/future* habits, often with frequency adverbs.

C CONNECTED SPEECH: contractions Listen to the examples of fast connected speech. Write *'d, 'll* or present simple (PS) for each sentence.

1 _____   2 _____   3 _____   4 _____
5 _____   6 _____   7 _____   8 _____

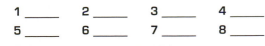

▶ page 134 **LANGUAGEBANK**

---

6 A Complete the readers' comments about the article on page 44. Use present and past habits. Write ONE word in each blank.

▶ I remember 1995, and it does seem like I had more free time then. I ¹_____ to meet friends a few times a week. Now we ²_____ get together once a month max.
Denise, Canberra

▶ Everybody is ³_____ blaming technology and work. So quit your job and turn off your cell! And stop whining. Remember, it didn't ⁴_____ to be like this.
Tatiana, Poznan

▶ I can identify with this article. In my twenties I ⁵_____ commute three hours a day to and from work, and I ⁶_____ worked on the train. I never seemed to switch off.
Craig, Edinburgh

▶ Young people don't understand. They ⁷_____ happily spend hours sitting next to each other in a café and never saying a word. When I was their age, my friends and I ⁸_____ talk for hours.
Scott, Los Angeles

▶ On a day off, I ⁹_____ nearly always check my work emails, and then I get into the whole Internet thing. But doesn't everybody ¹⁰_____ do this?
Steff, Berlin

B Work in groups and discuss. Which of the readers' comments can you identify with?

SPEAKING

7 A Work in pairs and look at the pie chart showing the hours spent on different activities in a working father's average weekday. Discuss the questions.

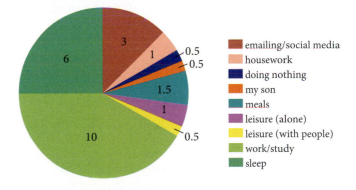

- emailing/social media
- housework
- doing nothing
- my son
- meals
- leisure (alone)
- leisure (with people)
- work/study
- sleep

1 Do you think this person has a balanced life?

2 Is there anything he should spend more or less time doing?

3 What would be similar or different on a pie chart of your average weekday?

B Draw a pie chart like the one above for your average weekday.

C Work with other students. Show each other your pie charts and discuss.

1 What are the differences between your pie charts?

2 How should other students change their lives?

3 Who has the most balanced average day?

45

WRITING

AN OPINION ESSAY; LEARN TO USE LINKERS

8 A Look at the essay title. Work in pairs and discuss the questions.

> **Most people fill their leisure time with meaningless activities. Do you agree?**

1 What do you consider a "meaningful" and a "meaningless" leisure activity?

2 What is your opinion of the statement?

B Read the essay. Do you agree with the writer's point of view?

1 It is said that technological development has given people more leisure time than they used to have and that this frees them up to concentrate on pursuing their interests or improving themselves. It seems to me, however, that most people spend their free time doing things that do not contribute to their development and are essentially unproductive.

2 **To start with**, the most popular free-time activities seem to be ones that people do alone. **For instance**, most people spend a large part of their time on the Internet, and, even when they are interacting with others, they are only doing so electronically. **In addition to this**, when people do go out, it is often to visit the shopping center; for some families, their main time together consists of a few hours walking, filling a shopping cart and eating at a snack bar in a shopping mall.

3 **At the same time**, there are examples of people making good use of their time. On weekends, there are parks, forests and beaches full of people doing sports or taking walks together. Some people do volunteer work for charity organizations for a few hours a week. Other people join theater or singing groups. All of **this supports the view** that there has been some positive change; sadly, however, this reflects a relatively small part of the overall population.

4 **In conclusion**, I agree that people use their free time wastefully, and I feel that the situation is getting worse. It is my hope that this might change in the future.

C Work in pairs. Identify the purpose of each paragraph.

D Underline three phrases for giving opinions.

9 A Complete the table with the linking words/phrases in bold in the essay.

first *to start with*	furthermore	to conclude
in contrast	for example	this shows

B Add the following phrases to the correct columns of the table.

> moreover   in the first place   to sum up
> this proves   as an example   as opposed to this

10 A Choose one of the essay titles below. Work alone and make notes on the questions.

> Adults need to play as much as children do.

> Leisure activities have become too expensive.

> Children need more play time in order to develop into healthy adults.

> Friendships formed over the Internet are as strong as ones formed in person.

- Do you agree with the opinion?
- Why/Why not? List three points.
- What examples can support your points?

B Work in groups and discuss your opinions. Note any new points you could include in your essay.

C Write a plan for your essay.

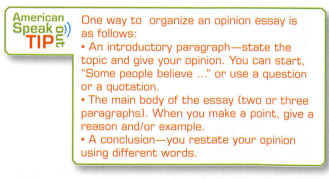

American Speak Out TIP

One way to organize an opinion essay is as follows:
- An introductory paragraph—state the topic and give your opinion. You can start, "Some people believe …" or use a question or a quotation.
- The main body of the essay (two or three paragraphs). When you make a point, give a reason and/or example.
- A conclusion—you restate your opinion using different words.

D Write the essay (120–180 words). Check your work for accurate grammar and use of linkers.

 shopping center / shopping cart   shopping centre / shopping trolley

4.2)) GREAT GETAWAYS

G future forms

P word stress; connected speech

V positive adjectives; uncountable and plural nouns

VOCABULARY

POSITIVE ADJECTIVES

1 A Work in pairs and tell each other about your last vacation. Did you enjoy it? How did you choose it?

B Read the website ads and answer the questions.

1 Which ads offer free vacations?

2 Which ones are vacations where you learn something?

3 Which, if any, appeal to you most?

2 A Underline eight positive adjectives in the ads. Circle the nouns they describe.

> **American Speak out TIP**
>
> Many adjectives with similar meanings are not interchangeable because they collocate with particular nouns, e.g., *a stunning view* but not *stunning fun*. Always make a note of typical adjective-noun collocations.

B Cover the text and complete the adjective-noun collocations. Then check in the text.

1 100% right: _____ opportunity/place/example

2 important and popular for a long time: _____ destination/car/movie

3 unusually good and more than expected: _____ results/talents/ability

4 giving a lot of pleasure: _____ city/village/yard

5 important and easy to notice: _____ progress/improvement/change

6 very good or beautiful: _____, _____, _____ views/location/scenery

C WORD STRESS Put the adjectives from Exercise 2B in the correct group. Then listen and check.

1 Oo

2 oO

3 Ooo

4 oOo

5 oOoo

D Work in pairs. Student A: say an adjective-noun collocation. Student B: give an example from your country and say why you chose it.

A: a delightful town
B: Trapani in Sicily because …

Alternative City Breaks

Tried all the classic destinations? Been to Rome, Paris and Lisbon? Take advantage of our hotel prices to explore lesser known cities such as Ljubljana, the jewel of Slovenia, or the delightful city of Seville.

Sail in the Sun

Spend a week with our instructors off the coast of Australia. Whatever your level, we guarantee you will make significant progress. We also promise breathtaking views from the yachts together with sunshine every day.

Help Out at a Festival

Traveling on a tight budget? Many arts and music festivals depend on volunteers to ensure they run smoothly in return for an entrance ticket. It's the perfect opportunity to plan a summer of partying or traveling around the world.

Top 10 Language Vacations

One-on-one language tutoring in a foreign country can achieve exceptional results. We round up 10 homestay language courses in superb locations ranging from learning Spanish in Guatemala to improving your English in the Lake District.

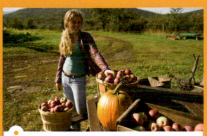

Volunteer on a Farm

If you're prepared to put in a few hours' work a day, you can stay in some stunning locations all over the world for next to nothing. Check out these volunteer placements in farms and small businesses.

LISTENING

3 A Listen to three conversations and match the people with the vacation ads above.

B Listen again to the three conversations and answer the questions.

1 In Conversation 1, what is the man likely to enjoy the most and least about his trip?

2 What does the other man think of the trip?

3 In Conversation 2, what three suggestions does the woman make?

4 Does the official agree to these suggestions?

5 In Conversation 3, what does the woman mention having done on her trip?

6 What does she want to do next summer? What could stop her?

tutoring   tuition

GRAMMAR

FUTURE FORMS

4 A Work in pairs and read the extracts from the conversations in Exercise 3A. Who is speaking?

1 A: When are you off?

  B: The taxi _____ me _____ (pick up) at seven tomorrow.

2 A: Not my idea of a vacation!

  B: Actually, I don't think it _____ (be) too hard.

3 A: I didn't know you were interested in gardening.

  B: I'm not really, but apparently there _____ (be) some building work on the house. They're not sure yet.

4 A: Bear with me a minute. I _____ just _____ (check) the latest information on the computer.

5 A: The plane _____ (arrive) at 10.30 at the earliest.

  B: But that's over three hours' time!

  A: I'm sorry, sir. And it _____ (be) later than that.

6 A: So are you hoping to go back?

  B: I'd love to. Maria's invited me, and I _____ (go back) next summer, but only if I can afford the flight. But I have a plan. I _____ (look for) a new job, with more money.

B Complete the extracts with the verbs in parentheses and one of the future forms from the box below. In several cases, more than one form is possible. In each case which forms cannot be used? Why?

> be going to   be likely to   present continuous   might
> be due to   will ('ll)

C Look at audio script S4.3 on page 167 and check the forms.

D Match rules 1–8 with the examples in Exercise 4A.

<table>
<tr><td rowspan="5">RULES</td><td>Intentions and Plans</td><td>Predictions</td></tr>
<tr><td>1 Use the present continuous for definite arrangements.</td><td>5 Use will ('ll)/won't + infinitive for general predictions often with adverbs such as definitely/possibly.</td></tr>
<tr><td>2 Use be going to/be planning to/be hoping to + infinitive for a general intention.</td><td>6 Use be due to when something is expected or scheduled to happen.</td></tr>
<tr><td>3 Use will ('ll) + infinitive for a decision made at the moment of speaking.</td><td>7 Use be likely/unlikely to for a prediction that is probable.</td></tr>
<tr><td>4 Use might/could + infinitive for an intention that is not certain.</td><td>8 Use might/could + infinitive for a prediction that is not certain.</td></tr>
</table>

5 A CONNECTED SPEECH Work in pairs and say sentences 1–4 out loud. Which pronunciation is more natural, a) or b)?

1 <u>What are you</u> going to do after class?   a) /wɒtɑːjuː/   b) /wɒtəjə/

2 <u>Who will</u> be there?   a) /huːwɪl/   b) /huːl/

3 <u>When will you</u> have time to talk?   a) /wenəljə/   b) /wenwɪljuː/

4 <u>When are you</u> meeting them?   a) /wenɑːjuː/   b) /wenəjə/

B Listen and check (✓) the pronunciation you hear. Then listen and repeat.

▶ page 134 LANGUAGE**BANK**

6 A Underline the best alternative in the sentences.

1 *We're going/We might go* to Venezuela on vacation this year. I booked yesterday.

2 *We'll probably/We're going to* go camping on the weekend, but we're not sure yet.

3 On Saturday, *I'm meeting/I'll meet* some friends for lunch.

4 In the future, *I'm using/I'm going to use* English to get a better job.

5 I think it *is raining/'ll rain* this weekend.

6 There's no class today? In that case, *I'm staying/I'll stay* at home and study.

7 I'm *hoping to/thinking of* travel to China at some point in the future.

8 *I might/I'm unlikely* to live abroad in the future.

9 We are due *getting/to get* our test results by the end of the week.

10 Our national team *definitely won't/won't definitely* win.

B Change five of the sentences so that they are true for you.

C Work in pairs and take turns. Student A: tell your partner your sentences. Student B: ask follow-up questions.

A: I might go to Croatia on vacation this year.

B: Sounds good. Whereabouts in Croatia?

SPEAKING

7 A Work in pairs and take turns. Ask and answer questions and make notes on:

- your partner's interests and hobbies.
- the type of accommodations and transportation he/she prefers on vacation.
- things he/she doesn't like on vacation.
- if he/she wants to spend a lot on a luxury vacation or wants something more reasonably priced or free.

B Work with a new partner. Use your notes to design an alternative vacation for each of your previous partners. Think about the following things:

- name of the alternative vacation
- location
- means of transportation
- length of time
- accomodations
- main activities
- other information (clothing, equipment, climate, health, preparation, items to bring)

C Tell your original partner about the alternative vacation you have designed.

Your vacation is called Patagonia by Horse. It's likely to be cold and rainy, so you should bring ...

VOCABULARY *PLUS*
UNCOUNTABLE AND PLURAL NOUNS

8 A Read the email. Why is Valerie enjoying her vacation?

To: Gabriel14@mailbox.com
....

Hi Gabriel,

Just a quick note from the middle of nowhere . . .

We got off to a bad start when Marianna fell down the (stairs) coming off the plane (no major injuries). Then our baggage got lost, along with all of my clothes and my reading glasses, as well as our toiletries. Things are pretty basic here—you can't buy soap for instance. We're staying on the outskirts of a tiny village, in a yurt, a sort of house made of cloth and wood (see attached picture). In fact, there's no concrete anywhere, only these yurts, except the remains of an old stone hut nearby. So how do we spend our time? Well, we do a little horseback riding during the day, and we play cards in the evening. The locals are incredibly friendly. You know, I've realized that simpler is better, and I really don't want to come home!

Valerie

B Work in pairs and discuss. Would you enjoy this type of vacation? Why/Why not?

C Look at the email again. Underline six uncountable nouns and circle eight nouns which are usually found only in the plural. Use a dictionary if necessary.

9 A Read the quiz below. Find and correct ten mistakes.

B Work in pairs and take turns. Ask and answer the quiz questions.

Travelers' quiz

1 When you travel, do you find informations and accommodations by asking at a tourist office?

2 What sort of facility do you expect hotels to have?

3 Do you ask friends for advices on what to see?

4 How many baggage do you usually carry for a two-week trip?

5 Do you ever carry any sports or camping equipments?

6 Has airport security ever gone through the content of your suitcases?

7 What mean of transportation do you like to travel by most— plane, train or car?

8 On vacation, what's your favorite type of sceneries?

9 Do you like looking at the remain of ancient buildings?

10 Do you always keep someone back home informed of your whereabout?

▶ page 151 **VOCABULARY**BANK

a little   a bit of

4.3)) HOW DOES IT WORK?

F describing procedures
P stress and intonation: mirror questions
V abilities

VOCABULARY
ABILITIES

1 Look at the pictures of game shows and quizzes and discuss the questions.

1 Do you enjoy watching shows like this? Why/Why not?

2 What are the most popular shows of this kind in your country?

3 Which type of show would you be best at? Why? Think about your personality, abilities and skills.

2 A Complete sentences 1–8 with the phrases in the box.

> understand human nature   in great shape
> know-how   inventive   cool-headed
> good with (words/my hands, etc.)   a sharp mind
> a good sense of humor

1 I have the practical knowledge needed. I have the necessary _____.

2 I know a lot about what people are like. I _____.

3 I can make people laugh. I have _____.

4 I don't get nervous under pressure. I'm _____.

5 I'm in good health and condition. I'm _____.

6 I can come up with new things easily. I'm _____.

7 I can think quickly. I have _____.

8 I'm talented or skilled in (various fields). I'm _____.

B Work in pairs and take turns. Student A: close your book. Student B: ask your partner about their abilities using the phrases in Exercise 2A.

Do you have know-how in any particular area?

C What type of game show or quiz would your partner be most suited to?

FUNCTION
DESCRIBING PROCEDURES

3 A Work in pairs and look again at the pictures. What exactly do you think happens in each show?

B Listen to the descriptions of two of the shows. Were your ideas correct?

C Listen again. For each show, make notes on these questions:

1 Is it an individual or team competition?

2 What is the aim?

3 What is the best thing about it?

> Game shows are one of the most popular TV formats in the world. In most countries, there are different types of shows that feature competitions: quiz shows, obstacle courses, talent shows, among others.

4 A Match the sentence halves to make phrases for explaining procedures.

1 The first thing they do

2 The key thing is

3 What happens next is

4 After they've finished, the team

5 Basically, the way it works is that

6 What you have to do is to

7 The point is to

a) that asked the questions decide if it was a lie or not.

b) twelve of the contestants stand on podiums over water.

c) is to tell a personal story.

d) jump over the arm when it gets to you.

e) that the other team grills the storyteller.

f) get around the course in the fastest time.

g) to say something that's so unbelievable that it's hard to imagine it's true.

B Which phrases from Exercise 4A are used:

1 to state the overall goal or aim?

2 to describe details of the procedure?

3 to highlight something particularly important?

▶ page 134 **LANGUAGEBANK**

5 A Complete the description of a game.

My favorite is *The Palate Test*. Basically, the ¹ __way__ it works ² _____ that one of the judges cooks a dish for the contestants. The ³ _____ thing they ⁴ __ is to taste it and try to work out what the ingredients are. ⁵ _____ happens ⁶ _____ is that they get the ingredients and try to make exactly the same dish. After ⁷ _____ done that, the two judges taste the dishes and choose the winner. The ⁸ _____ is to match the original dish as closely as possible. The ⁹ _____ thing is to work out the original ingredients— one thing missing, and the dish won't taste the same as the original.

B Think of a game/sport/show you know. Make notes on the number of players, the procedure and the aim.

C Work in groups and take turns. Student A: describe the game/sport/show but don't say its name.
Other students: guess the game/sport/show.

panelist   panellist

LEARN TO

USE MIRROR QUESTIONS

6 A Look at the extracts. Underline the word A says which B does not understand or does not hear properly.

1 A: There are two teams, with three celebs on each team.
   B: Er … **Three what?**

2 A: So a panelist tells a personal story …
   B: Sorry, **who tells a story?**

3 A: … the other team grills the storyteller.
   B: Um, **they do what?**

4 A: … twelve of the contestants stand on podiums over water …
   B: **They stand where?**

B Which question words or phrases can replace a noun? Which can replace a verb?

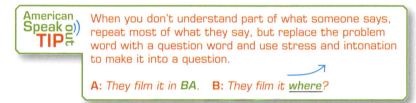

American Speak TIP When you don't understand part of what someone says, repeat most of what they say, but replace the problem word with a question word and use stress and intonation to make it into a question.

A: *They film it in BA.*   **B:** *They film it where?*

C STRESS AND INTONATION: mirror questions Listen to the questions in Exercise 6A and underline the main stress in each one. Then listen and say the questions at the same time, paying attention to the stress and intonation.

D Complete the mirror questions to check the words/phrases in bold. Then work in pairs and practice reading the conversations aloud.

1 A: You have to **sauté the potatoes**.
   B: _____?

2 A: The first player writes **an anagram of the word**.
   B: _____?

3 A: You go **to the webinar site**.
   B: _____?

4 A: Basically, the aim is to beat **the rival team**.
   B: _____?

SPEAKING

7 A Choose one of the situations below to explain to a partner.

- how to make a favorite dish
- one of your favorite websites and how it works
- the procedure for something practical, e.g., how to fold a T-shirt
- how you do one or more of the tasks in your job/studies
- a hobby, game or sport you enjoy
- how your phone or something in the room works

B Make notes on the main points, the procedure and key things to keep in mind.

C Work in pairs or groups and take turns. Student A: describe the procedure to the other students. Other students: ask mirror questions if you don't understand something.

▶ page 151 **VOCABULARY**BANK

DVD PREVIEW

1 Work in pairs and discuss. Which ways of completing the statement do you agree with? Check any new words with your partner or in a dictionary.

Money can't make you happy …
- but job satisfaction can.
- is a silly thing to say! Of course it can!
- but you can't be happy with none. You need a basic standard of living.
- but shopping does make me feel good.
- and neither can possessions or designer goods.
- but a good income gives you status in society.
- but I need enough for my leisure activities.
- but I would still like to be very, very rich!

2 Read the program information and answer the questions.

1 What does the program say about the relationship between money and happiness?

2 What are some of the theories that explain this, do you think?

3 What suggestions do you think the experts will make?

▶ The Happiness Formula

Happiness: everybody wants it, it's such a simple concept, so why is it so hard to get and to hold onto? Scientists have begun to look for answers, and this six-part series explores their findings. In tonight's installment, presenter Mark Easton looks at why consumerism has failed to increase our happiness and some theories and research that scientists use to explain this failure. He talks to experts who give us some ideas of how we might change our lives and become happier people.

DVD VIEW

3 A Watch the DVD. How similar were your answers for Exercise 2 to the ideas in the program?

B Work in pairs and try to complete the suggestions about topics 1–3 from what you remember. Then watch again to check.

1 the rat race: _____

2 the rich: _____

3 vacations: _____

C Check what you remember. Underline the correct words. Then watch the DVD again and check.

1 … does happiness come in a gift-wrapped *box/ package?* And if it doesn't, what on earth are we all doing?

2 … the standard of living has increased *dramatically/ hugely*, and happiness has increased not at all and, in some cases, has *fallen/diminished* slightly.

3 Then your neighbors drive up in two *top-of-the-line/ of the latest* BMWs. And suddenly your Mini just doesn't *do it for you/make you happy* anymore.

4 In our search for happiness, we work longer, *commute/travel* further, to get richer, to buy more. And yet the science of happiness suggests we should *do exactly the opposite/take a different direction*.

5 The next task, though, is to *persuade/convince* us all to change the way we live.

D Work in pairs and discuss the questions.

1 Did you find the program persuasive?

2 Which ideas do you agree with?

3 How might you go about making the changes that are suggested?

top-of-the-line   top-of-the-range

American Speakout a happiness survey

4 A Work in pairs and discuss. Look at the box below. What do most people consider the single most important "ingredient" of happiness? Which one is the least important?

> a life partner   peace and quiet   a nice car
> free time   friendship   sports or exercise   money
> clear goals   good food   music   other (what?)

B Listen to a man answering questions about happiness. Which topics from Exercise 4A does he talk about? Which are the most important for him?

C Listen again and check (✓) the key phrases you hear.

> **KEYPHRASES**
>
> [Could I/Do you mind if I] ask you some questions?
>
> Which would you find the [easiest/hardest/most difficult] to live without?
>
> Do you think that most people feel [money/a nice car/ …] is essential to happiness?
>
> How important are these things to you, on a scale of one to five, five being very important?
>
> Which is [the easiest/hardest] to achieve?
>
> What would you say is missing from your life?

5 A Work in pairs and prepare a short happiness survey using the key phrases.

B Talk to other students and ask your questions. Make notes on their answers.

C Summarize your findings to the class.

writeback tips for being happy

6 A A website asked its readers for tips for being happy. Work in pairs. Read two of the responses and discuss which you agree with.

Don't Read the News or Watch TV

The news is filled with negative images and stories, and each one contributes to your stress levels, making you feel more depressed. Following the news can also take up a great deal of your attention. Instead, use the time to do something you enjoy, such as cooking a meal, calling a friend or going for a walk.

Get a Pet

Studies have shown that people who have a dog or cat are happier and live longer. A pet can give companionship that, for some people, is almost as good as having a partner. Be realistic about what type of pet would be most suitable for you and for your accommodations. Remember, if you choose a dog, you'll have to take it for walks, whereas a cat is more independent.

B Work in pairs. Choose three topics from the box or your own ideas to write tips for being happy. Make notes using the headings below.

> exercise   friends   family   work   money   nutrition

Tip:

Why this helps:

How to do it:

C Write about your tips for the website (120–200 words). Use one paragraph for each tip.

D Read other students' tips. Whose tips would work best for you?

sports   sport

Ⓥ FREE TIME

1 A Add the vowels to complete the verbs.

Don't wait till it's too late!

These days, more than ever, it's important to know how to [1]r_ch_rg_ . But some people don't know how to relax and how important it is to do so before it's too late.

First of all, notice the danger signals. If you get [2]b_rn_d _p easily by the little annoying things people do, it's time for a break. It's time to [3]f_c_s _n yourself! Go and sit by a lake or on top of a hill. Don't think about anything, just [4]ch_ll _ _t. Don't listen to music or anything—music might be another way to [5]sw_tch _ff, but it's an artificial solution. So listen to the wind and the water. You'll feel your energy change; you'll feel yourself [6]_nw_nd.

B Work in pairs and discuss. Which part of the author's advice do you agree with?

Ⓖ PRESENT AND PAST HABITS

2 A Correct the mistake in each sentence. One sentence is correct.

1 When I was younger, I'd often went to clubs with my friends.

2 People are thinking always about the next task; of course, they can't pay attention to now.

3 I didn't used to check my email first thing in the morning, but now I do.

4 I used to get up early these days and go for a jog.

5 Most weekend mornings, I'll staying in bed till noon since I don't have a reason to get up.

6 As a child, I used to play board games a lot with my family.

7 My best friend always sending me texts. It's really annoying.

8 Years ago, I would believe I was always right. Not anymore.

B Work in groups and discuss. Which of the habits above are good and which are bad? Which of them do/did you share?

Ⓥ POSITIVE ADJECTIVES

3 A Rearrange the letters to complete the phrases.

1 a _____ place to relax (rpecetf)

2 a _____ book (aislcsc)

3 a _____ view of a city (rheabnikatgt)

4 a _____ restaurant (ubpesr)

5 someone with a/an _____ talent (lixeeoncpat)

6 a _____ improvement to public transportation (figistnican)

7 a _____ village (flughdielt)

8 _____ scenery (tnninsgu)

B Think of something, somewhere or someone for five of the phrases above. Then work in pairs and compare your ideas.

Ⓖ FUTURE FORMS

4 A Work in groups. Look at the headlines from a future newspaper. Which ones:

1 are likely to happen?

2 will definitely never happen?

3 could happen, but are not likely to?

A ITALIAN BECOMES UNIVERSAL LANGUAGE

B Average Lifespan Increases to 100 Years

C LAST WAR ENDS—WORLD PEACE ACHIEVED

D Gas Supply Exhausted— Price of Bicycles Soars

E INTERNET BANNED WORLDWIDE

B Which three predictions can you confidently make about the world in twenty years' time?

I think the average lifespan is likely to increase because …

5

A Write the conversations in full using different future forms.

1 A: What / you / do / Friday?
   B: I / go / Julia's party / or / maybe / go / movie theater.
   A: I / go / Julia's party / so / I / give you a lift / if / want.
   B: Thanks. / I / phone / if / I / need / a lift.

2 A: How / you / planning / use / your English / in the future?
   B: I / try / get a job / international company. How / you?
   A: I / hoping / get / into / American university / but / I / unlikely / get / my first choice.
   B: I / sure you /.

3 A: Hurry up or we / miss / the bus!
   B: What time / due?
   A: It / due / two minutes. Leave / coat. You definitely / not / need / it today.
   B: But it / rain. / I / take / umbrella just in case.

B Work in pairs. Use the prompts to practice saying the conversations.

Ⓕ DESCRIBING PROCEDURES

6 A Underline the correct alternatives.

The Oyster Card

The best way to get around London is with the Oyster Card. [1]*A/The* point is that you don't need a new ticket every time you travel. [2]*Basic/Basically*, the way [3]*it works/it's working* is that you put credit on your Oyster Card. What [4]*does happen/happens* is that, at the entrance to the subway, you swipe the card over a reader. The next thing [5]*what/that* you do is to swipe it again when you exit, and the cost is taken from your credit. The [6]*goal/main thing* is to add to your credit before it runs out. [7]*After/Afterward* you've left London, you can pass the card on to a friend!

B Write your own tips for getting around a town/city you know using five phrases for describing procedures.

movie theater / subway / add to   cinema / underground / top up

5)) ideas

BRIGHT IDEAS? p56

CONSUMER CRAZY p59

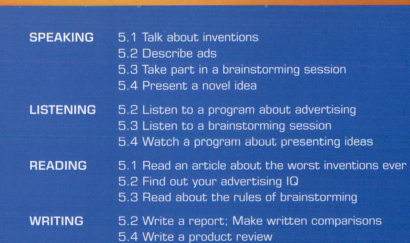

If you could start a business, what would it be?

INTERVIEWS

WHAT DO YOU THINK? p62

GENIUS p64

5.1)) BRIGHT IDEAS?

G articles
P weak forms and linking: *the*
V change; compound nouns

The world's worst inventions

Fast food and speed cameras are among the most hated inventions of all time. But what really gets you annoyed? Thousands of people voted and the results, published by the Discover science magazine, *Focus*, make for a surprising read.

7 FAST FOOD

Americans are the ultimate fast food eaters, spending an estimated $142 billion on it in one year. But it seems our days of carefree consumption of fatty, cholesterol-rich food may be limited, as we gradually wake up to the health risks. In 2002, some obese U.S. teenagers filed a lawsuit against McDonald's, accusing the fast food chain of fattening them up. A judge later threw out the lawsuit.*

*threw out the lawsuit—decided there was no reason for any legal action

6 TELEVISION

Many of us are probably surprised by this one. But it's actually reality TV that's the main offender with 3% of the total vote. Making its debut in 1948 with *Candid Camera* in America, reality television's popularity has risen in the 21st century; in the USA there are two TV channels devoted to it. Why it's so popular is anyone's guess.

5 CIGARETTES

Cancer-causing chemicals in cigarettes mean that men who smoke are twenty-two times, and women twelve times, more likely to develop lung cancer than those who don't. Smoking is also linked to other cancers and heart attacks. Pregnant smokers are at greater risk of giving birth to underweight babies. The World Health Organization says up to 29% of men and 19% of women smoke.

READING

1 Work in pairs and discuss. What do you think are the five worst inventions of all time?

2 A Look at the pictures. Were these the same as your ideas? Write down one reason why each is on the worst inventions list.

B Read the article. How many of your reasons were the same?

C Read the article again. Are the sentences true (T), false (F) or not given (NG)? Where possible, underline the phrase or word that helped you decide.

1 Americans consume the most fast food.

2 *Candid Camera* is famous for being the most popular U.S. reality show ever.

3 Smoking is more dangerous for women than men.

4 Cars being less expensive has meant that more people use cars.

5 Alternative fuels will probably replace gasoline in the near future.

6 Traditional power plants are less expensive to run.

7 Research has shown cell phones are not more dangerous as you get older.

8 People were equally negative about all types of weapons.

D Work in pairs and discuss. Which inventions should not be on the list?

VOCABULARY

CHANGE

3 A Complete the sentences. Then check your ideas in the reading text.

1 Nuclear accidents are rare but can _____ devastating effects.

2 [The cell phone is a gadget] that's _____ communication.

3 Innovations that go bang or _____ bodily harm were the most hated.

B Match 1–8 with a)–h) to make sentences.

1 We are already having to adapt *e*
2 Streaming services have transformed
3 It takes some people time to adjust
4 Hosting a global sports event can do harm
5 Coal and gas mining cause damage to
6 Online hotel reviews have a positive effect
7 E-learning courses have enabled millions
8 The appearance of female journalists in the media has revolutionized

a) their fight for equality.
b) to the change of seasons.
c) on travelers' experiences.
d) to access high-quality education.
e) to extreme weather events.
f) the environment.
g) the way we listen to music.
h) to a country's economy.

C Underline the verb phrases related to change in Exercises 3A and 3B and write them in the correct group according to their meaning. Include the part of speech that follows them.

1 react to change: *adapt to + noun*
2 make a positive change:
3 make a negative change:
4 make a big change:

D Work with other students and discuss. Which issues in Exercise 3B do you agree with or relate to personally? How many views or experiences do you have in common?

revolutionized   revolutionised

4 THE CAR

Car haters out-voted gasoline users. Developed in the late 1880s, the modern car was initially the toy of the wealthy, but falling prices have made it a key part of family life. The motor industry is now booming—over 60 million cars and light trucks are produced globally in a year. But a green fuel is unlikely to take over from gasoline soon, so the car continues to add to our growing carbon footprint.

3 NUCLEAR POWER

Nuclear accidents are rare but can have devastating effects. Nuclear power plants cost more to construct and operate than fossil fuel ones and are supported by large subsidies from the taxpayer. Waste storage is also a concern, but supporters promote nuclear power's green status because it produces no carbon dioxide directly.

2 CELL PHONES

A surprising silver medal for the gadget that's revolutionzed communication. Cells have been available since 1985 and have been widely used since the late 1990s. Almost three-quarters of the population now own one. Despite health scares linking cell phone use to brain tumors, most studies have found there is no increased risk. Maybe it's those annoying ring tones that have put cell phones here.

1 WEAPONS

Bombs, guns, biological weapons, you name it—innovations that go bang or cause bodily harm were the most widely hated in our survey. Nuclear weapons were the worst offender, getting 11% of the total vote. They've only been used twice in wars—in 1945, the USA dropped the bomb "Little Boy" on the Japanese city of Hiroshima, followed three days later by "Fat Man," which fell on Nagasaki.

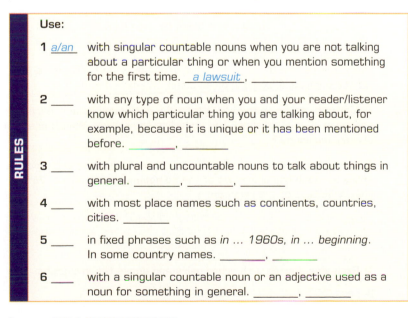

GRAMMAR
ARTICLES

4 A Check what you know. Complete the sentences with *a(n)*, *the* or – (no article). Then check your answers in the article.

1 In 2002, some obese U.S. teenagers filed _____ lawsuit against McDonald's, accusing _____ fast food chain of fattening them up.

2 In _____ America, _____ reality television's popularity has risen in the 21st century; in _____ USA there are two television channels devoted to it.

3 _____ World Health Organization says up to twenty-nine percent of _____ men and nineteen percent of _____ women smoke.

4 Developed in _____ late 1880s, _____ modern car was initially the toy of _____ wealthy, but falling prices have made it _____ key part of family life.

B Complete the rules 1–6 in the table with *a(n)*, *the* or –. Write a word or phrase from the sentences above as an example of each rule.

RULES	Use:	
	1 *a/an*	with singular countable nouns when you are not talking about a particular thing or when you mention something for the first time. _a lawsuit_ , _____
	2 ____	with any type of noun when you and your reader/listener know which particular thing you are talking about, for example, because it is unique or it has been mentioned before. _____, _____
	3 ____	with plural and uncountable nouns to talk about things in general. _____, _____, _____
	4 ____	with most place names such as continents, countries, cities. _____
	5 ____	in fixed phrases such as *in ... 1960s, in ... beginning*. In some country names. _____, _____
	6 ____	with a singular countable noun or an adjective used as a noun for something in general. _____, _____

▶ page 136 **LANGUAGE**BANK

▶ page 136 LANGUAGEBANK

5 A **WEAK FORMS AND LINKING:** *the* Look at sentences 1–3. Circle *the* where it is pronounced /ðə/ and underline it where it is pronounced /ði/. Then listen and check. What is the rule?

1 **The** interesting thing is that many of (the) people who hate it are **the** ones who watch it.

2 **The** automobile has done less well since **the** economic crisis.

3 Those who voted for **the** car mentioned **the** harm it does to **the** environment as **the** biggest problem.

B Listen to the pronunciation. What sound is used to link *the* and the following vowel? Listen and repeat.

the interesting thing

  /_/

the automobile

  /_/

the economic crisis

  /_/

the environment

  /_/

tumors   tumours

6 A Look at the headline. Why do you think people chose the bicycle? Read the article and check your ideas.

It's transformed the way …
It has enabled people to …

A wrist radio

B bottle cap

C pull tab

D jet pack

Bicycle Chosen as Best Invention

[1]_____ humble bicycle has won [2]_____ US national survey of [3]_____ people's favorite inventions.

Listeners to WKGE Radio U. & the *Universe* program were invited to vote in [4]_____ online poll looking at [5]_____ most significant innovations since 1800.

It was [6]_____ easy victory for [7]_____ bicycle, which won more than half of [8]_____ vote. Second came [9]_____ radio, with eight percent of the vote, and the electro-magnetic induction ring—the means to harness electricity—came third.

Despite the fact that you can find them everywhere, [10]_____ computers gained just six percent of the vote, and [11]_____ Internet trailed behind with only four percent of all votes cast. There were more than 4,500 votes cast in total.

People chose the bicycle for its simplicity of design, universal use and because it is [12]_____ ecologically sound means of transportation.

B Complete the text with the correct articles, a(n), the or —.

SPEAKING

7 A Work in pairs and discuss. For each pair of inventions, which one do you think is more important? Why?

1 the oven or the fridge
2 the pen or the pencil
3 fire or the wheel
4 the bicycle or the car
5 the zipper or Velcro
6 sunglasses or sunscreen

B Work with another pair.

Pair 1: say a number from the list, and choose one of the two items. Say why it's more important.

Pair 2: say why the other item is more important.

After two minutes, agree on which pair is the winner.

VOCABULARY *PLUS*
COMPOUND NOUNS

8 A Work in pairs and look at the pictures above. Which inventions do you think were the least successful? Why?

B Complete the encyclopedia entries with the names of the inventions in the pictures.

> The [1]_____ was expected to be a major **breakthrough** for transportation, but, in the **trade-off** between safety and efficiency, safety won. The **outlook** for its future remains poor.
>
> The [2]_____ was expected to revolutionize communication but had a serious **drawback**: it could not be used over a long range, and communication **breakdowns** were common.
>
> As glass bottles were replaced by cans, drink manufacturers needed a replacement for the [3]_____, and the **outcome** was the [4]_____. The **downside** of the move to cans was a huge increase in the amount of trash.

C Match definitions 1—6 with the words in bold above.

1 compromise *trade-off*
2 expectation
3 system failure
4 a discovery
5 disadvantage (2 words)
6 result

9 A Complete the information with examples from the entries in Exercise 8B. More than one answer is sometimes possible.

> Compound nouns are usually made of two words. They can be written as separate words, e.g., *bottle cap*, or a single word, e.g., [1]_____, or they can be written with a hyphen, e.g., [2]_____. The plural is made by adding an *s* to the end, e.g., *breakdowns*. Several common compound nouns are made of a verb + preposition, e.g., [3]_____, or a preposition or adverb + verb, e.g., [4]_____. If you understand both parts of the compound, you can often guess the meaning.

B Listen to seven sentences. Write the compound noun in each sentence in your notebook and underline the stress. Where does the stress usually fall?

C Work in pairs and choose three inventions. Write an encyclopedia entry for each one using two of the compound nouns above. Write *they/it* instead of the invention.

They were an important breakthrough in the 20th century. They give us relatively clean energy, but they also have some serious drawbacks, including the danger of a major breakdown.

D Exchange entries with other pairs and guess the inventions.

▶ page 152 **VOCABULARY**BANK

zipper — zip
pull tab — ring pull

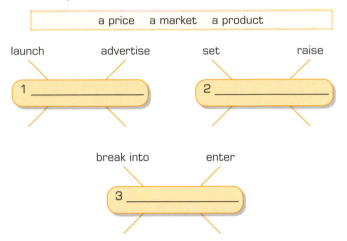

5.2)) CONSUMER CRAZY

G real and hypothetical conditionals
P sentence stress: conditionals
V advertising

LISTENING

1 A Work in pairs and discuss.

1 How do you make decisions about what you buy?
2 How much are you influenced by advertising?
3 What else influences you, e.g., people, brands, the Internet?

B Work in pairs and do the questionnaire. Note your answers.

C Listen to the radio program and check your answers.

D Listen again and answer the questions.

1 What one thing hasn't changed about marketing?
2 What is the effect of giving people choice?
3 In what two ways does pricing affect people?
4 What are the two advantages of a viral video?
5 What four things are important if you want a video to go viral?

E Work in pairs and discuss. Which ideas in the listening surprised you the most?

> Advertising has always been an important part of selling a product, but nowadays the Internet has changed the way products are marketed. Through social media, brands can now reach their desired market segment by using their listed preferences.

VOCABULARY
ADVERTISING COLLOCATIONS

2 A Complete the collocations with nouns from the box.

> a price   a market   a product

launch   advertise   set   raise

    1 _____   2 _____

break into   enter

    3 _____

B Add the verbs from the box to the word webs.

> increase   promote   dominate   reduce
> see a gap in   endorse

C Work in pairs and cover Exercise 2A.

Student A: say a noun from Exercise 2A.
Student B: say two verbs that go with it.
Student A: say another verb.

What's your advertising IQ?

1) There's a coffee shop downtown. It sells a thousand coffees a day. Imagine if a competitor opened another coffee shop right next door. After that, how many coffees would each shop sell?

2) You want to introduce a new product to the market, for example, chocolate. The product you want to compete with sells for two dollars. Should you price your product above or below your competition?

3) Which color (blue, green, orange, red or yellow) is best to use in an ad for:
a) high-tech products?
b) drugs and medical products?
c) energy drinks, games and cars?
d) food?

4) Out of 100 people, how many click off an online video before 10 seconds are up?

5) What times are the best for posting a video if you want it to go viral?

59

GRAMMAR
REAL AND HYPOTHETICAL CONDITIONALS

3 A Check what you know. Which sentences refer to real situations and which to hypothetical ones?

1 Experience shows that, if the price is higher, people think your product is better.

2 If a video goes viral, it will get millions of views.

3 People will click off unless the video is memorable.

4 Your brand name will travel around the world provided the video goes viral.

5 Supposing you wanted to sell a new brand of chocolate, ... what price would you set?

6 If another coffee shop opened next door ..., they'd sell at least a thousand cups each.

B In 1–6 above, circle the verb in the conditional clause and underline the verb in the result clause.

C Which words from the box could replace *provided* and *supposing* in sentences 4 and 5 above?

if	providing	suppose	imagine	let's say
	on condition that		as long as	

D Complete the rules. Use sentences 1–6 and the words in Exercise 3C above to help.

> **RULES**
>
> 1 Use a real conditional when...
> a) something is always or generally true:
> *if* + <u> present simple </u> + _____
> b) something is likely to happen in the future as a result of a possible action/situation:
> *if* + _____ + _____
>
> 2 Use a hypothetical conditional when something is unlikely to happen in the present or future:
> *if* + _____ + _____
>
> 3 As alternatives to *if*, it is possible to use:
> a) _____ to mean *if not*.
> b) _____, _____, _____ or _____
> to mean *if and only if*.
> c) _____, _____, _____ or _____
> to say that something is unlikely.

4 A SENTENCE STRESS: conditionals
Listen and write sentences 1–5 in your notebook.

B Underline the stresses in each sentence. Listen again and check. Then listen and repeat.

> **American Speak TIP**
> In many situations, especially in speaking, we use only one clause of the conditional structure, e.g.,
> A: *Do you think I should take this job?*
> B: *Well, I'd take it. But it's up to you.*

▶ page 136 **LANGUAGEBANK**

5 A Work in pairs and discuss. How could a company promote a new product? Give three ideas.

B Read the text. Does it mention your ideas?

If you wanted to launch a new product for a specific audience and only that audience, what [1]*would/will* you do? The answer is to get a vlogger to endorse your product. A vlog is a video blog, and a vlogger is the person who presents the videos. If your product were, for example, lipstick, you [2]*will/would* choose someone who gives advice on makeup—her followers are your perfect target audience. It works like this: you send the vlogger a sample of your product, and then, [3]*providing/unless* the vlogger likes your product, she [4]*will/would* mention it on one of her vlogs. OK, you pay her of course, but, [5]*as long as/unless* she's a vlogger with a large following (some have over a million), your investment [6]*will/would* be worthwhile and sales should boom. Just be sure that your suppliers have full stocks—if the vlog [7]*goes/went* online in the morning, your lipstick may be sold out by afternoon. Now supposing you [8]*make/made* your own vlog, you would be wasting your time. Even less-well-known vloggers have a bigger audience than you [9]*will/would* be able to get at first. Remember, [10]*unless/as long as* you reach your target audience, your product [11]*won't/will* go anywhere, and neither will you. And that [12]*will/would* be a shame.

C Underline the correct alternatives in the text.

D Work in pairs and discuss. What was new or surprised you in the text above? Do you follow a vlog or a blog?

SPEAKING

6 Work in pairs. Student A: turn to page 159. Student B: turn to page 160.

▶ page 152 **VOCABULARYBANK**

WRITING
A REPORT; LEARN TO MAKE WRITTEN COMPARISONS

7 A What influences you when you buy a new phone or a computer? Write a list of factors.

B Work in groups and compare ideas.

8 A Look at the chart on the right, which shows the results of a survey on why people choose a particular smartphone. What is the most and least important factor for each group of people?

B Read the report written by a student on the survey results and answer the questions.

1 Which factors are mentioned?

2 The student has made one factual error. What is it?

3 How would you complete the main headings?

C Look at the report and write true (T) or false (F).

1 A report has headings for the first and last paragraph only.

2 The first paragraph states the purpose of the report.

3 The last paragraph gives a final comment and sometimes a recommendation.

4 The language is formal.

D Read the report again and complete tasks 1–3.

1 Circle three phrases for saying that two things are the same or nearly the same.

2 Underline four different phrases for talking about differences.

3 Put a box around four linking phrases.

9 A Work in pairs. Look at the chart again and make notes on four points you could make about teenagers.

B Complete the report by continuing the paragraph about teenagers. Write 40–60 words. Include at least four of the phrases in Exercise 8D.

C Read your partner's text. Did you choose the same information to focus on? Did you both use a formal style?

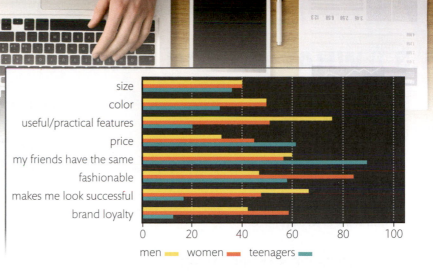

size
color
useful/practical features
price
my friends have the same
fashionable
makes me look successful
brand loyalty

0   20   40   60   80   100

men — women — teenagers —

Introduction
This report looks at the results of a survey of students and employees in our language school in relation to their reasons for buying a particular smartphone.

Men and Women: [1] _____
First of all, comparing the results for men and women, it can be seen that some factors affect both groups more or less equally. For example, there is no difference in how much size and color influence their choice of phone, and the results for "my friends have the same one" show only a slight variation.

Men and Women: [2] _____
There are, however, significant differences in the results for other factors. The usefulness or practicality of a phone's features is far more important for men than for women, as is the price and how much it makes the owner look successful. On the other hand, women place greater importance on brand loyalty.

[3]
_____

The results for teenagers showed an interesting contrast to those for men and women. First of all, ...

Conclusion
It appears that, despite the differences, there are two factors which have relatively high importance for all three groups: what smartphone their friends have, and what is fashionable. Given this, it can be concluded that people are more influenced by social factors than practical ones.

10 Complete the task below.

A group of adults were asked about how they choose a summer vacation destination, giving a score from 1–10 to each of a number of factors to indicate their relative importance. The graph below shows the results. Write a report of 120–180 words summarizing the results, highlighting the similarities and differences.

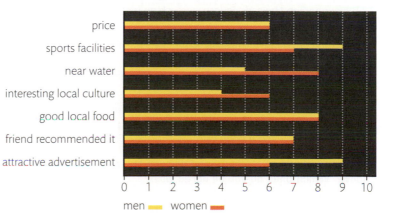

price
sports facilities
near water
interesting local culture
good local food
friend recommended it
attractive advertisement

0   1   2   3   4   5   6   7   8   9   10

men — women —

5.3)) WHAT DO YOU THINK?

F suggesting ideas
P intonation: showing reservations
V collocations with *idea*

VOCABULARY

COLLOCATIONS WITH *IDEA*

1 A Work in pairs and discuss. What do you understand by "brainstorming"? What is it used for?

B Read the article and check your ideas. Which rule do you think is wrong?

THE SIX RULES OF BRAINSTORMING

1 Quantity is more important than quality. Suppose you're looking for a way to get people to walk more. One brilliant idea isn't enough; you want five, ten, dozens to choose from. The goal of the brainstorming stage is to come up with as many ideas as possible.

2 No idea is too predictable or bizarre. In fact, sometimes these ideas can lead to the perfect solution.

3 Zero judgment. Never reject an idea because you think it's awful or unrealistic, because what you need is just ideas, ideas, ideas. The worst thing you can do in a brainstorm is to criticize an idea.

4 Everybody's equal. You have to identify shy people and encourage them. There's no hierarchy; it only works if you work as a team.

5 Have no time limit. People often get their best ideas if they have as much time as they need.

6 Write all the ideas down—each and every one. Have a secretary who records whatever anyone says. You can develop the ideas further after the meeting.

C Read the text again. Underline six verbs and circle six adjectives which collocate with *idea(s)*.

Come up with as many ideas as possible.

D Replace the words in bold with a word from Exercise 1C.

1 I **get** my best ideas when I'm in the shower.

2 Having a four-day work week is a **terrible** idea.

3 I would never **say no to** an idea completely unless I had slept on it.

4 It's OK if people **say** my ideas **are bad**.

5 People in my country are creative but are not so good at **expanding** their ideas into something with business potential.

6 Allowing teenagers to start school at 11 a.m. is a **crazy** but brilliant idea.

7 People's ideas about married life are **not** very **practical**.

8 When educational authorities want to measure progress, they usually suggest more testing. It's an **obvious** idea—and a good one.

E Work with other students and discuss the topics above. Which ones do you all agree with?

How about a competition?   Campaign
Brainstorm
Great idea!
Work as a Team

FUNCTION

SUGGESTING IDEAS

2 A You are going to listen to a brainstorm on ways to encourage people to walk more. Before you listen, work in pairs and write down three ideas.

B Listen to the first part of the brainstorm. Are any of your ideas included? Make notes on the other ideas.

C Check (✓) the three best ideas. Then listen to the second part. Which ideas are rejected and why? Which idea do they choose in the end?

3 A Complete the phrases with two words. Then listen and check your ideas.

1 How _____ feel about this idea?

2 Would _____ the opposite idea of scaring people into it?

3 How does the idea of closing public transportation _____?

4 I think it _____ be great if we _____ get celebrities to promote walking generally.

5 I think we should _____ the feet idea.

6 With that in mind, _____ try combining the two ideas?

7 Let's _____ that.

B Listen again and say the suggestions at the same time, copying the stress and intonation.

C Complete the responses to the suggestions. Then check in audio script S5.7 on page 169.

1 That could be a pr_____.

2 It wouldn't be my first ch_____.

3 It wouldn't wo_____.

4 I think we're on the wrong tr_____ here.

5 That's not a bad i_____ at all.

6 I'm t_____ between the video and the celebrity.

▶ page 136 LANGUAGE BANK

criticize   criticise

Get a TV Doctor or Celebrity

Healthy Eating

Exercise

Raise Money for Charity

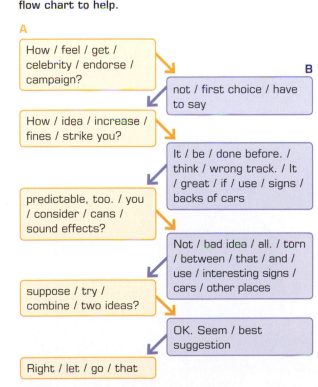

4 A Work in pairs and look at the ideas for getting people to stop littering. Which ones do you think are the best?

> **Getting People to Stop Littering**
> • get a celebrity spokesperson to promote the idea
> • have signs for the backs of cars: "Don't even think of throwing your trash out."
> • increase the fines for littering
> • have trash cans that make a fun sound when something's dropped in them

B Work in pairs and role-play the situation. Use the flow chart to help.

A
> How / feel / get / celebrity / endorse / campaign?

B
> not / first choice / have to say

> How / idea / increase / fines / strike you?

> It / be / done before. / think / wrong track. / It / great / if / use / signs / backs of cars

> predictable, too. / you / consider / cans / sound effects?

> Not / bad idea / all. / torn / between / that / and / use / interesting signs / cars / other places

> suppose / try / combine / two ideas?

> OK. Seem / best suggestion

> Right / let / go / that

C Change roles. Write two key words from each sentence and use these to practice again.

cans   bins

LEARN TO
SHOW RESERVATIONS

5 A Work in pairs. Cross (X) the negative comments and check (✓) the one that is neutral.

1 _____, that could be a problem.
2 _____, it wouldn't be my first choice.
3 _____, I don't think that would be effective.
4 _____, it wouldn't work.
5 _____, at the moment, I'm torn between the video and the celebrity.

B Listen to the phrases and write the missing words/phrases in comments 1–5 above.

C Which two phrases that you wrote signal a very negative comment?

> **American Speak TIP**
> We often use short phrases to prepare someone for a negative comment. Some phrases (*to be honest, actually, I have to say*) can also signal a positive or neutral comment, depending on the intonation and context.

D INTONATION: showing reservations
Listen and pay attention to the intonation. Does each one signal a positive (+) or negative (−) comment?

1 ____   4 ____
2 ____   5 ____
3 ____   6 ____

E Listen again and repeat the phrases. Pay attention to the intonation.

SPEAKING

6 A Work in groups. Choose one of the topics below and brainstorm at least five ideas.

• how to encourage people to learn a foreign language
• how to get people to visit your country or city
• how to improve one aspect of the building you are in
• how to encourage students to do their homework
• how to encourage young people to be more polite to older people
• how to get kids to eat more vegetables

B Look at your list of ideas and choose the best one. Give reasons for rejecting the other ones.

C Tell the class your best idea and briefly describe two other ideas you rejected.

We considered the idea of ... but we decided against it because ...

In the end we chose to ...

DVD PREVIEW

1 A Work in pairs. The name of the program you're going to watch is *Genius*. What do you think the program is about?

B Work in pairs. Read the program description and decide if the statements are true (T) or false (F).

1 Celebrity guests present their ideas.

2 The ideas are generally both funny and clever.

3 The audience decides which ideas are "genius."

▶ Genius

Can an idea be both silly and genius at the same time? That's what the program *Genius* is all about. Each week, members of the public present their wild and crazy ideas for a new product or service. Presenter Dave Gorman and a celebrity guest first interview each inventor to find out all about the invention, and, in the end, the celebrity guest decides whether the idea is truly genius or not. In this program, the suggestions include a new type of choir where each chorus member has very little to sing!

DVD VIEW

2 A Work in pairs. Look at the picture in Exercise 1B, which shows an idea from the program. What do you think the invention is?

B Watch the DVD and check your ideas. What did the show add to Dan's idea to make it work?

C Look at the sentences from the clip and underline the alternative you think they say. Then watch the clip again and check.

1 We invite the people with the *most potential/best ideas* to join us, and it's here that we *decide/work out* once and for all who really is a genius. OK, Stuart, let's see what you *think about/make of* our final idea tonight.

2 Someone playing the keyboard would then be *essentially/basically* playing a choir. I've never seen this done before, and I would really like *to/it*.

3 No, you couldn't have it at home, really, no, not unless … not unless you *by chance/happen to* live with a choir of some sort.

4 We thought it was *worth trying/worthy of investigation*, so …

5 Just hit anything you like *without thinking about it/at random*, a kind of …

6 And, well, I think that you should maybe *give it a go/try it* Laurie …

D Look at these ideas from the program. What are the benefits and drawbacks of each one? Which ideas are just silly? Which is the most "genius" idea?

- Sell socks in threes instead of pairs.
- Set up a "democrobus" bus service where the passengers decide where the bus goes.
- Have genetically engineered three feet-high mini-elephants as pets.
- Send food to houses via pipes for those times when you don't want to cook.

American Speakout a presentation

3 A Work in pairs and look at the invention below. Write three reasons why it might be a good idea.

Yummy Utensils: Knives, Forks and Spoons You Can Eat

B Listen to two students presenting the idea. How many reasons are the same as yours?

C Listen again and check (✓) the key phrases you hear.

> **KEYPHRASES**
>
> We would like to introduce to you an idea that …
>
> What makes our idea special is that it's not just … but it's also …
>
> We envision this product being sold [in supermarkets/on TV/via the Internet/ …]
>
> We think that … will be a hit with [single people/families/…] in particular.
>
> We differentiate ourselves from the competition by …
>
> In the future, we are planning to develop a [business/lightweight/diet/…] version.

4 A Work in pairs. Student A: turn to page 159. Student B: turn to page 161. Either choose one of the business ideas from your lists or think of an idea of your own to present to your classmates.

B Prepare your presentation. Discuss questions 1–3 below and make notes.

1 What is the product called?

2 Why is it such a good idea?

3 Where will it be sold?

C Join another pair and take turns. Pair A: practice your presentation. Pair B: give advice on improving the presentation.

D Present your product to the class and listen to the other presentations. Vote on the best one.

writeback a product review

★★★★★ EXCEPTIONAL   ★ VERY POOR

I'm now on my tenth pack of Yummy Utensils and have been delighted with their success. My four-year-old is a very picky eater, but now, even if he eats only part of his meal, he still insists on eating his knife, fork and spoon. What I like most is that they're not only good value for money, but they're also nutritious. The only downside is that Sergio has started to try and eat his real knife and fork at preschool! Highly recommended.

As a dedicated "green" supporter, I bought some Yummy Utensils after seeing them advertised in an eco-magazine. What a waste of money. They are supposed to be strong enough to cut vegetables. Mine broke on the first carrot, and the spoon half-melted when I was stirring sugar into my coffee. But the thing I really hated about them was the taste. They tasted like cardboard. I was very disappointed. Overpriced, over-hyped and not worth the money. Don't bother.

5 A Read the product reviews above. How many stars do you think each writer gave the product?

B Which of the following features occur in the reviews?

a) information about where the person first heard about the product

b) the things the person most liked or hated

c) a comparison of this product with other similar products

d) examples of the reviewer's experience using the product

e) a final short comment

C Write a review of either the product you have just heard about OR a product you have recently bought. Use the reviews above to help you with the language.

D Look at other students' reviews. How many stars do you think each writer has given the product?

envision / preschool   envisage / nursery school

V CHANGE

1 A Rewrite sentences 1–4 using the correct form of one of the words/phrases in the box.

> ~~adjust~~   revolutionize
> cause damage
> have a positive effect on

adjust — 1 People with many talents can (adapt) to it well and tend to find a new job quickly.

2 It's done harm to family relationships.

3 It has enabled people in the developing world to have a better quality of life.

4 It completely transformed the way people think about war.

B Work in pairs and discuss. What could "it" be in each sentence above?

G ARTICLES

2 A Complete the quiz questions with *a/an*, *the* or no article (—).

Fun & Games

1 ¹_____ game of ²_____ BASKETBALL was invented by:

(a) ³_____ teacher in America.
(b) ⁴_____ Chinese general Zhao Tuo.
(c) ⁵_____ prisoners of war in Korea.

2 Originally, basketball was played by throwing … into a fruit basket.

(a) ⁶_____ first peach of the season
(b) ⁷_____ soccer ball
(c) ⁸_____ apples

3 WINDSURFING was invented by:

(a) ⁹_____ Ukrainian sailor.
(b) ¹⁰_____ American.
(c) ¹¹_____ head of ¹²_____ Australian Imperial Navy.

4 It was developed:

(a) in ¹³_____ 14 BC.
(b) during ¹⁴_____ First World War.
(c) in ¹⁵_____ 1960s.

5 SCRABBLE® was developed by a former architect who was:

(a) ¹⁶_____ unemployed.
(b) ¹⁷_____ designer of the Eiffel Tower.
(c) ¹⁸_____ blind.

B Work in pairs and answer the quiz questions. Then check your answers on page 160.

V ADVERTISING

3 A Add vowels to complete the words.

> Seven key questions when you l_ _nch a new version of a product:
>
> **1** Is the market for the product difficult to br_ _k into?
>
> **2** Is there a g_p in the market?
>
> **3** How would you s_t the price?
>
> **4** If sales are poor, will you _ncr_ _s_ or r_d_c_ the price?
>
> **5** What are the best ways to pr_m_t_ the product?
>
> **6** Where is the best place to _dv_rt_s_ the product?
>
> **7** What famous person could best _nd_rs_ the product?

B Work in pairs. Choose a product and discuss the questions above.

G CONDITIONALS

4 A Complete B's answers in two different ways. Use conditional structures.

1 A: Have you decided whether to get that car?

B: I'm not sure yet. But it _____ save money on fuel.

B: Well, it _____ save money on fuel, so yes.

2 A: Should we go ahead with the ad?

B: I _____ wait a little longer. But it's up to you.

B: I _____ wait a little longer. It's my decision.

3 A: I'm not sure which color to choose.

B: Let's ask Anne. What do you think she _____ say?

B: A shame Anne's not here. What _____ she say?

4 A: Can we have the meeting away from the office?

B: Yes, provided we _____ (be) back by four.

B: No, because we _____ (not be) back by four.

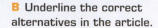

Should 🇺🇸 Shall

B Underline the correct alternatives in the article.

Seducing Shoppers

¹*Provided/Supposing* you wanted to sell a product in a store; exactly where ²*would/do* you place it to promote it best? Research shows that if there ³*are/would be* two similar products, identical in quality, but different in price, the store ⁴*will put/put* the more expensive one on the shelf you see first and put the cheaper one around the corner. That way, ⁵*provided/imagine* you want to buy the product, you ⁶*put/will put* the expensive one in your basket; and then, even if you ⁷*saw/would see* the cheaper one later, you probably ⁸*wouldn't/won't* go to the trouble of swapping it. Similarly, if a product was on the bottom shelf, consumers ⁹*are/would be* less likely to buy it (they're often too lazy to bend over ¹⁰*unless/if* they're really short).

C Work in pairs and discuss. Which of the ideas in the article above do you think are true?

F SUGGESTING IDEAS

5 A Find and correct ten mistakes in the students' conversation.

A: It's be great if we could have the class party at a four-star hotel.

B: That wouldn't be my last choice. How much do you feel about the school cafeteria?

C: The school cafeteria? To be honest, wouldn't work. What does Pizza Rizza strike you?

B: That's no a bad idea at all.

A: Actually, I think we're on the wrong truck here. I think we should go for somewhere nicer.

B: OK. Supposed we try the Four Seasons or the Hilton?

A: I'm tearing between the two, but the Four Seasons is closer.

C: OK. Let go with that.

B Cover the conversation and try to memorize the phrases.

C Work in groups and plan a party for your class.

1 Brainstorm the place, kind of food, activities/games, live music and dress. Remember the rules of brainstorming—just say ideas and write them down but don't criticize.

2 Discuss the different ideas and come to an agreement for each.

6 age

SPEAKING   6.1 Discuss different ages and generations
6.2 Talk about your future
6.3 Discuss the right age for different things
6.4 Hold a debate

LISTENING   6.2 Listen to a program about letters to your future self
6.3 Listen to a call-in radio show about life's milestones
6.4 Watch a program about living longer

READING   6.1 Read an article about early and late successes
6.2 Read emails making arrangements

WRITING   6.2 Write an informal email; Focus on informal style
6.4 Write a forum comment

What was the best period of your life?

INTERVIEWS

call-in radio show   phone-in show

G modal verbs and related phrases
P connected speech: elision
V age; word-building: prefixes

SPEAKING

1 Work in pairs and discuss. What are the advantages and disadvantages of being the ages in the box?

| 10 | 15 | 20 | 30 | 45 | 65 |

VOCABULARY

AGE

2 A Match the words/phrases in bold in questions 1–8 with meanings a)–h).

1 If someone looks young **for their age**, is that good? *f*

2 When is someone **in their prime**?

3 If you tell a twenty-five-year-old person, "**Act your age!**" what kind of thing might they be doing?

4 At what age do people generally **come of age** in your country: seventeen, eighteen, twenty-one?

5 Are eighteen-year-olds too **immature** for college?

6 At what age does a person have the **maturity** to make a decision about marriage or a career?

7 At what age is a person **elderly**?

8 Does **age discrimination** affect people looking for jobs in your country?

a) behave in a more adult way

b) "old" (said in a more polite way)

c) in the best period of their life

d) treating people unfairly based on age

e) reach the age when legally an adult

f) in relation to how old they are

g) wisdom that comes with age

h) childish

B Choose three questions that interest you from Exercise 2A and discuss them in pairs.

READING

3 A Work in pairs and discuss. What do you think it means to "peak early" or to be a "late bloomer"? Read the first two paragraphs of the article and check.

B Work in pairs and discuss the questions. Make notes on your ideas.

1 In the photographs, who do you think are late bloomers? Who peaked early?

2 In which of these fields is someone more likely to peak early: acting, singing, writing, sports, business?

3 One author says that sometimes a late bloomer seems to be a failure. Why do you think this is?

4 How do these change as one gets older: freedom, obligation, expectations? What is an example of each?

C Read the article and check your ideas.

EARLY PEAKERS AND LATE BLOOMERS: WHO HAS IT WORSE?

We're all familiar with the story of the movie star or singer who peaks early, finds fame at a young age and then seems to disappear. Or the novelist whose brilliant debut at age 22 is followed by works of increasing **mediocrity**. Sports are particularly **biased** toward youth; how many teenagers have a moment of glory at the Olympics only to fade away in their 20s when they are no longer able to compete?

And then there are the late bloomers who discover their talent relatively late in life: the actress who gets her first big part in her 40s, the office clerk who **pens** a bestseller at 50, and the businessman who starts a multi-million dollar **enterprise** in his 60s. Late bloomers might spend decades struggling to find their passion or be noticed, and that can be painful. As author Malcolm Gladwell wrote, "On the road to great achievement, the late bloomer will resemble a failure."

Wherever in the world you are born, society sets out a timeline for your life. You start out confronted by rules and restrictions: you must not cross against a red light; don't talk back to the teacher. There are **milestones** of freedom: the age at which your mother says you can stay out late, the point at which you're allowed to take public transportation alone or to drive a car. Later, the fruits of your work give you other freedoms, for example, you don't have to worry about money for a nice vacation or a meal at a fancy restaurant. And there are the **ever-shifting** sands of obligation and expectations. A teenager complains because her parents make her do her homework and don't let her stay out after 10 o'clock. The 30-year-old suffers because he's supposed to be earning more than his **peers**, but he isn't; he has to work all hours but can't find himself in his profession, and meanwhile feels he should give everyone the impression that he's successful, even if he isn't.

Early peakers and late bloomers have all made a name for themselves because in some way they managed to break out of the timeline that society had set for them. Perhaps we can all take a lesson from them and break out of our own timelines.

Director Ang Lee had his first global breakthrough at the age of 41 with *Sense and Sensibility* in 1995. Since then, with movies like *Brokeback Mountain* and *Life of Pi*, he has become a worldwide success.

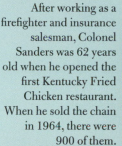

After working as a firefighter and insurance salesman, Colonel Sanders was 62 years old when he opened the first Kentucky Fried Chicken restaurant. When he sold the chain in 1964, there were 900 of them.

Wang Yani is a Chinese child prodigy whose work was first exhibited in China when she was four and later became a stamp. Her work now appears in galleries internationally.

It was in 1605, after a career as a soldier and then a tax collector, that Cervantes' novel *Don Quixote* was published, destined to become one of the greatest novels of all time. He was 58.

Romanian Nadia Comăneci, winner of three Olympic gold medals, was the first female gymnast to be awarded a perfect score of 10 in an Olympic gymnastic event. She was only 14. She retired at the age of 23.

As a child, Jocelyn Lavin was a natural mathematician and a gifted oboe and piano player. She later discovered she lacked the discipline for college work and eventually became a teacher.

4 A Work in pairs. Guess the meanings of the words in bold in the text.

B Check your ideas. Match meanings 1—7 with the words in bold.

1 a company or business
2 constantly changing
3 important events in the development of something
4 average quality
5 supporting one group in an unfair way
6 writes
7 people who are the same age or have the same job as you

C Work in pairs and discuss.

• What timeline and milestones do you think society sets out for you?
• Do you feel pressured by this, or is it not a problem for you?

I think I'll be expected to … People tend to … It bothers me that …

GRAMMAR
MODAL VERBS AND RELATED PHRASES

5 A Check what you know. Complete the table with the modal and semi-modal verbs underlined in sentences 1—6 below.

1 You <u>must not</u> cross against a red light.
2 Your mother says you <u>can</u> stay out late.
3 You <u>don't have to</u> worry about money for a nice vacation.
4 He <u>has to</u> work all hours.
5 He <u>can't</u> find himself in his profession.
6 He feels he <u>should</u> give everyone the impression that he's successful.

RULES				
	Obligation (strong)	—————	Prohibition	*must not*
	Obligation (weak)	——————	Permission	——————
	Lack of Obligation	——————	Ability/Lack of Ability	——————

B Look at the phrases in bold and think about their meanings. Which category in the table are they closest to?

1 They **are** no longer **able to** compete.
2 There are milestones of freedom: … the point when you **are allowed to** take public transportation alone …
3 A teenager complains because her parents **make her do** her homework and don't **let her stay** out after 10 o'clock.
4 The 30-year-old suffers because he**'s supposed to** be earning more than his peers …
5 … they **managed to** break out of the timeline that society had set for them.

6 A Listen and write the sentences you hear.

B **CONNECTED SPEECH: elision** Cross out a *t* or a *d* that isn't pronounced at the end of a word in each sentence. Then listen again and repeat.

We must go home now.

▶ page 138 **LANGUAGEBANK**

7 A Complete the sentences with a modal verb or related phrase in the correct form. In some cases there is more than one possibility.

1 Parents ____should____ be strict with babies, or they _____ to control them later.

2 The worst thing about school was that I _____ do what I wanted to.

3 When I was a child, my parents often _____ me stay over at my friends' houses.

4 When I was younger, I _____ help clean our apartment, but I never did.

5 The best thing about being an adult is that no one can _____ you do something if you don't want to.

6 And the worst thing is that you just _____ to get the apartment neat, and then the family messes it up again!

7 When I am older, I _____ afford an apartment downtown.

8 A good thing about being retired is that you _____ work anymore.

B Choose four sentences and change them to give your opinion. Then discuss with a partner.

SPEAKING

8 A Make notes on your answers to questions 1–3.

1 Are most of the people you spend time with your age or a different age? Why?

2 How is your generation different from older or younger ones? What sort of misunderstandings or conflicts can this cause?

3 Is the "generation gap" greater or smaller than it used to be? Why?

B Work in groups and discuss the questions.

VOCABULARY *PLUS*
WORD-BUILDING: PREFIXES

9 A Check what you know. Add a negative prefix to the words in bold to make them negative. Use *dis-, in-, il-, im-, ir-, mis-* or *un-*.

1 You have __un__realistic expectations of life.

2 Your behavior is ____predictable and sometimes ____logical.

3 You are ____satisfied with how your life has turned out.

4 You aren't very eager about ____familiar situations.

5 You are ____patient with people who don't understand technology.

6 You think you are ____mortal.

7 You are ____willing to change your mind about your opinions.

8 You ____behave to get people's attention.

9 You sometimes feel ____secure in groups and ____interpret what people say to you.

10 How much money you have is ____relevant. You're just happy not to be ____healthy.

B Listen and check your answers to Exercise 9A. Then listen and repeat. Are the prefixes stressed or unstressed?

C Work in pairs and discuss. Are any of the sentences above truer for younger people and/or older people? Give examples to support your ideas

> **American Speak TIP** A dictionary can help you find which negative prefix a word takes. Look at this listing below for the adjective *mature*. How is the negative shown? How does your dictionary show negative prefixes?

> **M** **mature** *adj* **1** behaving in a reasonable way like an adult [≠ immature] *She's very mature for her age.*

from Longman Active Study Dictionary

10 A Answer each pair of questions with words that share the same prefix. Use the prefixes in the box and the words in bold to help.

over-	post-	pre-	under-

What do you call:

1 a) the generation who were born before the **war**? (adj)

   b) the period of **history** before written records? (adj)

2 a) the generation born after the **war**? (adj)

   b) a college program taken after you **graduate** from your initial program? (adj)

3 a) the **time** you spend working in your job in addition to your normal working hours? (n)

   b) people who are forced to **work** too much or too hard? (adj)

4 a) someone who isn't the minimum **age** to see an X-certificate movie? (adj)

   b) someone who doesn't have enough **qualifications** to get a job? (adj)

B Work with other students and brainstorm other words that begin with these four prefixes. Which group came up with the longest list?

▶ page 153 **VOCABULARY**BANK

eager about keen on

6.2)) FUTURE ME

G future perfect and continuous
P weak forms: auxiliaries
V optimism/pessimism

LISTENING

1 A Over the next four years, what are you definitely going to do, what do you think you might do and what do you hope you'll do?

B Work in pairs and compare your ideas. Do you have any plans or hopes in common?

2 Read the program information below and answer the questions.

1 How does the website work?

2 Do you think it would be uplifting or depressing to get a letter from your younger self?

Letters to Myself

The idea is simple:

write a letter to yourself, and futureme.org will keep it and send it back to you at a point in the future–you pick the date. What will you discover, looking back? In this BBC radio program, people read aloud and comment on their letters.

3 A Listen to Laura reading a letter she wrote to herself four years ago, when she was sixteen. Answer the questions.

1 Which topics did she write about?

2 Is the letter down-to-earth or romantic? Is it generally optimistic or pessimistic?

B Listen again and correct the mistakes.

1 I envision myself at Oxford University, ... sitting under a tree ... and watching something floaty.

2 I know, I'm practical. I hope that hasn't changed.

3 I hope I'll have married someone.

4 ... I think I'll have three children with long brown hair and blue eyes.

5 ... I have to write everything I can down, but I'm running out of time.

6 Don't worry too much, and be happy with who you are.

C Listen to the second part of the program and underline the two correct alternatives.

1 Laura now sees her sixteen-year-old self as *shallow/really mature/unrealistic*.

2 She feels *very happy/ecstatic/amazed* at the way her life has turned out.

GRAMMAR
FUTURE PERFECT AND CONTINUOUS

4 A Look at sentences a) and b) from Laura's letter. Which one talks about:

1 things that will be completed before the moment she opens the letter?

2 things that will be in progress around the moment that she opens the letter?

a) I'll have changed so much.

b) I bet when I get this, it'll be raining.

B Complete the rules.

> **RULES**
>
> 1 To talk about something that will finish before a specific time in the future, use *will* + _____ + _____.
>
> 2 To talk about something that will be in progress at or around a specific time in the future, use *will* + _____ + _____.

C Underline the correct alternative in the sentences and explain your reason.

1 In ten years' time, I expect *I'll be owning/I'll own* an apartment.

2 I'll have finished the report *by/until* 12 and certainly no later than that.

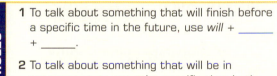

D **WEAK FORMS: auxiliaries** Listen and write the sentences. Underline examples of the future perfect and future continuous. Circle the auxiliary verbs.

E Listen again and say the sentences at the same time as the speaker.

▶ page 138 LANGUAGEBANK

5 A Look back at the rules on page 71 and complete the questions with the correct form of the future perfect, future continuous or the future with *will*.

1 By the end of the day, do you think _____ (you/receive) more than fifty emails?

2 At 9 p.m. tonight, _____ (you/watch) TV? If so, what?

3 Do you think _____ (you/fall) asleep by midnight tonight?

4 This time next year, _____ (you/still/study) English, and _____ (you/pass) any English exams?

5 Do you expect _____ (you/still/like) the same kind of music a few years from now?

6 In twenty years' time, _____ (you/live) in the same town, do you think?

B Work in pairs and discuss the questions in Exercise 5A. Use words and phrases from the box.

> Possibly   Yes, definitely
> That's pretty likely   I doubt it
> No, definitely not   Perhaps
> I expect so   I don't suppose so

SPEAKING

6 A Work alone and think about your plans for ten years' time. Make notes on three of the areas below.

studies or work   *achievements*

travel   **English**

relationships and/or family

home   *activities/experiences*

B Work with a partner and discuss your ideas.

A: What would you say about "achievements"?

B: Well, in ten years' time, I hope I'll have become fluent in English. I'd like to be working abroad somewhere, maybe Australia. How about you?

C Work in pairs. Would you say you are generally an optimistic, "glass half full," type of person or a pessimistic, "glass half empty," one? Give examples.

Glass half full or half empty?

1 How do you feel about your English?
   a) It's going well.
   b) You **have your ups and downs**.
   c) You're stuck and **going nowhere**.

2 This weekend, you're going to a party with lots of people you don't know. How do you feel?
   a) You're **looking forward to** it.
   b) You **have mixed feelings about** it.
   c) It's the last thing you feel like doing.

3 Your partner calls you and asks to meet as soon as possible because they have something important to tell you. What do you think?
   a) You **look on the bright side**; the news will be good.
   b) It'll just be news, nothing particularly positive or negative.
   c) You're **dreading** it; you're sure they want to break up with you.

4 When you think about the next year or two in your life, how do you feel?
   a) really **upbeat** about it
   b) cautiously hopeful
   c) really pessimistic about the prospects

5 How does the future in general make you feel?
   a) It fills you with great hope.
   b) It has its fair share of positive and negative prospects.
   c) It **fills you with despair**.

VOCABULARY
OPTIMISM/PESSIMISM

7 A Work in pairs and read the quiz. Guess the meaning of the words/phrases in bold.

B Match the phrases in bold in the quiz with the meanings below. Put the phrase in the infinitive.

1 feel both positive *and* negative about something

2 think about a future event and feel good about it

3 sometimes go well and sometimes go badly

4 make no progress

5 be really worried and fearful about something

6 makes you feel extremely negative

7 optimistic

8 see things in a positive way

C Work in pairs and complete the quiz questions. Then read the key on page 159 and work out your partner's score. Do you think the analysis is accurate?

▶ page 153 **VOCABULARY**BANK

WRITING

AN INFORMAL EMAIL; LEARN TO FOCUS ON INFORMAL STYLE

8 A Imagine you could go anywhere and do anything you like on vacation next summer. Complete the sentence below, and then compare with other students. Did any of you have the same idea?

In the middle of next summer, I'd like to be _____-ing (activity) and _____-ing (activity) in _____ (place).

B Read the email about someone's suggestion for next summer and the email reply from her friend. Does Corinna answer Louise's questions? What do you notice about the style?

Hi Corinna!

I've just heard there's an Irish dance and music festival in Dublin in July. [1]How about coming over to visit me, and we can go to it together?

[2]Tickets are already on sale, and I'll get us some as soon as I know you're coming for sure. [3]Check out the festival website (I'll paste the address below) and let me know which concerts you'd like to see.

[4]My cousin has a apartment in Dublin—how about if we stay there? His family will have left for their summer vacation, so it'll be just us staying there. Is there anything else you'd like to do in or around Dublin while you're over here?

[5]Let me know how many days you can stay. Can't wait to see you!

Louise

Dear Louise,

[6]I was **delighted to receive** your email **regarding** the music festival, and **I would like to accept the invitation**. I have always wanted to visit Dublin, and this seems like **the perfect occasion to do so**.

You asked me about concert choices, but I didn't get the link. [7]**I would be most grateful** if you could send it again. [8]**My preference would be for** dance rather than music. **I will inform you** of my specific choices once I see the program.

Your cousin's apartment sounds excellent. [9]**I would be interested to know** if it is downtown or on the outskirts.

[10]I'll be able to stay for three days, and I will reserve a flight once I know the concert dates. **I look forward to receiving further information** about it all.

Yours sincerely,

Corinna

C Read the emails again and write the number of the sentence next to the functions below. One sentence has two functions.

a) acknowledge email
b) request information (x4)
c) invite someone   *1*
d) accept an invitation
e) make a suggestion
f) providing information (x3)

9 A Read Corinna's reply again. Work in pairs and discuss how to replace the formal phrases in bold with informal ones.

B Complete the table with the phrases in bold.

Informal	Formal
1 a great time for it	*the perfect occasion to do so*
2 about	
3 Can't wait to hear more	
4 Do you know	
5 happy to get	
6 I'd love to come	
7 I'd rather see	
8 All the best,	
9 I'll let you know	
10 It'd be great	

C Rewrite Corinna's reply in an informal style.

10 A Read the email extract from a friend. Write an informal reply accepting the invitation in 120–180 words.

I'm glad to hear that you're coming next month. This'll be only your second time in this city, won't it?

We could spend Wednesday walking in the hills nearby or perhaps just drive out and look at the scenery. Then would you like to go to the theater in the evening?

On Thursday, some friends of mine are having a party. We could go to that or, if you like, just stay in and watch a DVD or walk around town.

Let me know what you prefer. Can't wait to see you!

B Swap your reply with your partner. Check each other's work using the table in Exercise 9B.

C Read other students' replies. Who sounds the most excited about their visit?

VOCABULARY
COLLOCATIONS

1 A Underline the correct alternative.

1 *making/doing* a part-time job
2 *owning/belonging* a smartphone
3 *wearing/putting* make-up
4 *keeping/staying* home alone
5 *getting/making* your ears pierced
6 *going/using* social networking sites
7 *having/signing up* your own credit card
8 *driving/riding* a scooter
9 *babysitting/taking care* for a toddler
10 *journeying/traveling* solo
11 *staying/keeping* up as late as you want
12 *being in charge/running* your own business

B Work in pairs. Which of the activities above can you see in the pictures?

C Work in pairs and discuss. What age is appropriate for someone to do activities 1—12?

D Tell the class anything you disagreed about.

FUNCTION
PERSUADING

2 A Listen to a radio call-in show and check (✓) the three activities in Exercise 1A that the people discuss.

B Listen again and make notes about the callers' problems and the D.J.'s opinions. Then check with a partner.

Problem	D.J.'s Opinion

C Work in pairs and discuss. What's your opinion about each of the situations from the call-in show?

3 A Match examples 1—4 with meanings a)—d). Which two are often used to persuade people to agree with you?

1 Is it better to talk it over with her?
2 It's better to talk it over with her.
3 Surely it's better to talk it over with her.
4 Isn't it better to talk it over with her?

a) an opinion
b) a genuine question—the listener can answer *yes* or *no*
c) an opinion where the speaker is inviting the listener to agree with them
d) a strong opinion where the speaker thinks the listener *should* agree with them

B Complete the sentences from the call-in show.

1 _____ up to the parents to set guidelines. (Surely/it/be)
2 _____ it better to talk it over with her? (not/be)
3 _____ just normal nowadays. (Surely/that/be)
4 _____ it's just a stage he's going through? (you/not/think)
5 _____ to be like her friends? (she/simply/not/want)

C Listen and check.

D INTONATION: persuading Listen again and repeat. Copy the intonation pattern.

▶ page 138 LANGUAGEBANK

LEARN TO
CLARIFY IDEAS

5 A Read the extract from the radio call-in show. Find two phrases where people ask for clarification of an idea.

DJ: So basically you think she's too young for a phone.

Ed: Yeah, yeah, that's right.

DJ: Surely it's up to the parents to set guidelines.

Ed: So what you're saying is I should give her some rules?

B Read audio script S6.6 on page 170 and find two other phrases to ask for clarification.

> **American Speak TIP** Clarify an idea by repeating something in your own words (paraphrasing). This also "buys" time while you think about how to react.

C Complete the sentences to paraphrase 1—4.

1 It's unfair. Rich kids don't have to work.
So what you're saying is all kids should __*have to work*__.

2 Elderly people don't get enough respect from younger people.
So, in other words, younger people should _____.

3 Why is it that students who cheat on tests often don't get punished?
So basically you think students who cheat should _____.

4 It makes me angry that men are paid more than women.
So what you mean is women should _____.

D Work in pairs. Student A: read out a statement from Exercise 5C. Student B: cover the exercise and clarify the idea.

6 A Complete statements 1—4 with your own ideas.

1 The biggest problem with young people today is …

2 It's not fair that …

3 I think it was a mistake to …

4 One thing I learned from my parents is …

B Work in pairs and swap your sentences. Write a paraphrase of your partner's sentences.

C Work in pairs. Student A: read out your idea. Student B: clarify the idea. Then practice again without looking.

A: The biggest problem with young people today is they can't concentrate.

B: So, what you're saying is they can't focus on just one thing?

A: That's right.

SPEAKING

7 A Work in pairs. For each statement, think of two points that support the opinion and two points against it.

- Thirteen is too young to join a social networking site.
- A sixteen-year-old shouldn't be allowed to get a tattoo.
- An eighteen-year-old who has just passed their driving test isn't ready to drive the family car alone.

B Student A: turn to page 159. Student B: turn to page 160. Student C: turn to page 162.

---

4 A Work in pairs. Do you know anyone who has had a "gap year" either before they went to college or between college and work? What do you think of the idea?

B Work in pairs and role-play the situation. Use the flow chart to help.

Student A

> not / you / think / everyone / a gap year?

Student B

> I / not / agree. / not / be / better / start / work as soon as possible?

> Yes / but / not / gap year / give people / different kind of experience?

> gap year / just / long vacation. Surely / year / work / more useful?

> I / disagree. / year off / give / people / chance / think about / career.

> not / most 22-year-olds / decide / by that age?

> Not always. People / often / end up / job they hate. / Anyway, surely / worth trying?

> I / still / not convinced. / I think / a waste of time.

> Gap years or years off have become so popular in the last few years that many colleges have included them in their curriculums. Some organizations such as AmeriCorps offer students help with tuition in exchange for taking gap years where they do volunteer work.

DVD PREVIEW

1 Work in pairs and discuss the questions.

   1 Who is the oldest person you know or have known?

   2 What do you think they would say is the secret to a long life?

2 A Match 1–8 with a)–h) to make collocations.

1	keep	**a)**	some gentle exercise
2	follow	**b)**	into monotonous routines
3	do	**c)**	a sensible diet
4	don't fall	**d)**	mentally active
5	avoid	**e)**	a positive attitude
6	stay	**f)**	healthy
7	maintain	**g)**	depressed
8	don't become	**h)**	stress

B Work in pairs and discuss. Which two factors do you think are the most important for a long life?

3 Read the program information. Which three places are mentioned and what do they have in common?

▶ Horizon: How to Live to 101

The quest to live longer has been one of humanity's oldest dreams, but, while scientists have been searching, a few isolated communities have stumbled across the answer. On the remote Japanese island of Okinawa, in the California town of Loma Linda and in the mountains of Sardinia, people live longer than anywhere else on earth.

A group of scientists who study the science of longevity have dedicated their lives to trying to uncover the secrets of these unique communities. Tonight's documentary travels to Okinawa to meet some of its long-living and remarkably healthy inhabitants.

DVD VIEW

4 A Watch the DVD. What are the two main reasons mentioned for why Okinawans live such long lives?

B Work in pairs. What does the underlined word refer to? Watch again and check your ideas.

   1 It's four times higher than in Britain and America.

   2 The Okinawans don't really think about this.

   3 Bradley and Craig think that one of the main reasons for the Okinawans' longevity can be found here.

   4 They contain antioxidants, which protect against cell damage.

   5 The Okinawans only fill it to 80 percent of its capacity.

   6 If you do this, you may die sooner than you might if you didn't do it.

C Watch the DVD again and underline the word you hear.

   1 Without thinking about the latest diet or lifestyle *fad/ fashion*, Mr. Miyagi has developed his own way of slowing the aging process.

   2 The explanation for this extraordinary *phenomenon/ miracle* begins in the most ordinary of places.

   3 They've identified a number of important *qualities/ properties* that protect the Okinawans from disease.

   4 You go and you load up at the ... at the, the all-you-can-eat restaurant, and you, you walk away with this *swollen/bloated* feeling.

D Work in pairs and discuss. How easy do you think you would find it to live on Okinawa? Is there anything you would find difficult?

American Speakout a debate

5 A Look at the topic for a debate. Work in pairs and write two ideas in favor of the statement and two ideas against it.

Employers should give preference to younger applicants when hiring.

B Listen to part of the debate. Did either speaker mention any of your ideas? Which speaker do you agree with most?

C Listen again and check (✓) the key phrases you hear.

> **KEYPHRASES**
>
> The first point I'd like to make is that …
> I would like to start off by saying that …
> I would like to support the point made by …
> Going back to what [Junko] said …
> I would like to pick up on the point made by …
> In [answer/reply] to the point made by …

6 A As a class, choose one of the topics for a debate.

1 Politicians should be young—younger adults understand the changing world better.
2 Junk food can shorten lives and should be made illegal.
3 Children should take care of their parents when they get old.
4 Workplaces should require employees to do an hour of exercise a day.
5 It's better to live at a very high standard for 50 years than at an average standard for 100.
6 Some younger people think they have nothing to learn from older people, and they're right.

B Work in pairs either for or against the statement. List at least four points to support your opinion.

C Work in groups and debate the topic. At the end, have a vote.

writeback a forum comment

7 A Read the forum comment and discuss in pairs. Do you agree with the writer?

I strongly feel that children should take care of their parents when they get old, and I'm shocked that anyone disagrees. I grew up in a traditional society, where my grandparents lived with us and were always in the house. When I came to this country, it surprised me how unusual it was for three generations to live together. I accept that most young people's lifestyles don't fit with those of grandparents. However, in my opinion, we are fully responsible for taking care of our aging parents and grandparents. My reasons are that:

- our parents and grandparents invested a lot in caring for us, and it's our duty to do the same for them.
- elderly people can experience loneliness and helplessness. If we care about someone, we should protect them from these feelings.
- it's more expensive and wasteful for people to live in separate homes.

I definitely think that everyone should reconsider the way they live and move towards a more traditional family structure, even in a modern context.

B Number parts a)—d) in the order they occur in the forum comment.

a) summary statement
b) reasons for opinion
c) statement of opinion
d) personal background

C Choose one of the topics from Exercise 6A and write a forum comment giving your point of view.

D Read other students' forum comments and tell them which parts you agree and disagree with.

V AGE

1 A Add the vowels to complete the sentences.

1 Society, not families, should take care of the _ld_rly.

2 People _n th_ _r pr_m_ should simply enjoy life and not work.

3 The key sign of someone c_m_ng of _g_ is when they earn enough money to pay their own rent.

4 It's embarrassing when an older man or woman dresses too young f_r th_ _r _g_. People should dress and act th_ _r _g_.

5 _g_ d_scr_m_n_t_ _n is necessary in certain types of jobs.

6 M_t_r_ty comes from experience, not from age.

B Work in pairs and discuss. Which sentences do you agree with?

G MODAL VERBS AND RELATED PHRASES

2 A Underline the correct alternatives in the website forum.

⭐ My Worst Job

My current job is the worst ever. I'm a waiter in an amusement park restaurant, and the manager [1]*makes/lets* us dress up as bears. The costume is the worst, and, when I'm wearing it, I [2]*can't/'m not able* to see properly. I can't believe some of the things children [3]*are allowed to/should* do. We [4]*don't have to/aren't supposed to* get angry with them but I'm sure one day I [5]*can't/won't be able* to keep my temper and will do something awful! Thankfully, we [6]*don't have to/aren't allowed* wear the costumes for more than two hours at a time. Fortunately, because of the masks, my friends [7]*don't have to/oughtn't to* know about my job. Once, I [8]*could/managed to* serve two of my friends without them realizing it was me!

32 answers • 2 days ago

B Work in pairs and discuss. What's the worst job you've ever had or that you can imagine? What was or would be so bad about it?

G FUTURE PERFECT AND CONTINUOUS

3 A Complete the sentences with the correct form of the words in parentheses.

1 Ten minutes from now, I _____ here. (not sit)

2 In two hours' time, the class _____. (definitely finish)

3 By the time you read this, I _____ in New York. I'll be in touch! (arrive)

4 A year from now, all of us in this group _____ regularly. (still communicate)

5 By 2025, the Internet _____ by an alternative technology. (replace)

B Work in pairs and discuss. Which of the sentences above are true?

C Work in pairs and write five predictions about yourself/a classmate/a country/a famous person/the world.

D Work with another pair and discuss your ideas.

V OPTIMISM/PESSIMISM

4 A Correct eight mistakes in the words/phrases in bold.

I've **had my downs and ups** at work, but I will never forget my first job: teaching French to a group of sixteen-year-olds in a public school. I **had fixed feelings** about taking the job, since I was very young myself, but I'd learned to always **look on the light side** of things. I went in the first day feeling **beat-up** and really **looking backward to** meeting my group. But they turned out to be difficult, and, for a long time, I truly **dread** those lessons. No matter what I tried, I always felt I was **coming nowhere**, and it **filled me up with despair**. Then, one day, something amazing happened. One of the students brought a ...

|Comment

B Work in pairs and discuss. How do you think the story ended?

F PERSUADING

5 A Complete the conversation by adding the missing words from the box to the phrases in bold.

> what   surely   isn't   agree
> can   clearly   shouldn't

A: **Don't you that** everyone should be vaccinated against flu?

B: **But** people ought to be able to choose for themselves.

A: **Why? Anyone see that** the community needs to be protected, and that means everyone has to be vaccinated.

B: **But** parents decide what they think is best for their children? What about some of the side effects of vaccination?

A: **So you're saying is that** you think parents know more than the medical profession?

B: **But it obvious that** it's the companies who make the vaccines that are actually making money?

A: **Well**, we'll have to agree to disagree.

B Practice the conversation above in pairs. Look only at the phrases in bold to help.

C Work in pairs. Use the phrases in bold in Exercise 5A to discuss the following topics.

1 People who drink and drive should never be allowed to drive again.

2 The ideal world language is _____, not English.

3 Everyone should do one day a week of community service work.

A: Don't you agree that everyone should do community service?

B: Why? Anyone can see that wouldn't be fair ...

public school   state school

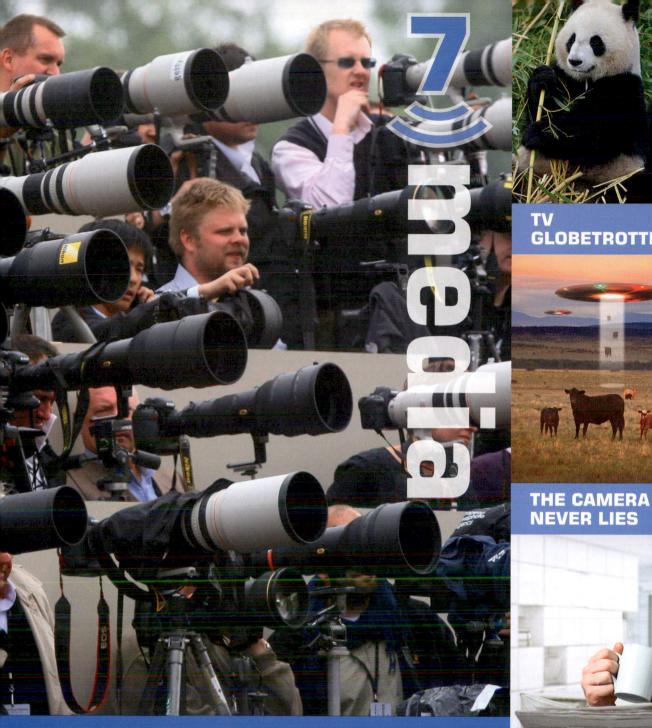

7 media

SPEAKING
- 7.1 Talk about TV programs
- 7.2 Talk about celebrity and media
- 7.3 Express strong reactions
- 7.4 Retell a news story

LISTENING
- 7.2 Listen to an expert talking about hoax photographs
- 7.3 Listen to people talking about recent news stories
- 7.4 Watch a program about live news

READING
- 7.1 Read about TV with a global appeal
- 7.2 Read an essay on celebrities and the media
- 7.3 Read about tabloid topics

WRITING
- 7.2 Write a discursive essay; Use linkers of contrast
- 7.4 Write a short news article

What kind of news stories interest you?

INTERVIEWS

7.1)) TV GLOBETROTTERS

G quantifiers
P connected speech: linking
V television; multi-word verbs

VOCABULARY
TELEVISION

1 A Work in pairs. Think of one similarity and one difference between the TV programs. Use your dictionary to help if necessary.

1 a wildlife program—a reality show
2 a period drama—a soap opera
3 a sketch comedy show—a sitcom
4 a documentary—a docudrama
5 a series—a miniseries
6 a thriller—a detective series
7 a game show—a quiz
8 a current events program—the news

B Work in pairs and discuss. Which program types above do you like the most/least? Give some examples.

READING

2 A Work in pairs and look at the pictures of five programs produced in the U.K. What type of program is each one? Why do you think each one is a global hit?

B Read the article and check your ideas.

C Why are sentences 1–8 false? Underline the relevant phrase or sentence in the article.

1 While nature programs might be expected to be popular worldwide, period dramas are only popular in the U.K.
2 For a car program, *Top Gear* has surprisingly few cars in it.
3 Viewers loved seeing the bullet train hit the supercar in *Top Gear*.
4 A lot of people thought *The Office* would be successful.
5 *The Office* is actually a serious documentary.
6 Everyone thought that people who liked Sherlock Holmes would welcome a new version.
7 Chinese viewers lost interest in *Sherlock* after the second season.
8 The only dancers on *Strictly Come Dancing* are professionals.

> **American Speak out TIP**
> Good writers use a range of vocabulary to refer to similar ideas, for example, *quirky humor* and *slightly strange humor*. This makes a text more interesting for the reader.

D Find words in the article with similar meanings to the following. The numbers in parentheses show the paragraph.

1 very good outcome(s) *successes* (1) _____ (2)
2 crazy or unconventional _____ (2) _____ 2)
3 worldwide extraordinary event _____ (2) _____ (3)
4 attracted _____ (2) _____ 4)
5 transmitted _____ (4) _____ (4)
6 brought back to life _____ (5) _____ (5)

E Discuss. Which of the programs would you most like to watch?

NATURAL WORLD

UNLIKELY GLOBAL SUCCESSES

What sort of TV program would you make if your goal was to appeal to the whole world? Obviously a well-made wildlife program such as the BBC's *Natural World* series would travel well, with its visual content and cross-cultural appeal. Period dramas and historical miniseries also seem to survive the transition to a different culture. But how about a car program, a quirky British comedy or an old-fashioned dance competition? Recent years have seen **quite a few** unlikely successes for programs with an appeal beyond their intended audience.

Would it surprise you to know that the most downloaded program ever is *Top Gear*, which regularly attracts over 350 million viewers worldwide in 170 countries **every** week? And, yes, we are talking about a car program headed up by three middle-aged men. True, there are **a large number of** cars, very fast cars, but its appeal lies more in the jokey relationship between the three hosts and also in the crazy challenges that are a key feature of **each** program. On one occasion, for example, the hosts' bizarre search for the source of the Nile pulled in millions of viewers, and a race between a supercar and a bullet train was **another** huge hit. Like it or loathe it, *Top Gear* truly is a global phenomenon.

THE OFFICE

period drama / sketch comedy show
miniseries / current events program
costume drama / sketch show
serial / current affairs programme

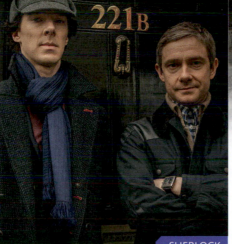

STRICTLY COME DANCING

SHERLOCK

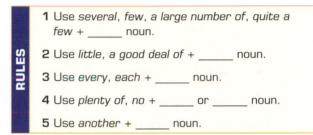

Comedies rarely travel well, and **many** people predicted *The Office* would flop because of its slightly strange British humor. Instead, the American version of the sitcom attracted 11.2 million viewers during its first showing in 2005. Since then, this "mockumentary" has become an international sensation and has been copied **several** times. The French call it *Le Bureau*, while those living in Chile have *La Ofis* and, in Germany, it's *Stromberg*. It enjoys **a good deal of** popularity despite the fact that it features characters who aren't particularly funny and survive mundane office life by acting a little cooler than they really are. The boss is a deeply unattractive character who is respected by no one. However, *The Office* is a sitcom with a heart, centered around the romantic relationship between two main characters. Perhaps that's one reason why it has proved such a success.

There are **few** fictional characters as well-known as Sherlock Holmes, and, when the BBC decided to give him a makeover, there was a real risk of alienating fans of the much-loved classic tales. The stories were updated to twenty-first century London, used state-of-the-art graphics and had two relatively unknown actors in the main parts. The BBC now has a worldwide hit on its hands. *Sherlock* is broadcast in more than 200 territories, and the long-awaited first episode of the third season was viewed almost seven million times in China only a couple of hours after it was initially aired in the UK. As with *The Office*, people are drawn in by the intriguing relationships between the main characters, so maybe there's a theme developing here. However, this doesn't explain the appeal of our final program.

Whoever could have imagined that *Come Dancing*, an old-fashioned dance competition popular in the 1960s, would be resurrected as *Strictly Come Dancing* in the UK and *Dancing with the Stars* in over forty-five countries that have bought the format? What's not to like? Show-stopping dances, celebrities, **plenty of** glamorous dresses, big band music, popular hosts and viewer participation, this program has it all. Celebrity contestants with **little** or **no** experience with dancing pair up with professional dancers and perform in front of a live audience to impress the voting viewers and judges. A tired old format has been revitalized and gone global in a most unexpected way.

It all goes to show that, when it comes to picking favorites, the audience will surprise you every time.

TOP GEAR

centered / experience with revitalized

centred / experience of revitalised

GRAMMAR
QUANTIFIERS

3 A Check what you know. Which of the quantifiers in bold in the article refer to: all; a lot; a moderate or small number/amount; an additional one; zero?

B Complete the rules with the type of noun: *singular*, *plural* or *uncountable*. Use the article to help.

RULES	
	1 Use *several, few, a large number of, quite a few* + _____ noun.
	2 Use *little, a good deal of* + _____ noun.
	3 Use *every, each* + _____ noun.
	4 Use *plenty of, no* + _____ or _____ noun.
	5 Use *another* + _____ noun.

C In sentences 1–4 below, do the quantifiers *few* and *little* mean *some* or *not many/not much*?

1 There are <u>few</u> fictional characters that are as well-known as Sherlock Holmes.

2 There are <u>a few</u> programs I never miss, perhaps three or four every week.

3 Celebrity contestants with <u>little</u> or no experience with dancing …

4 I always try to spend <u>a little</u> time watching the news each day, at least half an hour.

▶ page 140 **LANGUAGE**BANK

4 A Listen and write sentences 1–5 in your notebook.

B CONNECTED SPEECH: linking Draw links between final consonants and initial vowels in the quantifiers.

1 All of us watch lots of TV.

C Listen and check. Then listen again and repeat.

5 A Find and correct one mistake in each sentence.

1 I watch very little sports programs.

2 Every programs have a commercial break every ten minutes.

3 The weekend schedules usually include few talent shows, at least three or four.

4 I like each programs about hospitals or emergencies.

5 I once spent quite few days watching a box set of the series *24*.

6 I think a large number of TV has been dumbed down.

7 We have plenty detective shows; we don't need more.

8 I think little news is OK, but not 24-hour news non-stop.

B Make the sentences true for you or your country.

C Work with other students and compare your answers. How many points do you have in common?

D Report back on three interesting results.

SPEAKING

6 A Work in pairs and discuss the questions.

1 What are the benefits of watching TV online as opposed to on a TV?

2 What types of TV shows do people tend to watch online?

3 What types do you watch online?

4 Would you allow a child online access to a TV or a computer? If not, how would you limit it?

B Work alone. Read the following statements and put a check (✓) if you agree and an (✗) if you disagree.

1 TV and online news is the best way to stay accurately informed about current events.

2 TV programs and online video hits are a vital part of people's shared cultural experience.

3 Watching TV is bad for you because it robs you of time you might spend exercising.

4 The negative effect of violence in TV programs and online media is exaggerated. Violent people will do violent things anyway.

5 Watching online video or TV has a negative effect on your concentration span.

6 Sitcoms often provide positive role models for children.

C Talk to other students. Find out how many statements you disagree about. Give reasons.

VOCABULARY *PLUS*
MULTI-WORD VERBS

7 A Which programs in the box might the quotes below come from?

> *Natural World*   *Top Gear*   *Dancing with the Stars*   *Sherlock*
> *The Office*   *World News*

1 "The company has just brought out an electric version of the 408. It's superb! I take back everything I've said about electric models."

2 "We've just come across a herd of elephants on our way through the jungle. The rain is making it difficult to film, but we'll have to put up with it for a few more days."

3 "Over five hundred turned out to cheer the runners to the finish."

4 "A marvellous couple! And that dress! It takes me back to my teenage days! And it brings out the color of your eyes."

5 "He comes across as a helpful member of the public, but it turns out that he's the mastermind behind the crimes. Clever!"

6 "I've lost the key to my apartment. Could you put me up for the night? Otherwise I'll have to sleep at my desk. Like I do most of the day!"

B Underline ten multi-word verbs in quotes 1–6.

C Match meanings 1–10 with the multi-word verbs in Exercise 7A. Add *something* (sth) or *somebody* (sb) in the correct place if the verb takes an object. One verb is a three-part verb.

1 introduce (a product) or make something available   *bring sth out*

2 emphasize, or make something easier to notice

3 tolerate

4 let someone stay in your home for a short time

5 meet by chance

6 seem to have particular qualities

7 make somebody remember

8 accept you were wrong to say something

9 go to watch or be involved in an event

10 happen in the end

8 A Cover the exercises above and complete the sentences.

1 What's one sound, smell or taste that takes you _____ to your childhood?

2 Do you think you come _____ as an extrovert or an introvert?

3 What sort of person do you find it most difficult to put _____ with?

4 Do you always turn _____ to vote in an election?

5 What situation brings _____ the best—and worst—in your English?

6 Imagine you've been dating someone for a year and it turns _____ that they've lied about their age. What would you do?

7 Have you ever come _____ an old friend in an unexpected place?

8 When they brought _____ 3D movies, did you think they were worth it?

9 Would you ever put _____ a stranger in your home?

10 If you criticized someone and later found out you were wrong, would you take _____ what you said and apologize?

B Work in pairs. Take turns asking and answering the questions.

▶ page 154 VOCABULARY BANK

7.2)) THE CAMERA NEVER LIES

G reported speech
P word stress
V reporting verbs

A Abandoned Bicycle Swallowed Up by Tree

B Man Survives Cross-Channel Journey on Landing Gear

C Sharks Infest Flooded Suburban Town

LISTENING

1 A Look at pictures A–C. Do you think the news events really happened or are they hoaxes?

B Listen to the interview and check.

C Listen again and check (✓) the true statement(s) in each sentence.

1 The guest wants to remain anonymous because
   a) he thinks mystery is important.
   b) he doesn't want to get sued.

2 Police pay him to
   a) work out if a picture is a hoax.
   b) find out who did it.

3 He says the bike picture
   a) is easy to put together from two pictures.
   b) was put together by a friend of his.

4 The guest says the plane picture
   a) could be real.
   b) is well done.

5 He laughs at the shark picture because
   a) hoax pictures with sharks are common.
   b) this one looks so fake.

6 People who produce hoax pictures do it because
   a) they can make good money.
   b) they feel excited when the hoax succeeds.

D Check (✓) the statements you agree with. Then discuss your ideas with a partner.

1 When I see a picture in the media, I assume it's real.

2 It should be illegal to publish hoax pictures. It's the same as publishing false news.

3 It's unfair to show a famous person in an embarrassing situation in a hoax picture.

4 It's more fun to be tricked by a hoax picture than to find out that it's fake.

GRAMMAR

REPORTED SPEECH

2 A Check what you know. Which sentences below report a) a statement, b) a request or c) a question?

1 I asked you before the show if you'd ever earned money for your hoax work.

2 A friend told me he had seen it with his own eyes a number of years before.

3 You said that you often work with the police.

4 Sometimes the police ask me to look at it.

B For the sentences in Exercise 2A, write the exact words each person said.

1 "Have you ever earned money for your hoax work?"

C Work in pairs and complete the rules.

> **RULES**
>
> **1** In reported statements and questions, the verbs usually shift back if the reporting verb (*say, tell, etc.*) is in the *past/present*.
>
> **2** This doesn't happen in sentence *1/2/3/4* because the reported information is *always true/still true*.
>
> **3** In reported questions the word order is the same as *a question/an affirmative statement*.
>
> **4** To report a request, use ask *somebody* + infinitive with *to/gerund*.

▶ page 140 **LANGUAGEBANK**

3 A Work in pairs. Who says each of these sentences, the interviewer (I) or the hoaxer (H)?

1 Can you explain why you want to remain anonymous?

2 What exactly do you do for the police?

3 Talk us through the photographs if you would.

4 I wasn't sure myself, but I found out it was near Seattle, Washington.

5 Is there a technical reason why you know it's a hoax?

6 I'm thrilled when people believe one of my pictures.

B Write the sentences in reported speech. Start with *He/She said/asked.*

VOCABULARY
REPORTING VERBS

4 A Read the news story and discuss with a partner. Do you think Les Brown is telling the truth?

Insurance hoax?

An insurance company has accused a Louisville man of faking injuries from an on-the-job accident in order to get a large insurance payment. Les Brown, 49, denies lying to authorities about his injuries and has promised to prove that pictures showing him playing tennis are fake. Brown has refused to speak to journalists about the matter.

B Read the update to the story below. Have you read about any similar stories in the news?

Faced with clear evidence, Les Brown has admitted faking his injuries to cheat the insurance company. His ex-wife persuaded him to stop lying about the situation after authorities warned Brown to tell the truth or face a long jail sentence. Brown has apologized for embarrassing his family and has agreed to pay a large fine.

C Look again at the texts and underline all the reporting verbs.

D Write each reporting verb next to the pattern that follows it.

1 -*ing* Form	
2 Preposition + -*ing* Form	
3 Object + Preposition + -*ing* Form	*accuse sb of doing sth*
4 Infinitive	
5 Object + Infinitive	

5 A Check what you know. Add the verbs in the box to the table above. If you are not sure, use examples in a dictionary to help.

> tell   invite   suggest   advise   remind   threaten   offer

B WORD STRESS Work in pairs. Which reporting verbs in the completed table have the stress on the first and which on the second syllable? Listen and check.

C Complete the sentences so they are negative.

1 He accused them _____ (take) his injuries seriously.

2 He persuaded his doctor _____ (talk) to the media.

3 His wife told him _____ (lie) about the situation.

4 He apologized _____ (tell) the truth.

5 The authorities warned him _____ (do) it again.

6 A Complete the questions with the correct form of the verb in parentheses.

Questions of Trust

Situation 1

A co-worker has a picture of you at an office party doing something embarrassing. He threatens to show it to your boss unless you pay him a small sum of money. Would you:

a) agree _____ (pay) the money since it's a small amount, just to avoid trouble?

b) deny _____ (do) anything wrong and tell your co-worker to do whatever he wants?

c) talk to your boss and apologize _____ (act) stupidly?

Situation 2

Someone shows you a printout of an email written by your best friend. It's full of negative comments about you and also contains a few secrets that you told your friend. Would you:

a) accuse your friend _____ (betray) you?

b) refuse _____ (believe) that the email is real and do nothing?

c) make your friend admit _____ (write) the original email and warn him/her _____ it again (never do)?

Situation 3

A year ago, you promised to take a friend out to dinner for her birthday at an expensive restaurant. She's just reminded you, but now you don't really have the time or money. Should you:

a) promise _____ (take) her, but next year?

b) persuade her _____ (go) to a cheaper restaurant?

c) tell her the situation and apologize _____ (not keep) your promise?

Situation 4

Your boss has offered to give you a bonus if you write a report that will have her name on it and that she will take full credit for. Would you:

a) offer _____ (do) it, but only if she gives you credit, too?

b) suggest _____ (ask) someone else?

c) say no and threaten _____ (report) your boss to her boss?

B Work in pairs. Take turns asking and answering the questions in Exercise 6A.

jail sentence / co-worker   jail term / colleague

SPEAKING

7 A Work in pairs. Look at statements 1–4. Choose two statements and write one reason for and one reason against each one. Give examples to support your ideas.

1 Manipulation of images in advertising is justified in order to make a message stronger.

2 Idealized images of models in media can have a positive effect on ordinary people.

3 The media should be free to examine the lives of public figures.

4 The media should focus more on the lives of ordinary people rather than on famous people.

B Work with other students and compare your ideas.

WRITING

A DISCURSIVE ESSAY; LEARN TO USE LINKERS OF CONTRAST

8 A Read the essay and discuss. Which topic in Exercise 7A is it about? Do you agree with the writer's point of view?

These days, the media is full of stories of celebrities' private lives: their relationships, arguments, problems with weight and so on. In fact, the public seems to have a never-ending appetite for this type of gossip.

It could be argued that celebrities invite publicity despite knowing that this will leave them open to public attention. Therefore, it is hypocritical for them to complain when the media shows interest in other aspects of their lives. Also, celebrities are influential role models for many people, and, because of this, their private lives should be open to public examination. Additionally, the public has the right to know about the rich and famous since it is our money that supports them.

However, there are several reasons why celebrities deserve a certain level of privacy. First, while some people actively seek fame, others do not. For example, a person might want to be a great tennis player, but not wish to suffer media intrusion into their family's private life. Second, although reporters might claim an item is "in the public interest," often, in fact, they are more interested in selling a sensational story. Last, the unwelcome attentions of reporters and photographers can put celebrities under great stress.

On balance, I believe that celebrities have the right to the same kind of privacy as anyone else. Just because, on some occasions, they invite interest in order to publicize their work, this does not mean that they should not be able to say "no."

B Read the essay again and underline the correct alternative.

1 The introductory paragraph *explains why the topic is of interest/gives the writer's opinion about the topic*.

2 Paragraph two gives points *for/for and against* the idea.

3 Paragraph three gives points *against/for and against* the idea.

4 The conclusion *asks the reader's/gives the writer's* opinion.

9 A Look at sentences 1–4. Circle the linker which is used to show a contrasting idea.

1 Celebrities invite publicity (despite) knowing that this will leave them open to public attention.

2 While some people seek fame, others never want or plan for it.

3 Although a reporter might claim that a story is "in the public interest," often they are more interested in selling a sensational story.

4 However, there are a number of reasons why celebrities deserve our sympathy.

B Work in pairs and answer the questions.

1 What punctuation follows *However*?

2 Which form follows *despite*?

3 In sentences 1, 2 and 3, which is the main clause?

4 Do the linkers in 1, 2 and 3 introduce the main clause or the subordinate clause?

C Use the linkers in parentheses to connect the ideas in two different ways.

1 some celebrities are good role models for young people / others set a negative example (however, although)

2 anonymously published Internet news is unreliable / many people rely on it as a main source of information (despite, while)

3 false reports of celebrity deaths are common / some people still believe them (while, however)

4 the scandal damaged his reputation / he still has millions of fans (although, despite)

10 A Write notes for the four sections of a discursive essay on one of the other topics in Exercise 7A.

B Write the essay (250–300 words).

Though tabloids are still popular, most people watch entertainment programs or morning shows on television. The E! Channel is entirely dedicated to celebrity news and gossip.

idealized idealised

7.3))) WHAT'S IN THE NEWS?

- **F** adding emphasis
- **P** sentence stress
- **V** the press

VOCABULARY
THE PRESS

1 A What do you think are the most popular topics in newspapers? Read the article below and check your ideas.

Six Topics That Keep the Tabloids in Business

In an age when quality newspapers are seeing a serious drop in **circulation**, tabloid journalism is in no danger of dying out. Six topics always guarantee sales:

1 Scandal—the public loves glimpses into the lives of the rich, famous and powerful, and scandal fuels **tabloid** sales.

2 Money—everyone wants it, and some people will stop at nothing to get it. Many tabloids have a regular **feature** about money.

3 Babies—whether it's because they were born in a taxi or can speak two languages from birth, it seems we can't get enough of them.

4 Animals—flip through any tabloid, and you'll find a heart-warming story about a brave dog or a cat that's befriended a mouse.

5 Celebrities—hardly a day goes by that a "celeb" doesn't make an appearance in a morning **edition**.

6 Winners—from lottery winners to Olympic gold medallists, a winner on the front cover guarantees high sales.

Bold headlines, plenty of appealing pictures, a low price and a color **supplement** or two make tabloids the perfect escape from real life. They aren't afraid to be **biased** and show their opinion, most strikingly on the **editorial page**, which tends to be direct and aggressive in stating the editor's position on major issues. The public wants excitement and **sensationalism**, and tabloids deliver.

B Match meanings 1–8 with the words in bold in the article.

1 a popular newspaper, half the size of a standard newspaper, with few serious stories   *tabloid*

2 the section that gives the paper's opinion

3 a special report or article about a topic

4 giving a single point of view, unfairly

5 an extra section of a newspaper that can be pulled out, often a magazine

6 reporting news to make it sound as exciting as possible

7 the set of newspapers that are published at the same time

8 the number of newspapers sold in a day or week

C Work in pairs and discuss the questions.

1 Which paper in your country is the most sensationalist/biased?

2 Which sections of a newspaper or online news do you read first, e.g., sports, etc.?

3 Which sections or stories do you never read?

▶ page 154 **VOCABULARYBANK**

A Store Clerk Cheats Lottery Winners

B GAME FIXING SHOCK

FUNCTION
ADDING EMPHASIS

2 A Work in pairs and look at tabloid headlines A–F above. What do you think the stories are about?

B Listen to the conversations. Which headlines do they talk about?

C Listen again. What surprises the woman most in each story?

3 A Work in pairs. Underline the phrases that the speakers use to add emphasis.

1 The amazing thing is that the tiger ran off.
2 Wow, there's no way I'd do that!
3 You're the one who's always telling me to stop.
4 That is so wrong!
5 That's totally outrageous!
6 I do think they should do something about it.
7 That is a good idea.
8 How on earth did he catch it?
9 That's such an amazing thing!
10 Absolutely incredible!

B Work in pairs and discuss the questions.

1 What is the difference between so and such?
2 In sentence 6, what is unusual?
3 In sentences 5 and 10, what other modifiers could be used with the adjectives?
4 How is the beginning of sentence 3 different from "You're always telling me …"?
5 In sentence 8, what expression is added to a question word to show surprise?

C SENTENCE STRESS Work in pairs and mark the main stresses in the sentences in Exercise 3A. Listen and check. Then listen and repeat.

American Speak out TIP The words that show surprise are usually stressed and said with high intonation (pitch). It's a good idea to exaggerate when you practice this to help you get it right.

▶ page 140 **LANGUAGEBANK**

D Prince Takes First Steps

E WIFE'S LADLE SAVES MAN FROM TIGER

F POP STAR LOVE TRIANGLE

4 A Rewrite the sentences to add emphasis using the words in parentheses and making any other changes necessary.

Conversation 1

A: I'm ~so~ angry with you. Why didn't you tell me about the party? (so)

B: But I told you. A few minutes ago. (did)

A: That's helpful! How am I supposed to get ready in time? (really)

B: But you said you never want to go to parties. (one)

Conversation 2

A: Dave's good-looking, but she's crazy about Will. (absolutely)

B: It's sad. Dave adores her. (the sad thing)

A: Yeah, and he's really kind; a nice man. (such)

B: What do you want me to say if he asks me about Will? (earth)

Conversation 3

A: I'm quitting my job. It's badly paid, and it's hard work. (so, such)

B: I think you'll regret it. (do)

A: You always say I should do what I want. (one)

B: But you shouldn't just quit. (no way)

B Work in pairs and add two more sentences to each conversation. Add emphasis to one of your sentences in each conversation.

C Cover and practice the conversations.

LEARN TO

MAKE GUESSES

5 A Work in pairs and try to complete the extract. Then check your ideas in audio script S7.4 on page 171.

A: It's lucky the men noticed the baby.

B: Yeah, I [1]_____ they saw some movement.

A: Or [2]_____ they heard something.

B: What's that? The woman's bringing something.

A: It's [3]_____ to say, but it [4]_____ like a cushion.

B: Yeah, it [5]_____ be a sofa cushion.

A: I [6]_____ they thought the baby might fall on it.

B: That [7]_____ be the luckiest baby alive.

B Which words in 1–7 above could be replaced by words in the box?

> difficult   seems   perhaps   think   might
>   's   surely   imagine

6 A Listen to the sound. What do you think it is? Write down two ideas.

B Use the prompts to discuss the sound.

A: What / you / think / it / be?

B: hard / say / but / might / be (your first idea)

A: think / sound / like (your first idea)

B: suppose / could / be (another idea)

A: Or / perhaps / be (another idea)

B: Well / think / it / be (final decision)

C Listen to five more sounds. Practice the conversation after each one.

SPEAKING

7 A Work in pairs and look at the categories. What do you think the top five are for each category?

> The top five ...
> 1 most dangerous animals
> 2 countries with the tallest people
> 3 cities for art lovers
> 4 friendliest countries

A: I imagine the most dangerous animal is a tiger. What do you think?

B: I'm not sure. I suppose it could be, but ...

B Work in groups and take turns. Student A: turn to page 158, Student B: turn to page 160, Student C: turn to page 161, Student D: turn to page 162. Student A: tell the other students your category and see how many items they can guess. Tell them the answers they don't guess. Discuss which answers are the most surprising.

What do you want me to say...?   What shall I say...?

DVD PREVIEW

1 A Work in pairs and discuss the questions.

1 How often do you watch the news? Are the newscasters in your country always serious?

2 What are the pros and cons of working as a TV newscaster?

3 The name of the program you're going to watch is *The Funny Side of the News*. What do you think it's about?

B Read the program information and answer the questions.

1 Why are there more mistakes on TV news than there used to be?

2 How many different types of mistakes are mentioned?

▶ The Funny Side of the News

The Funny Side of … is a series that looks at all the things that can go wrong on TV, from talent shows to wildlife programs. Tonight it takes a look at TV news. As serious as news can be, mistakes and blunders are unavoidable. And with the introduction of 24-hour rolling news, mistakes have become more frequent and more visible with newscasters stumbling over their words and endless technical hiccups. From microphones malfunctioning to the wrong guest being brought into the studio for an interview, disaster is waiting to strike at any moment.

C Look at the program information again and match the words/phrases in bold with 1–6 below.

1 hesitating or making mistakes when speaking

2 happen suddenly and cause damage

3 small problems with machines

4 continuous

5 mistakes

6 going wrong (for a machine)

DVD VIEW

2 A Watch the DVD and make notes on which blunder:

• you found the funniest.

• you didn't find funny or didn't understand.

B Work in pairs. Number the blunders in the order they appear in the program. Some have more than one example (there are seven). Then watch the DVD again and check.

malfunctioning equipment   *1*

people stumbling over their words

the wrong guest in an interview

an accident on a live program

A: There was the bit where the woman …

B: Yes, and there was the part where the guy …

C Complete extracts 1–5 from the DVD. Then watch again and check.

1 So, if it starts going _____, you're going to see it.

2 The _____ about rolling news _____ that you have to fill an awful lot of time …

3 I'm afraid we obviously have the wrong guest here. That's deeply _____ for us.

4 But the undisputed _____ of the wrong guest division is the BBC News 24 incident _____ the charming but inappropriate Guy Goma.

5 It goes to _____ just how much the public loves a good news blunder.

D Discuss. Which incident do you think was the most embarrassing for the newscaster?

newscaster 🇺🇸🇬🇧 newsreader

American Speakout a news story

3 A Listen to someone retelling a news story about a man who swapped a paper clip for a house. Number the things he traded in the correct order.

a paper clip   *1*

a snow globe

a pen shaped like a fish

a house

a door knob

a part in a movie

B Listen again and check (✓) the phrases you hear.

> **KEYPHRASES**
>
> Did you [hear this story/see the news] about … ?
>
> I [heard this story/read this article] about …
>
> Apparently what happened was …
>
> According to [the report/the guy on the news] …
>
> Anyway, so he …
>
> I don't remember all the details, but …
>
> The [weird/strange/interesting thing] was …

C Think about a recent news story. Make notes listing the events in the story and think about which key phrases you can use.

D Work in groups and tell each other your stories. Ask follow-up questions and take notes. Which story was the most interesting?

writeback a short summary

4 A Read the article and write down the one thing that the man traded that is mentioned in the article but not in the recording.

Man Trades Paper Clip for House

A Canadian man has made headlines by trading a paper clip for a house. Bored blogger Kyle Macdonald started by exchanging small objects—a pen, a door knob, a neon sign—but, step by step, the 26-year-old built up to items of larger and larger value, and, after one year, his journey from paper clip owner to homeowner was over.

B Read the article again and do the tasks.

1 Circle three different ways that Kyle Macdonald is referred to in the story apart from *he* or *his*.

2 Underline two places where the writer uses two different words for the same thing.

3 Put a box round two places where a word is repeated. What effect does this have?

C The article is exactly 60 words. Imagine your editor tells you to cut it to exactly 45 words. Which words could you omit without losing important details (hyphenated words count as one word)?

D Write an article of exactly 60 words about one of the stories your group told in Exercise 3D. You may need to invent some details.

E Student A: read your article aloud. Other students: is it a summary of the story you told in Exercise 3D? If so, is it accurate?

V TELEVISION

1 A Find fifteen kinds of TV program in the wordsnake.

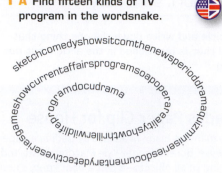

sketchcomedyshowsitcomthenewsperioddrama
show currentaffairsprogramsoapoperar
gramdocudrama
minideriesdocumentarydetectiveseriesg
gameshowrealityshowthrillerwildlifepr

B Work in pairs. Which type of program would you choose if you wanted to:

- laugh?
- learn something?
- just relax and watch real people?
- catch up on the news?
- test your knowledge?

G QUANTIFIERS

2 A Work in pairs and underline the correct alternative. The sentences are about two people.

1 *Both/Few* of us enjoy spending time in airports.
2 *None/Neither* of us plays a musical instrument.
3 We remember *a large amount of/quite a few* of our dreams.
4 Both of us take *a few/a little* sugar in our coffee.
5 We both got *hardly any/very few* sleep last night.
6 *Neither/Both* of us is allergic to anything.
7 We like *all/every* type of music.
8 We would like to live in *other/ another* country.
9 We spend *several/a great deal of* hours in the gym every week.
10 We both like having *few/a few* minutes' sleep in the afternoon.

B Which sentences are true for you and your partner? Change any that are not true.

A: Do you enjoy spending time in airports?
B: No.
A: Me, neither. OK, so neither of us enjoys spending time in airports.

G REPORTED SPEECH

3 A Rewrite the sentences in reported speech.

1 Last week, an interviewer asked me, "What's your biggest weakness?"
2 The other day, a complete stranger walked up to me and asked, "What have you been doing lately?"
3 Once, I was trying on pants, and the sales clerk asked, "Would you like to try a bigger size?"
4 Every day, my roommate says, "Could you do the dishes?" and then says, "I'll do them next time."
5 At the end of a first date, the girl asked me, "So when do you want to get married?"
6 At 3 a.m., my phone rang, and the caller asked, "Are you sleeping?"

B Which question would make you feel the most uncomfortable?

V REPORTING VERBS

4 A Complete the questions with the correct form of a verb in the box. Add any necessary words.

> ~~help~~   quit   lend   make
> do   pay   be (x2)

1 When was the last time you offered *to help* someone?
2 Do you find it easy to admit _____ a mistake?
3 Would you ever agree _____ a friend a large amount of money?
4 Have you ever refused _____ a bill?
5 Would you always apologize _____ late?
6 Have you ever threatened _____ your job?
7 Have you ever been accused _____ too serious?
8 Do you often promise _____ something and then simply forget?

B Work in pairs and discuss the questions above.

F ADDING EMPHASIS

5 A Find and correct the mistakes. There is one extra word in each sentence.

1 My hometown is such a so boring place.
2 I so do think that some people are very generous.
3 It's totally very ridiculous that people have such short vacations.
4 Why on the earth am I learning English?
5 Really, there's that's no way I would ever borrow money from a friend.
6 My teacher was the one who she had the most influence on me when I was young.
7 Sometimes learning English is so such difficult that I want to give up.
8 I like cooking, but the surprising thing that is that I never do it.

B Work in pairs and take turns. Student A: read one of your sentences from Exercise 5A. Student B: continue the conversation using some of these follow-up questions.

> How do you mean?

> In what way?

> Why (not)?

> For example?

> What makes you say that?

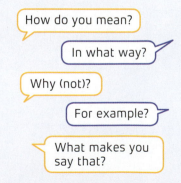

sales clerk   shop assistant

o 24 hour booth

8 behavior

IT'S A TOUGH CALL   p92

FAIR SHARE   p95

DO YOU HAVE A MINUTE?   p98

THE HUMAN ANIMAL   p100

What kind of behavior gets on your nerves?

INTERVIEWS

G past and mixed conditionals

P connected speech: weak forms

V collocations: decisions; compound adjectives

READING

1 A Work in pairs. Look at the pictures and read the headlines. What do you think happened in each situation? Write two predictions about each one.

B Read the articles and check your ideas.

C Look at statements 1–8 below. Who do you think said each one?

1 I'm looking for something to support my family.
Delroy Simmonds

2 Her face wasn't covered so I recognized her immediately.

3 She said, "I have a lot of money in that couch, and I really need it."

4 I'm incredibly grateful, and my three other kids are, too.

5 It was hard for him. I think that's why he came in with his brother.

6 Look, there's something in here.

7 You shouldn't have done that.

8 We laid it all out, and we were screaming.

D Work in pairs and discuss. Who had the most difficult decision: the three roommates, Simmonds or McQuinn's father? Do you think you would have behaved in the same way?

2

Man Misses Job Interview to Save Baby from Train

An unemployed Brooklyn man missed a job interview for the best of reasons: He was saving the life of a nine-month-old boy who was blown into the path of an oncoming subway train by a gust of high wind. Like a superhero without a cape, Delroy Simmonds jumped onto the tracks and lifted the bleeding child—still strapped into his stroller—to the safety of the platform as the train bore down on them. "If he hadn't jumped down there, the baby wouldn't be alive," said a worker at the station. "Everybody thinks I'm some sort of superhero," the father of two said. "I'm just a normal person. Anybody would have done the same." A friend of Simmonds thought differently. "If that had happened to me, I might not have jumped."

The out-of-work Brooklyn native was on his way to apply for a maintenance position at a warehouse. "A strong gust of wind blew," he recalled. "There was a woman with four kids. One was in a stroller. The wind blew the baby onto the tracks." He had no time to assess the situation. "The train was coming around the corner as I lifted the baby from the tracks. I really wasn't thinking."

1

New York Roommates Find $40,000 in Sofa

Three roommates who bought a used couch for $20 found $40,000 in cash stashed inside and returned the money to the 91-year-old widow who had hidden it there.

Cally Guasti said that she and her friends had bought the beat-up couch and a chair for $55 at a Salvation Army thrift store. They noticed the arm cushions were weirdly lumpy. Then roommate Reese Werkhoven opened a zipper on one arm and found an envelope. It contained $4,000 in bubble-wrapped bills. Guasti, Werkhoven and roommate Lara Russo opened the other arm zipper and started mining the treasure stashed inside. They counted it up: $40,800.

Later on, Guasti found a deposit slip with a woman's name on it and then called her. They drove to the home of the woman, who cried in gratitude when they gave her the cash she had hidden away.

Guasti said the three had considered the option of keeping the money, but decided they couldn't do that. It went against their principles. "At the end of the day, it wasn't ours," Guasti said. "I think if any of us had used it, it would have felt really wrong."

3

FATHER TURNS IN BANK-ROBBING DAUGHTER

An Adelaide man made the hardest choice of his life this weekend: he turned his own daughter into police after recognizing her picture from a police report about a recent string of bank robberies. Neighbor Bill Baugely says the heartbroken dad was trying to protect his daughter. "It's a really tough situation," Baugely said, "But I would have done the same thing."

Twenty-seven-year-old Anne McQuinn was allegedly seen at the St. George Bank in King William Street, at the Suncorp Bank in Grenfell Street, and at a bank in nearby Elizabeth in the past few months. Sergeant Tom Landers of the Adelaide police said, "The father came into the station with the woman's uncle. They'd seen the pictures on TV and the Internet and were sure it was McQuinn."

Police say the father didn't want to put off the decision once he saw it was his daughter and came in immediately. "The surveillance pictures were clear," said police. "He really had no doubt it was her."

The father said most of his friends were supportive, but not everyone. Local resident Gerry Comber said, "OK, the guy wants to do the right thing, but who turns in their own daughter?"

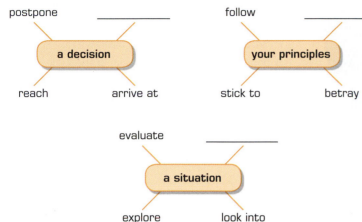

VOCABULARY
COLLOCATIONS: DECISIONS

2 **A** Find verbs in the articles to complete the word webs.

postpone _____   follow _____

a decision   **your principles**

reach   arrive at   stick to   betray

evaluate _____

a situation

explore   look into

B Each word web has two pairs of words with similar meanings. Draw a line to connect each pair.

C Match two collocations from Exercise 2B to each definition.

1 choose to do one thing or another   *arrive at a decision,*

2 delay deciding

3 be faithful to what you believe is right

4 do something that you don't believe is right

5 look at a situation in detail

6 judge a situation

3 **A** Read the extracts from a web forum below. Complete the texts with the correct form of the verbs from Exercise 2A. More than one answer is possible.

⭐ At the store, my food came to $10. I gave the cashier $20, but she gave me $100 in change. Obviously, she thought she'd given me a $10 bill. I ¹_____ the situation—I needed money badly; it was her mistake. Should I ²_____ my principles and keep the money, although I knew she might have to pay the missing cash back herself? In the end, I ³_____ a decision ...

⭐ The night before my final school exams, a classmate sent me an email with the exam answers in an attachment. What should I do? Ignore the email or ⁴_____ the situation by asking him why he'd sent it and who else he'd sent it to? I really wanted to ⁵_____ my principles and do the exam without cheating. I ⁶_____ the decision by going to bed. In the morning, it was clear to me what to do ...

B Work in pairs and discuss.

1 What do you think each person did? Do you think that was a good decision?

2 Can you remember a time when you took a long time to reach a decision or where you decided to stick to your principles?

bill 🇺🇸 note

GRAMMAR
PAST AND MIXED CONDITIONALS

4 **A** Look at the sentences and underline all the verbs.

1 I think if any of us had used it, it would have felt really wrong.

2 If that had happened to me, I might not have jumped.

3 I would have done the same thing.

4 If he hadn't jumped down there, the baby wouldn't be alive.

B Work in pairs and answer the questions about sentences 1—4 above.

1 Do they refer to real or hypothetical situations?

2 Does each sentence refer to the past or to the past and present?

3 Sentence 3 has only one (result) clause. Why is it unnecessary to have a conditional clause? In the second text find another example of a result clause on its own.

C Complete the rules with the words in the box.

> modal (x2)   past perfect   *have*
> infinitive   past participle

RULES

1 In the conditional clause use: the _____ to talk about the hypothetical past.

2 In the result clause use:

a) _____ + _____ + _____ to talk about the past.

b) _____ + _____ to talk about the present.

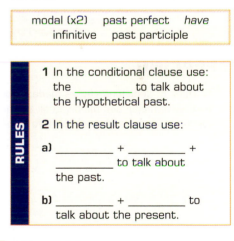

5 **CONNECTED SPEECH: weak forms**
Listen and match the words in bold in sentences 1—4 with the weak forms a)—d). Then listen again and repeat.

1 I **would have** done the same.

2 I **might have** behaved differently.

3 I **wouldn't have** been so brave.

4 I **couldn't have** done what he did.

a) /ˈmaɪtəv/

b) /ˈkʊdəntəv/

c) /ˈwʊdəntəv/

d) /ˈwʊdəv/

▶ page 142 **LANGUAGEBANK**

93

6 Read the situations 1–3 and complete the sentences a) and b) with the correct form of the verbs in parentheses.

1 A hiker saved two strangers lost on a snowy mountain by sharing his food and water with them and risking his own life.

a) If they _____ (be) more prepared when they set out that morning, he _____ (not need) to risk his own life.

b) They _____ (be) dead now if he _____ (leave) them there.

2 A 39-year-old man saved a woman by pulling her out of her burning car, which exploded moments later.

a) They both _____ (could die) if it _____ (take) any longer to pull her out.

b) Most of the other people there _____ (not do) that.

3 A woman found a winning lottery ticket and used the money to buy a house. Later she had to return the money to the original owner of the ticket, who still had the receipt proving he had bought it.

a) I _____ (feel) pretty bad if I _____ (do) what that woman did, and if I'd been caught.

b) If the man _____ (not save) the receipt, he _____ (might never recover) the money.

SPEAKING

7 A Think of decisions you've made: good and bad, easy and hard, major and minor. Look at the topics for ideas, and make notes about two situations.

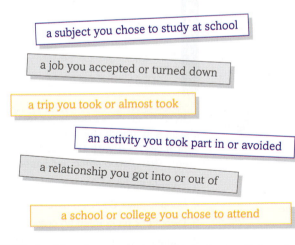

a subject you chose to study at school

a job you accepted or turned down

a trip you took or almost took

an activity you took part in or avoided

a relationship you got into or out of

a school or college you chose to attend

B Work with other students and take turns. Ask and answer questions 1–5 about each situation. Who had the most difficult decision?

1 Where did it happen?

2 What happened leading up to the situation?

3 How did you feel, and what did you do?

4 What else could you have done?

5 Would you do the same again?

VOCABULARY *PLUS*
COMPOUND ADJECTIVES

8 A Work in pairs and discuss. How could you reword these phrases without using the compound adjectives?

1 the 91-year-old widow

2 $4,000 in bubble-wrapped bills

3 bank-robbing daughter

B Work in pairs and find a compound adjective above which is formed with:

1 a past participle

2 a present participle (verb + *-ing*)

3 a number and measure of age/time

American Speak out TIP)) — Compound adjectives are made up of two or more words that form a single idea. They often have hyphens. With phrases expressing quantity, do not use a plural: *nine-month-old baby* NOT *nine-months-old baby*.

C Complete the sentences using a compound adjective formed from the underlined words.

1 The baby is <u>three days old</u>. She's a …

2 I like clothes that people <u>make</u> by <u>hand</u>. I like …

3 That wall is <u>49 feet high</u>. It's a …

4 That moment <u>changed</u> my <u>life</u>. It was a …

5 The TV series has <u>run</u> for a <u>long</u> time. It's a …

6 The course is <u>five years long</u>. It's a …

7 Elaine Jones has very <u>good qualifications</u>. She's very …

8 Research is an activity that <u>consumes</u> a lot of <u>time</u>. It's a …

9 A Rewrite the sentences using a compound adjective that expresses the meaning in parentheses.

1 A _____ child shouldn't be left alone at home. (one who is twelve years old)

2 All outdoor cafés should be _____. (you can't smoke there)

3 A _____ vacation is too long. (it lasts two months)

4 It's hard for me to remember names, especially _____ names. (ones that sound odd)

5 Auto manufacturers should spend more money developing a _____ car. (solar energy powers it)

6 I would never live at the top of a _____ building. (it's twenty stories)

B Check (✓) the statements you agree with, and put an (✗) if you disagree. Then discuss with a partner.

▶ page 155 **VOCABULARY**BANK

 stories / storeys

8.2)) FAIR SHARE

G -ing form and infinitive
P connected speech: intrusive /w/
V values

The Ultimatum Game
You have been given $10. You have to offer some of this money to your partner. If your partner accepts your offer, you split the money as agreed. If your partner rejects the offer, neither of you keep anything. You must decide how much money to offer to your partner.

THE SHARING EXPERIMENT

The Dictator Game
You have been given $10. You have to offer some of this money to your partner. Your partner has no choice and has to accept your offer. You must decide how much money to offer to your partner.

SPEAKING

1 **A** Work in pairs and discuss. Read the instructions above for The Sharing Experiment, two games that test people's behavior. What do you think the games show about people?

B Work alone. Imagine you are playing the games. Write an amount from $0—$10.

1 The Ultimatum Game:
I would keep $_____ and offer my partner $_____. The lowest I would accept from my partner is $_____.

2 The Dictator Game:
I would keep $_____ and offer my partner $_____.

C Compare your ideas with other students and discuss the questions.

1 How different are your results?
2 What did the two games show about your personality?
3 Do you think you would behave differently in a real-life situation than you did in the game?

VOCABULARY
VALUES

2 **A** Work in pairs. Match 1—6 with a)—f) to make sentences.

1 I think it shows that you have a sense of **fairness**, *d*
2 It brings out **aggression** in people. In fact,
3 I enjoyed being in **control**
4 Here there's no **equality** because
5 I imagine some people give more than they have to,
6 There's no **justice** in this game,

a) just as there's none in real life. I felt cheated and short changed.
b) and that's why I kept all the money for myself. I'm surprised at my own **greed**.
c) one person has less **power**.
d) especially if you split it 50-50, even though you don't have to.
e) and that sort of **generosity** always surprises me.
f) I think someone might try to hurt the other person.

B Write the words in bold in Exercise 2A next to their meanings.

1 being kind and willing to give
2 threatening behavior
3 a situation where people have the same rights
4 the ability to make someone do something (2 words)
5 being reasonable in judgement (2 words)
6 strong desire for more money, food or other things

C Discuss in pairs. Does each sentence in Exercise 2A refer to the Ultimatum Game, the Dictator Game or both?

LISTENING

3 **A** Listen to two people, Heather and Dominic, play the Ultimatum Game and answer the questions. (S8.2)

1 How much did Dominic offer Heather?
2 Did she accept?
3 What reasons does Dominic give for his decision?
4 What does Heather say about the decision?
5 What was the lowest amount Heather would have accepted?

B Discuss in pairs. Did anything surprise you about the outcome of the game? How do you think Heather and Dominic will behave in the Dictator Game?

C Listen to them play the Dictator Game and answer the questions. (S8.3)

1 How much did Dominic offer Heather?
2 What reasons does he give for his decision?
3 What does Heather say about the decision?

D Work in groups and discuss.

1 How different were Dominic and Heather's results from yours in Exercise 1B?
2 How much do you identify with the reasons Dominic gave for his decisions in either game?
3 How much do you identify with Heather's reaction? Were your reactions very different?

Contrary to the idea that most people are selfish, many would argue that generosity is more common nowadays. Crowdfunding, through websites such as Kickstarter and Gofundme, has become a popular way to help out others in need of funds for things like medical operations or just capital to start their own business.

GRAMMAR
-ING FORM AND INFINITIVE

4 A Check what you know. Complete the article using the correct form of the verb in parentheses. Use the *-ing* form, the infinitive or the infinitive + *to*.

AN EXPERT COMMENTS ON
▶ The Ultimatum Game

Research shows that people tend [1] _to respond_ (respond) differently depending on their cultural context and other factors. In Japan, players offered twice as much as those in Peru. But don't make the mistake of [2] _____ (think) that the Japanese are more generous than Peruvians. Perhaps [3] _____ (be) generous in the game means you want people [4] _____ (think) you are in real life. The game gives you the chance [5] _____ (act) unselfishly or not; some people are playing [6] _____ (impress) people. If it's important to someone [7] _____ (see) as fair, it's easy [8] _____ (act) that way in the game because it's just a game.

The Dictator Game is very interesting because no one would imagine a genuine dictator really [9] _____ (share) money. True, some players would [10] _____ (keep) everything, but most people let their partner [11] _____ (have) a share of the money. Interestingly, most five-year-olds will [12] _____ (share) at least half of the money—they're not interested in [13] _____ (have) the most. My opinion is that, deep down, most human beings would rather [14] _____ (cooperate) and avoid [15] _____ (exploit) others in the game and in real life.

B Work in pairs and discuss. What surprised you the most? Do you agree with the last sentence?

C Work in pairs. Look at the verb forms 1—15 in the article and complete the table.

	-ing Form, Infinitive or Infinitive + *to*	Example
After a Preposition		
To Express Purpose		
After *let someone* or *make someone*		
As Part of a Semi-fixed Phrase, e.g., *It's important/easy* and *the chance*		
As a Subject or Object (or Part of One of These)		
After Modal Verbs		
After Certain Verbs e.g., *enjoy, avoid, imagine*		
After Certain Verbs e.g., *want, would like, tend*	infinitive + *to*	1
After *had better, would rather*		

▶ page 142 LANGUAGE**BANK**

5 A Work in pairs. Complete each sentence with an alternative that means the same as the modal verb in parentheses. Then listen and check.

1 I don't want _to have to_ refuse. (must)

2 I hate _____ argue to get my way. (must)

3 I don't seem _____ to stand up for myself. (can)

4 I enjoy _____ offer people help. (can)

B CONNECTED SPEECH: intrusive /w/
Work in pairs. In sentences 1–4, circle *to* where it is pronounced /tə/ and draw a box around it where it is pronounced /tuw/.

C Listen again and check. What is the rule? Then listen and repeat.

6 A Cross out the incorrect forms in the sentences.

1 I would rather *being/to be/be* a victim of unfairness than an unfair person.

2 It's good that some parents make their children *working/to work/work* from an early age.

3 Everyone is capable of *cheating/to cheat/cheat* another person, given the right circumstances.

4 Beware of anyone who says they can't stand *losing/to lose/lose* because they'll do anything to win.

5 A child should *being/to be/be* taught when and how to be generous …

6 … but not just *earning/to earn/earn* the praise of others.

7 It's better *giving/to give/give* than *receiving/to receive/receive*.

8 *Being/To be/Be* good is easy; what is difficult is *being/to be/be* just. (Victor Hugo)

B Look at the sentences above. Check (✓) two that you agree with, and put an (✗) next to two you disagree with.

C Work in groups and compare your ideas. Who in your group agreed with you the most?

> **American Speak**out **TIP**
> Record patterns after verbs and phrases, e.g., *would rather (do)*, and write an example: *I'd rather stay at home.* How might you record these phrases: *look forward to …, had better …* ?

ATTITUDE

WRITING

AN INFORMAL ARTICLE; LEARN TO USE LINKERS OF PURPOSE

7 A Read the article and choose the best title.

a) Learn to Be Aggressive

b) Life Isn't Fair

c) Change the Things You Can

Do you hate it when people treat you unfairly? If you get a lower grade than you deserve, or you miss out on a promotion, do you lie awake all night fuming? Well, here are some things you can do about it to help you get past all that negativity.

First of all, it's important to remember that, **for** a positive outcome, you need to maintain a positive attitude. It's much more difficult to change something if you're feeling angry or upset. If you know you're in the right, develop a can-do attitude **so as to** bring some positive energy to the situation.

Second, you have to get yourself to think rationally **so that** it's your head not your heart that dictates what you do. Don't get emotional **because** that'll only result in you making the situation worse; I've often made that mistake and lived to regret it. If you want to stand up for yourself or for someone else, you need to stay calm. That's how I managed to get a promotion recently after a long fight for justice.

Finally, you need to recognize the difference between things you can do something about and things you can't. For example, once someone bumped into my car and drove away, and I couldn't really do anything about it; I had to accept the situation **in order to** move on. If, on the other hand, you see someone being unkind to someone else, you can say something to the person **to** change their behavior as long as you do it clearly, firmly and unemotionally. They may not respond exactly as you'd like, but you'll have a better chance of influencing them.

With these ideas in mind, you can become much better at dealing with unfairness, and you might even have a positive influence on situations as well as people.

B Underline the correct alternative and give a reason.

1 The article is probably for a *student magazine/ serious newspaper*.

2 The aim of the article is to *describe/give advice*.

3 The topic sentence is at the *beginning/end* of each main paragraph.

C Work in pairs and read the guidelines. Are they true (T) or false (F)? Find examples in the article.

In an informal article you should:

1 give personal examples.

2 use the pronouns I and you.

3 avoid contracted forms.

4 use conversational language.

5 use linkers to help structure the article.

6 use questions to the reader.

7 avoid multi-word verbs.

8 use the passive where possible.

8 A Work in pairs. Look at the linkers of purpose in bold in the article and answer the questions.

1 Which linkers are followed by:

a) an infinitive? *so as to (bring)*

b) a subject + verb?

c) a noun?

2 Which two linkers can also be used in more formal situations?

3 How do you change the following underlined linkers to make the sentences negative?

Count to ten in order to lose your temper.
Control your emotions so as to act with aggression.

B Rewrite the sentences replacing the underlined linkers with the ones in parentheses.

1 A good leader treats everyone equally in order to make everyone feel valued. (so that)

2 When I'm upset, I usually call my sister to chat. (for)

3 It's important to check everyone on a team reaches a decision together because, if you don't, someone will be left behind. (so as not to)

4 In a good relationship, it's important to sit down together from time to time so that you make sure everything is OK. (to)

5 Never make a decision late at night. Sleep on it to let your brain continue working overnight, and you'll wake up knowing what to do. (because)

6 In a family, it's good to have a list of tasks for each person because then no one is given the feeling they are doing more than their fair share. (in order not to)

9 A Work in pairs and brainstorm a list of main ideas for an article about one or two of the following topics:

• how to control your temper

• how to make decisions

• how to work as a team or a family

• how to have a good marriage or relationship

• how to do something that you know a lot about

• how to be a good leader or teacher

B Choose the topic you like and discuss ideas for opening/closing paragraphs. Then write the article (250–300 words).

8.3)) DO YOU HAVE A MINUTE?

BEWARE
Awkward Moments
NEXT EXIT

F handling an awkward situation
P sentence stress and intonation
V behavior

VOCABULARY
BEHAVIOR

1 A Look at the pairs of adjectives. Are they similar (S) or different (D) in meaning? Use a dictionary to check.

1 supportive—unhelpful
2 diplomatic—tactful
3 sensitive—sensible
4 confrontational—collaborative
5 aggressive—assertive
6 direct—focused

B Which adjectives in Exercise 1A become opposites by adding/removing a prefix/suffix?

*supportive—**un**supportive*

C Work in pairs. Which adjectives above describe your manner when:

• you break bad news to someone?
• a friend is down or in trouble?
• making a complaint?
• you work on a project with someone?
• you are driving or cycling?
• trying to sort out a problem between two friends?

I think I'm tactful but also really direct if I have to break bad news to someone.

▶ page 155 VOCABULARY BANK

FUNCTION
HANDLING AN AWKWARD SITUATION

2 A Work in pairs. Look at situations 1–3 and pictures A–C. What would be the best way to handle each situation?

1 Your co-worker has loud, personal conversations on the phone when you're trying to work.
2 A roommate of yours keeps borrowing money and never pays you back.
3 You're the manager of an elegant restaurant and a waitress has come in with purple hair.

B Work in pairs. Read the tips and discuss.

A

Q |Search

Tips for Talking Things Through

Sometimes we have to raise topics with someone that we find embarrassing or awkward. Following these five tips will help smooth the process and minimize hurt feelings.

1 Say clearly why you want to talk to them at the start.
2 Give the message clearly. Be specific.
3 Don't tell them what other people say or think.
4 Give them space to say what they think and feel.
5 Suggest a solution (if they don't).

3 A Listen to the conversation. Are the statements true (T) or false (F)? Correct the false statements.

1 Liz owes Jim a small amount of money.
2 She wants to pay him back immediately.
3 She doesn't always keep her promises.
4 Jim wants her to pay a set amount of money each week.

B Listen again. Check (✓) the tips in Exercise 2B that the man follows.

4 A Complete phrases 1–5. Then look at the audio script on page 173 and check.

Preparing the Listener
There's something I've been ¹_____ to talk to you about.

Giving the Message
It's ²_____ that …
I hope you don't ³_____ this the wrong way, but …
I don't want you to get the wrong idea, but …

Getting the Other Person's Point of View
Do you know ⁴_____ I mean?
Do you see where I'm coming from?
How does that ⁵_____?

B SENTENCE STRESS AND INTONATION Listen and underline the stresses in the phrases. Does the voice rise or fall at the end of each phrase? Why?

1 There's something I've been meaning to talk to you about.
2 I hope you don't take this the wrong way, but …
3 I don't want you to get the wrong idea, but …

C Listen again and repeat.

▶ page 142 LANGUAGE BANK

minimize   minimise

C

LEARN TO
SOFTEN A MESSAGE

6 A Work in pairs. Read the sentences below. When speaking, how could you soften the messages? What extra words or sounds could you add?

1 It's not that. I hope you don't take this the wrong way, but it's just that this isn't the first time I've lent you money and you haven't paid it back. I know it's not a lot, just small amounts each time, but it adds up quickly. I don't know. Do you know what I mean?

2 Actually, you've said that once before. I don't want you to get the wrong idea, but it never happened. And it makes things awkward. It makes me feel annoyed. Do you see where I'm coming from?

S8.7 B Listen to the sentences and add the extra words or sounds you hear.

> **American Speak out TIP**
> Fillers can help you sound less confrontational and allow thinking time. Some fillers (e.g., *um, er, well, you know, I mean, kind of*), are used instead of a pause. Modifiers (e.g., *just, a bit, slightly, really*) often go before an adjective and soften a strong message (e.g., *I'm just a bit concerned = I'm VERY concerned*).

SPEAKING

7 A Work in pairs. For each situation below, write the first two sentences of the conversation.

1 You've been driving your co-worker to work for over a month. He/She has never offered you money for gas.

2 Your neighbor in a apartment building leaves bags of trash in the hall for days. He/She eventually takes them out, but there's always a bad smell in the hall as a result.

3 Your friend has long conversations on her cell when you're out together.

4 A friend often gives you a lift on his/her motorcycle, but his/her driving is scary.

B Role-play one of the situations.

C Work with another student and role-play a different situation.

8 Work with other students. Decide on the three most annoying things people do a) in your place of study or workplace b) at home.

5 Work in pairs and role-play the situation. Use the flow chart to help.

Student A

> there / something / I / mean / talk / you / about.

Student B

> Yeah. What / up?

> Well, look / don't / get / wrong idea, but ...

> But what?

> It / just / I / very busy / you / always / call.

> Oh, right.

> It / really / annoying. / know / I / mean?

> sorry / I / not / thinking.

> I / suggestion. / Why / you / not / ask friends / call your cell / instead of / land line?

> You / mean / I / use / phone / different room?

> That / right. / How / sound?

> seem / reasonable. / really / sorry.

> No problem. / Forget.

apartment building / motorcycle block of flats / motorbike

DVD PREVIEW

1 A Work in pairs. Which gestures do you know? Show your partner.

1 shrug your shoulders
2 cross your fingers
3 tap the side of your head
4 give the thumbs up sign
5 hold your hands out, palms up
6 nod
7 shake your head
8 rub your thumb and first two fingers together

B What do these gestures mean in your country? Do people there use any other gestures?

2 Read the program information and correct the sentences.

1 Desmond Morris observed human behavior even though he's a bird-watcher.
2 He created a classification system for words people use with animals.
3 His project took him over sixty years, and he traveled to many countries to complete it.
4 The program looks at sign language.

▶ The Human Animal

Desmond Morris is widely known for his study of human behavior, customs and rituals, a "man-watcher" in the same way as some people are bird-watchers. Originally a zoologist, Morris decided to observe and classify human behavior in much the same way as he would observe animals—in his words "to do for actions what dictionary makers had done for words." His project of cataloging human gesticulation and movement took him to over 60 countries and engrossed him for many years. In this program in the series, Morris focuses on fascinating customs connected with greeting and on the meaning of different gestures.

DVD VIEW

3 A Before watching, discuss:

1 How many ways of shaking hands do you know?
2 How do you say "You're crazy!" with your hands?

B Watch the DVD. Does Morris mention or show any of the things you talked about in Exercise 3A? Which handshake and "You're crazy!" sign did you find the most interesting?

C Match the types of gesture to the countries. Then watch the DVD again and check.

Shaking Hands:
1 Masai elders   a) shake and kiss hands
2 Mali, West Africa   b) continue until a deal is struck
3 Morocco   c) briefly touch the forearm
4 Kurdish farmers   d) give a quick palm touch

Saying "You're crazy!":
1 Rome   a) twist finger round and round
2 England   b) circle finger counterclockwise
3 Japan   c) put fingers together and tap forehead
             d) tap side of head with finger

D Watch the DVD again and underline the correct alternative.

1 I *drew/directed* his attention to the fact that, over the other side of the road, there were two men who were *gesturing/gesticulating* in a particular way.
2 … a major new project, one that was to *keep my interest/engross me* for many years to come …
3 I began making huge charts naming every facial *gesture/expression*, every gesticulation, every movement, every *position/posture*.
4 Even the simplest human action such as the handshake has countless *differences/variations*.
5 The essential feature of handshaking is that it's an *equal/egalitarian* act.
6 They're all *exactly right for/fine-tuned to* the precise *context/situation* in which they occur.

cataloging   cataloguing
counterclockwise   anticlockwise

American Speakout advice for a visitor

4 A Listen to some advice for visitors to the USA. Is there anything that surprised you?

B Listen again and check (✓) the key phrases that you hear.

C Work in pairs or groups. Choose a country both of you know and prepare advice for visitors.

• Choose from the topics below and make notes on Do's and Don'ts for visitors.

• For each point, say why it is important and what can go wrong if a person doesn't know about the particular behavior.

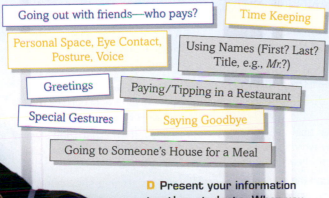

Going out with friends—who pays?

Time Keeping

Personal Space, Eye Contact, Posture, Voice

Using Names (First? Last? Title, e.g., *Mr.*?)

Greetings

Paying/Tipping in a Restaurant

Special Gestures

Saying Goodbye

Going to Someone's House for a Meal

D Present your information to other students. When you listen to other students, make notes of anything you didn't know before.

writeback cross-cultural article

5 A Read the short article giving advice on an aspect of behavior in the USA. Which topics in Exercise 4C does it mention?

B Which things are the same as in your country?

Body Language in the USA: Play It by Ear

People from the United States are friendly, but there are some important things every visitor should know when spending time with them.

When you meet someone for the first time, it's normal to shake hands firmly, regardless of gender, both in formal and semi-formal situations. On subsequent meetings, this is not usually expected, unless you haven't seen someone for a while. Exchanging kisses is usually reserved for family and loved ones. It should not be initiated by visitors; however Americans are usually open to and respectful of new customs. So, don't worry if you forget, people will understand if you explain yourself.

In terms of personal space, Americans feel uncomfortable if you stand too close, so try to respect personal space. Also, it's important to make eye contact when talking to Americans, but don't overdo it or you'll make people feel uncomfortable.

Gestures such as hugging and backslapping are common between friends and people you know well. Get to know people first, and, after time, they'll warm up to you. Be aware though, in a formal environment, Americans do not raise their voices or use gestures a lot to emphasize a point, and shouting is never acceptable.

If you keep these points in mind, you'll have a much more comfortable, enjoyable visit to the United States.

C Write a short article (150–200 words) giving advice to a foreign student or business person coming to your country. Choose one or two topics from Exercise 4C to focus on.

D Read other students' articles. What information did you find that you didn't know before?

V COLLOCATIONS

1 Underline the correct alternative in each sentence.

1 I had no time to *evaluate/stick to* the situation and had to act quickly—it was too dangerous to *postpone/reach* the decision till later.

2 I always try to *betray/stick to* my principles and never go *against/arrive at* them.

3 You should *explore/follow* the situation thoroughly and not be afraid of *doing/putting off* the decision.

4 We would like to take more time to *betray/assess* the situation before we *arrive at/follow* a final decision.

G PAST AND MIXED CONDITIONALS

2 A Underline the correct alternative in each sentence.

1 If I hadn't started studying English,
   a) I *might study/might have studied* another language.
   b) I *wouldn't go/wouldn't have gone* to college.
   c) I *wouldn't be/wasn't* able to watch movies in English.

2 If I'd had the chance to live in a different country,
   a) I *wouldn't take/would have taken* it.
   b) I *would find/would have found* it very hard to make a decision about where.
   c) I *would choose/would have chosen* to live in Spain.

3 If computers hadn't been invented,
   a) the world *would be/had been* a less open place.
   b) people would *spend/have spent* more time together now.
   c) my parents would *end up/have ended up* in different jobs.

B For each sentence, circle the ending a), b) or c) that is most true for you.

C Work in pairs and compare your ideas.

V VALUES

3 A Add the vowels to complete the questions about values.

1 Is it possible to have f__ __rn__ss without __q__ __l__ty? How about when a disadvantaged person is given special treatment?

2 If kids play team sports, are they more likely to learn cooperation or __ggr__ss__ __n?

3 How can g__n__r__s__ty be used as a way of gaining c__ntr__l over people or a situation?

4 If you were a judge with total p__w__r, would you be able to practice perfect j__st__c__ and never show favor toward anyone— even family and friends?

5 You can press a button and eliminate either gr__ __d or ignorance from the face of the earth. Which one would it be?

B Work in pairs and ask and answer the questions.

G -*ING* FORM AND INFINITIVE

4 A Complete the sentences with the correct form of the words in parentheses.

1 The most difficult thing about my day is _____ to and from work. (travel)

2 I've always been able _____ new words just by _____ them. (learn, hear)

3 It's not very good for a person _____ alone when they're depressed. (be)

4 I never have time _____ the things I really want to do. (do)

5 _____ a bike is one of my favorite ways of relaxing. (ride)

6 I study English for an hour a day, but I keep _____ the same mistakes! (make)

7 I enjoy _____ movies in English. (able / watch)

8 _____ a uniform is the worst part of my job. (have / wear)

B Check (✓) any sentences you agree with. Make the others true for you.

C Work in pairs and take turns. Student A: read one of your sentences. Student B: ask follow-up questions.
   A: The worst part of my job is …
   B: Oh, why is that?

F Handling an AWKWARD SITUATION

5 A Correct the mistake and add the missing word in each sentence.

1 Excuse me, Wendy. Do ^*you* have a *moment* ~~monument~~?

2 There's nothing I've meaning to talk to you about.

3 Look, I want you to get the right idea, but …

4 It that just I've noticed that …

5 I feel brighter if …

6 How you fill about that?

B Work in pairs. Choose one of the situations below and practice the conversation. Student A: use all of the sentences from Exercise 5A in order. Then choose another situation and exchange roles with Student B.

• telling a co-worker that their clothing isn't appropriate for the workplace

• telling a friend that they always forget your birthday, and it bothers you

• telling a student they didn't pass an important exam

Excuse me, Juan. Do you have a moment? There's something I've been meaning to talk to you about …

9))) trouble

Do you have any phobias?

INTERVIEWS

9.1)) WITNESS

G -ing form and infinitive
P connected speech: elision
V crime; dependent prepositions

VOCABULARY
CRIME

1 A Work in pairs and discuss. What crimes are the most common in your city/town?

B Work in pairs and complete the newspaper extracts with the crimes in the box.

> kidnapping   hacking   stalking   vandalism
> identity theft   bribery   counterfeiting   mugging
> arson   shoplifting

1 A teenager has been accused of _____ after he was seen setting fire to an empty factory.

2 He was jailed for five years for _____ into government computer systems.

3 There has been a reduction in _____ in stores after the introduction of more security guards.

4 A man has been found guilty of _____ movie star Halle Berry. He followed her everywhere.

5 There have been several cases of _____ of foreign journalists. In the latest case, a demand was made for $500,000.

6 _____ is a problem, with officials accepting money from companies that want to do business in the country.

7 There were no witnesses to the act of _____ in which a statue was damaged.

8 Police arrested three people for _____ dollars. More than a million fake $50 bills were found.

9 Banks revealed that cases of _____ have doubled. Customers are warned to keep PIN numbers more secure.

10 The increase in CCTV cameras has cut cases of late-night _____ in town centers.

C Complete the table for the words in Exercise 1B. Use your dictionary to help if necessary. Add any other crime vocabulary you know.

Crime	Person	Verb
arson	arsonist	to commit arson
hacking		

D Work with other students and discuss.

1 Which ones do you think are the most serious crimes and which are more minor offences?

2 Are any of the crimes serious problems in your country?

3 Do you know anyone who has had experience with any of these crimes?

Memories **on Trial**

Even in these days of DNA tests and other forensic techniques, witness testimony still plays an important part in court cases. But how reliable are our memories? *Science Today* magazine's Andy Ridgway finds we know less than we think ...

READING

2 A Work in pairs and discuss. Do you have a good memory? What do you remember easily? What do you have difficulty remembering?

B Read the article and find two examples of false memories.

C Read the article again. Are statements 1–6 true (T) or false (F)? Underline any words/phrases that help you decide.

1 In court, evidence from a witness is not important if there are other kinds of evidence.

2 Forty percent of people in one study were able to give a full description of the movie of the bus exploding in Tavistock Square.

3 A poor memory doesn't usually matter in day-to-day life, according to the article.

4 In 1998, in the USA, almost all major criminal cases depended entirely on witness evidence.

5 The rumor about the white van was started by one witness.

6 One in five witnesses makes a mistake in line-ups.

D Look at the article again. What do the six highlighted words refer to? Draw an arrow backwards or forwards to the word/phrase.

Most of us have some recollection of the 2005 terrorist attacks in London. It could well be a mental image of ...

E Work in pairs and discuss. Who/What does the author blame for false convictions? Would you make a good witness?

rumor / line-ups   rumour / ID parades

> In line-ups, forty percent of witnesses identified the police's suspect.
> In forty percent of cases, no identification was made.
> In twenty percent of cases, they pointed to a volunteer.

Most of us have some recollection of the 2005 terrorist attacks in London. It could well be a mental image of a red double-decker bus in Tavistock Square with its roof ripped off by the force of the explosion. That's not surprising given the number of photographs of the damaged bus that were carried in newspapers in the days after the attack.

But what about CCTV footage? Do you remember seeing a video of the bus exploding? What can you see in that video?

Well, the truth is, you shouldn't be able to see anything in your mind's eye because such CCTV footage simply doesn't exist. But don't worry. If it only took a suggestion that you may have seen a video of the explosion to create an image in your mind, you're not alone. In fact, in a study carried out by Dr James Ost at the University of Portsmouth, forty percent of people claimed to have seen this nonexistent footage. Some even went on to describe what happened in vivid detail.

Many of us think we have a good memory. After all, it's gotten us through the occasional test. But what Ost's study clearly demonstrates is just how easily influenced our memories are. "Facts" from the past can become confused in our minds. And it can simply be the fact that we've been asked about something, such as a nonexistent video clip, that can alter our memory.

In many cases, an unreliable memory is not a problem. It just means we forget to send a birthday card on time or a story we tell at a party is not one hundred percent accurate. But sometimes the contents of our memories can have huge consequences—putting people behind bars or even, in the USA, on death row.

In 1998, an American study calculated that in ninety-five percent of felony cases—the more serious crimes—witness evidence (in other words, people's memories) was the only evidence heard in court. In the UK, despite DNA and other forensic evidence being used more regularly, witness memories are still a vital part of court proceedings.

Even before a case gets to court, a few false memories can get an investigation off to a bad start. In the sniper attacks that took place in the Washington, D.C., area in 2002, witnesses reported seeing a white van or truck fleeing several of the crime scenes. A white vehicle may have been seen near one of the first shootings, and the media began repeating this. When they were caught, the sniper suspects were actually driving a blue car. It seems many witness memories had been altered by the media reports. ∎

GRAMMAR

-ING FORM AND INFINITIVE

3 A Underline the correct alternative in sentences 1–3. Then check in the article.

1 Do you remember *to see/seeing* a video of the bus exploding?

2 Some even went on *to describe/describing* what happened in vivid detail.

3 It just means we forget *to send/sending* a birthday card on time.

B Work in pairs and check what you know. What is the difference in meaning between the pairs of phrases in bold?

1 a) I **remembered to set** the alarm before I left.

   b) I **remember thinking** the building was quiet.

2 a) I **forgot to buy** tickets for the Adele concert.

   b) I'll never **forget seeing** Adele in concert.

3 a) Henri **stopped to drink** some coffee.

   b) Then he **stopped driving** because he still felt tired.

4 a) After lengthy training, Billy **went on to become** a famous dancer.

   b) Billy **went on practicing** every day even when he was famous.

5 a) He **tried to recall** her name, but couldn't.

   b) He **tried going** through the alphabet to remember it.

6 a) We **regret to inform** you that the concert has been canceled.

   b) And I **regret spending** so much on the ticket!

C Match rules 1–12 below with meanings a) or b). Use the examples in Exercise 3B to help.

RULES		
1 remember doing	a) do something that is one's responsibility
2 remember to do	b) have a memory of something
3 forget doing	a) not do something that is one's responsibility
4 forget to do	b) not have a memory of something
5 stop doing	a) finish an action
6 stop to do	b) finish an action in order to do something else
7 go on doing	a) do something after finishing something else
8 go on to do	b) continue an action
9 try doing	a) experiment with an activity
10 try to do	b) make an effort to do something difficult
11 regret doing	a) be sorry about something you are about to do
12 regret to do	b) be sorry about something you did in the past

4 CONNECTED SPEECH: elision Listen and write the sentences. Cross out letters at word endings that are not pronounced. Then listen and repeat.

I remembered to lock up.

▶ page 144 LANGUAGEBANK

canceled   cancelled

5

A Complete the questions with the correct form of the verbs in the box.

~~get~~   study   buy   write   hide   take   help   become   witness   think   inform   do

1 If someone stole your wallet, would you run after them and try _to get_ it back?

2 Have you ever forgotten _____ a ticket for a train journey, then got caught?

3 If you were in a hurry and you saw an accident but there were lots of people around, would you stop _____?

4 Is there an event in your country you'll never forget _____, because it was so significant?

5 Is there anything thing you regret not _____ when you were a child?

6 Do you ever stay awake at night because you can't stop _____ about a problem?

7 Do you always remember _____ breaks when you're studying hard?

8 Has anyone you knew as a child gone on _____ famous?

9 Have you ever tried _____ on your hand as a way of reminding yourself to do something?

10 You open a letter that says, "I regret _____ you that your application has been refused." What's it referring to?

11 How long do you think you'll go on _____ English?

12 Do you sometimes remember _____ something "in a safe place" but find you've forgotten where you put it?

B Work in pairs and ask and answer the questions.

SPEAKING

6

A Work alone. How would you have acted if you'd witnessed a crime? Read situations 1—4 and make notes on what you would have done. Use questions a)—c) to help you.

1 You caught a pickpocket trying to take your cell and he threatened to hurt you if you called the police.

2 You saw a friend shoplifting in a department store.

3 You noticed a co-worker stealing office supplies from your place of work.

4 You witnessed your neighbor's teenage children committing an act of vandalism, e.g., spraying graffiti on the wall of their school.

a) Would you have intervened or try to stop the person?

b) Would you have reported the person to the authorities?

c) If you'd been questioned by the authorities, would you have told the truth?

B Work in groups and compare your ideas.

VOCABULARY *PLUS*
DEPENDENT PREPOSITIONS

7

A Work in pairs. Complete the headlines with a preposition and the correct form of the verbs in parentheses.

> **1** FAKE POLICE OFFICER CHARGED _____ $600 NECKLACE (steal)

> **2** Woman Accuses Con Artist _____ Bag and PIN (take)

> **3** Gang Arrested _____ One Car Nine Times (sell)

B Write the headlines in full. Which are active and which passive?

1 A fake police officer has been charged with stealing a $600 necklace. passive

C Complete the headlines using a dependent preposition and the correct form of the verbs in parentheses. Then check with a partner or in a dictionary.

1 Hacker Suspected _____ Government Computers (access)

2 Student Apologizes _____ on Test (cheat)

3 President Blames "Greedy" Banks _____ Crisis (cause)

4 Local Girl Dreams _____ Top Talent (become)

5 Agency Criticized _____ Size-zero Models (employ)

6 Train Company Bans Teenager _____ for One Year (travel)

7 Mother Thanks Toddler _____ Her Life (save)

8 Animal Rights Activists Rescue Lobster _____ (be eat)

9 Jury Clears Actress _____ Husband Number Three (murder)

10 Dolphin Saves Swimmer _____ (drown)

8

A Work in pairs. Choose two of the headlines above and write a news article in three sentences.

B Work in groups and take turns. Student A: read out your article. Other students: close your book and say the appropriate headline.

▶ page 156 VOCABULARY BANK

G past modals of deduction
P connected speech: past modals
V synonyms

VOCABULARY

SYNONYMS

1 A Read the dictionary extract. Think of an example of a scam.

> **S** **scam** /skæm/ *n* [C] *informal* a clever but dishonest way to get money

from Longman Active Study Dictionary

B Work in pairs. Read the infographic and answer the questions.

1 What are your answers to the first two questions in the text?

2 Which of the five scams can be done by one person?

C Match meanings 1–6 with two of the underlined verbs or verb phrases in the infographic. Write the verb phrases in the infinitive.

1 act as if you're someone else *pretend to be,*

2 trick someone

3 cause somebody to <u>not</u> notice something

4 take something quickly

5 believe a trick

6 exchange one thing for another

> **American Speak TIP**
> Use synonyms to improve your speaking and writing. You can a) notice synonyms when you read b) record them in your notebook c) look up synonyms in a thesaurus or on the Internet d) use synonyms when writing to avoid repetition.
> Rewrite the following, using synonyms for *nice: Yesterday was very nice. I had a nice meal at a nice restaurant with some nice people*

LISTENING

2 A Listen to the conversations. Which two scams from the infographic happened to the people?

B Work in pairs and try to complete the statements. Then listen again and check your ideas.

1 The thieves distracted Lise by …

2 She trusted the man because …

3 She thought she was talking to the bank on the phone because …

4 The thieves got her PIN code by …

5 The man in the jewelry store was posing as …

6 He accused the woman of …

7 He left the store with …

8 Dan thought that the man was going to …

3 Work in pairs and discuss the questions.

1 What should/shouldn't the people have done in each situation?

2 Why do you think people fall for scams?

3 Have you read or heard about any other scams (over the phone, Internet or face-to-face)?

> Even though street scams are still common, computer scams have become a leading form of fraud. Con artists send emails offering fake prizes or high-paying jobs as a way to commit identity theft, this is known as "phishing."

Scam-proof Yourself

How easily do you think you could <u>be taken in</u> by a professional con artist? Is it easy for a well-dressed but ill-intentioned stranger to <u>deceive</u> you and walk away with your money, credit cards or phone? Once you understand the basic principles of street scams, you'll never <u>fall for</u> a scam again.

1) The Shoulder Surf

You're standing at the ATM, and some nice person asks if that's your 20 dollars on the ground. An innocent question or a trick to <u>distract</u> you so they can <u>snatch</u> your card out of the slot?

2) The Fake Police Officer

If a man walked into a store where you worked and <u>pretended to be</u> a police officer, would he <u>fool</u> you?

3) Escalator Jam

As you reach the bottom of the escalator, suddenly there's a jam of people, and you get bumped into. You drop your cell, but a kind woman picks it up and gives it back to you. Are you sure she hasn't <u>switched</u> it for an identical (but broken) one?

4) The Tourist Picture

"Can you take our picture?" It's just one of many ways to <u>divert your attention</u> so the hustlers can easily <u>grab</u> your wallet or cell or <u>swap</u> it for an identical one.

5) The Squirt

A stranger bumps into you and gets ketchup all over your jacket! How nice that some people are helping you wipe it off … or are they just thieves <u>posing as</u> helpful passersby?

jewelry store   jewellery shop

GRAMMAR
PAST MODALS OF DEDUCTION

4 A Match sentences 1–7 with meanings a)–c).

1 It can't have been the young couple because I was looking at them all the time.

2 So it must have been stolen when I was taking the picture.

3 He must have taken my bag when I wasn't looking.

4 He could have hidden it in his briefcase.

5 The woman must have been working with the guy.

6 She couldn't have been a real customer.

7 But she might have had fake money.

a) I'm almost certain this happened.

b) I feel it's possible this happened.

c) I'm almost certain this didn't happen.

B Complete the rules. Use the sentences in Exercise 4A to help.

> **RULES**
>
> 1 To speculate or make a deduction about something that happened in the past, use the modals:
> must /_____ /_____ /_____ /_____ + have + _____.
>
> 2 To emphasize that an activity was in progress, use modal + have + _____ + _____.
>
> 3 In the passive, use modal + have + _____ + _____.

5 A **CONNECTED SPEECH: past modals** Listen to the pronunciation of the past modals in connected speech. Then listen again and repeat.

must have   could have   might have   can't have   couldn't have

/mʌstəv/   /kʊdəv/   /maɪtəv/   /kɑntəv/   /kʊdəntəv/

B Listen to the phrases and repeat.

must have, must have been, It must have been great!

▶ page 144 LANGUAGE**BANK**

6 A Complete the accounts of two scams. Use modals of deduction and the verbs in parentheses.

> I was taking out money at an ATM. Just as my card came out, a guy behind me said I'd dropped some money. Sure enough, there was a twenty-dollar bill on the floor. I bent down, picked it up and my card was gone ... and so was the man! He ¹_____ (drop) the twenty-dollar bill and pretended it was mine, or the bill ²_____ (fall) out of my wallet, and he simply took advantage of the situation. He ³_____ (pull) my card out of the ATM when I bent down.

> A real state agent was showing me a apartment when she got a phone call from another customer who wanted to put down a deposit on that same apartment. So I gave the agent my deposit, signed the contract and was given the key. When I went back later to move in, the key didn't work ... and the agent didn't answer her phone number! The woman ⁴_____ (be) a real state agent. She ⁵_____ (be) an imposter, and the other customer ⁶_____ (work) with her.

B Discuss in pairs. Which scam in Exercise 6A would be most likely to fool you?

real state agent   estate agent

SPEAKING

7 A Work in pairs. Student A: turn to page 162. Student B: imagine the following situation happened to you. Add some details about the place, time, the amount of money spent on the gifts and your feelings. Prepare to tell Student A.

> It was [name of a festival] and everyone was buying presents. I was in a shopping mall, and I'd bought some games and a camera for people in my family. In the middle of the mall, there was a big sign saying "Free Gift Wrapping," so I left the presents with a woman there and picked them up half an hour later. On the morning of [name of festival], the kids opened their presents, and, inside the boxes, there were just oranges and straw.

B Tell Student A the situation and discuss these questions.

1 Who swapped the presents?

2 How did they trick people into giving them the presents?

3 Why didn't people notice that the presents felt different?

4 How do you think the scam was done?

C Now listen to Student A's situation and discuss his/her questions.

D Turn to page 161 to see if your ideas were right.

HOW TO AVOID TROUBLE ON VACATION

Taxis

Be careful when taking taxis, especially at the airport. As an unsuspecting tourist, you may find yourself charged up to three times the normal fare or in a taxi with a driver who claims to have no change.

- Never **take** a taxi without a company name on its side.
- Always **ask** the approximate fare before getting in.
- **Call** for a taxi ahead of time rather than catching one in the street.
- Make sure you **carry** plenty of change with you.

Money

Be careful around any major tourist site. Pickpockets often work in gangs and will come up behind you while you're walking and unzip your backpack or may "accidentally" bump into you and steal your money or cell before passing these immediately to a partner. Also, take care when using an ATM. A tiny hidden camera may have been installed to steal your card number and PIN.

- **Keep** your credit cards and larger sums of money in a money belt under your clothes.
- Be sure to **keep** any money that you think you'll use that day loose in your pocket, so that you don't need to pull out large bills.
- Be particularly careful to **cover** the keypad when you enter your PIN into an ATM machine.
- **Use** ATMs inside a bank where they are less likely to have been interfered with.

Tours

If someone offers a "budget" tour, you may find that the price is cheap, but you'll spend more time at shopping places not on your itinerary than the places you intended to visit. This is because your "guide" is being paid by the storekeepers for taking you there.

- **Book** tours only with reputable companies.
- Try to **check** with other visitors or with your hotel before booking a tour.
- Take time to **look** on the Internet for reviews and recommendations.

WRITING

A "HOW TO" LEAFLET; LEARN TO AVOID REPETITION

8 A Work in pairs. What advice would you give a visitor to a city about how to avoid getting into trouble?

B Read the extract from a "how to" leaflet for tourists. Which ideas are different from the ones you discussed?

C Complete the guidelines for writing a "how to" leaflet with the words in the box.

> bullet points   title   fonts   sections   contracted   subheading   underlining

1 Give the leaflet an overall _____.
2 Divide the leaflet into different _____, each with its own short _____ .
3 Use different _____ or _____ so that it is easier for the reader to see the main points before they start reading.
4 Use _____ when you are writing a list.
5 To make your leaflet more direct and informal, use "you" and _____ forms.

9 A Look at the verbs in bold in the leaflet and:

1 put a box around two adverbs used before the verbs.
2 underline five verb phrases used before the verbs.
3 circle the remaining four imperatives.

B Complete the rules and examples with words from the leaflet.

To avoid repetition when giving a list of advice:

1 use the adverbs ____always____ and _____.
2 use a range of synonyms (words/phrases) in the imperative:

a) Make _____ you
b) Be _____ to
c) Be particularly _____ to
d) Try _____
e) Take _____ to

10 Write a "how to" leaflet (200–250 words) on one of the following topics. Use a variety of ways to give advice and avoid repetition.

- advice for people traveling solo
- advice for Internet banking
- advice for passing exams
- advice for joining a particular social networking site
- advice for (your own idea)

storekeepers   shopkeepers

9.3)) IT'S AN EMERGENCY!

F reporting an incident
P sentence stress
V incidents

SPEAKING

1 A Work in pairs and look at the pictures. What would you do if you witnessed these situations?

B Work in pairs and discuss.

1 List three situations in which you think you should call emergency services.

2 Read the reasons for calling emergency services below. Which reason do you think is the most ridiculous?

3 Do you think the person was justified in calling the police in any of the situations?

Police are becoming concerned because a significant percentage of calls to emergency services are about everyday inconveniences and problems or are simply ridiculous. Some of the silliest calls include:

- I need help with my math homework.
- I'm having a bad dream. In fact, this is part of it.
- My husband's snoring, and I can't sleep.
- There's a squirrel on my porch, and it's acting suspiciously.
- The weather report was wrong. And now I'm stuck in the snow.
- I'm stuck in traffic and need to get to the bathroom.
- My boyfriend promised to marry me, and now he won't.
- I'm locked in a house. Not my house—I'm a burglar.

VOCABULARY
INCIDENTS

2 A Complete sentences 1–10 with the correct form of a verb phrase in the box.

> fall off   get stuck   knock over   break down   lock out
> run over   get knocked out   be on fire   steal   rob

1 "My card has _____ in the machine."

2 "The house _____—there's smoke coming from the windows."

3 "We crashed into a lamppost and _____ it _____."

4 "My car has _____ on the motorway."

5 "My wallet has _____."

6 "A workman on my roof has just _____ the ladder."

7 "I've _____ myself _____ of my house."

8 "I fell down, but I don't remember anything after that. I think I _____."

9 "Someone's just _____ my cat, and I think they've killed it."

10 "I've just _____! Someone's taken my bag from the changing room."

B Work in pairs. Look at the sentences above and discuss.

1 Whom might the person be calling in each case?

2 What two questions might the other person ask the caller?

3 Which situations would you find the easiest to deal with?

1 In number one, they might be calling the security department in a bank.

▶ page 156 VOCABULARY**BANK**

FUNCTION
REPORTING AN INCIDENT

3 A Listen to the phone conversation. What happened to the man?

B Listen again and complete the report form.

INCIDENT REPORT 2047561A

Name: _____

Date and time of incident: _____

Location of incident: _____

Description of incident (what exactly happened?): _____

_____

Description of stolen or damaged property (serial number, bank card type, value of property, color, make, model of car, etc.): _____

_____

Description of suspect or offender (age, sex, ethnicity, build, clothing, distinguishing marks or features, etc.):

_____

Witnesses: _____

Contact details: _____

_____

bathroom   toilet

EMERGENCY PLAN

 4 A Complete the phrases. Then listen and check.

1 _____ I realized what _____ _____ , he had run off.

2 It was _____ about thirty seconds _____ _____ I realized my wallet _____ _____.

3 But did it _____ your _____ that it wasn't just an accident?

4 It never _____ to me _____ he'd done it on purpose.

5 My mind just went _____.

6 He looked _____ _____ he were just out jogging.

7 It _____ _____ so quickly.

8 He just _____ _____ a normal guy.

9 He _____ me a little _____ that actor.

10 I didn't _____ what he said. It was too quick.

B Work in pairs. Which phrases above a) describe impressions of a person b) refer to time?

C SENTENCE STRESS Underline the main stressed syllables in sentences 1–10 in Exercise 4A. Listen and check. Then listen and repeat.

Before I realized what had happened, he had run off.

▶ page 144 LANGUAGEBANK

5 Work in pairs and role-play the conversation between a police officer and a caller whose bag has been stolen from a store changing room. Use the flow chart to help.

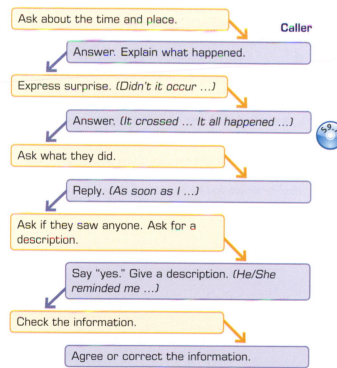

Police Officer

Ask about the time and place.

Caller

Answer. Explain what happened.

Express surprise. (Didn't it occur …)

Answer. (It crossed … It all happened …)

Ask what they did.

Reply. (As soon as I …)

Ask if they saw anyone. Ask for a description.

Say "yes." Give a description. (He/She reminded me …)

Check the information.

Agree or correct the information.

6 Work in pairs.

Student A: choose a situation from Exercise 2A and call the police to report what happened.

Student B: you are the police officer. Use the report form in Exercise 3B to ask questions.

LEARN TO

REPHRASE

7 A Look at the extract. Underline two places where the police officer (A) rephrases something to help the caller (B) understand.

A: Could you tell me exactly when the incident happened?

B: Just now. About an hour ago.

A: Could you be more precise?

B: Excuse me?

A: Could you give me the exact time?

B: I think at 2:50 or 2:55.

A: And where did it happen?

B: Park Avenue.

A: Can you pinpoint the exact location?

B: Pinpoint?

A: Tell me exactly where.

B Match the meaning of the words in bold in 1–5 with phrases a)–e) below.

1 I'll need **to take a statement**.

2 And he **ran into** me **hard** …

3 … a sweater, **gray** color, with a—you know— something you put over your head.

4 … some sort of dark **pants, for running or for the gym.**

5 And were there any other people **in the vicinity**?

a) in the surrounding area—nearby

b) tracksuit bottoms

c) a hood … a hoodie

d) to write down some details

e) collided with

C Listen and check your answers.

American Speak out TIP Using familiar words to explain unfamiliar vocabulary not only helps communication but can also be an opportunity to learn more sophisticated vocabulary.

SPEAKING

8 A Work in pairs. There was a burglary in your house last night. Student A: turn to page 162. Student B: turn to page 161.

B Work in pairs. Student B: ask Student A how the burglar got into the house. Draw a line showing his route. Help Student A with difficult vocabulary.

A: The burglar first climbed the … thing for rainwater … going down …

B: It's like a pipe, right? Which one?

A: Yes, like a pipe. The one on the left.

C Change roles. Student A: ask Student B how the burglar got out of the house. Draw a line showing his route. Help Student B with difficult vocabulary.

gray   grey

DVD PREVIEW

1 A Work in pairs and discuss.

1 What are different ways that people react in a disaster situation? Think about a building on fire, a sinking ship or a plane making a crash landing.

2 What do you think survival in a disaster depends on?

3 Which factors are connected to the character of the survivor?

B Read the program information. What factors for survival does it mention? What do you think it means by "how your brain reacts"?

▶ Horizon: How to Survive a Disaster

When disaster strikes, who lives and who dies is not purely a matter of luck. In every disaster, from those people face once in a lifetime, to those they face every day, there are things that can be done to increase the chances of getting out alive. Some of these things have to do with planning ahead, some have to do with how your brain reacts, and some are simply down to luck. In this program, we look at the sinking of the car ferry *Estonia* in 1994 through the experience of Paul Barney, a passenger on the *Estonia*, and examine why it is that he ended up among the survivors.

DVD VIEW

2 A Watch the DVD. Why did Paul Barney survive while others didn't?

B Are the statements true (T) or false (F)? Watch the DVD again and check your ideas.

1 Paul Barney slept in the cafeteria below the waterline.

2 He said he wasn't scared on board the ship, but was in the life raft.

3 One hundred and thirty-seven people died on the *Estonia*.

4 His tunnel vision caused him to focus on saving himself.

5 Professor Silke said that tunnel vision is not always a good thing.

6 Paul doesn't understand why some people didn't try to escape.

7 Most people keep a clear head in a disaster.

C Work in pairs. Complete the extracts by writing three words in each blank. Then watch the DVD again to check.

1 … I say to them, really, that there was no time _____, there was literally no time.

2 It was a very scary place to be because you never knew whether the next wave was going to _____ from the life raft.

3 I'm purely thinking of what's going to _____.

4 … our brain is focusing on whatever the threat or danger is, and it's focusing on that to the exclusion _____.

5 One of the things I remember clearly is the water actually coming into the cafeteria and seeing lots of people around just _____ spot.

D Work in pairs and discuss. How do you think you would react in a disaster like this? Would you be like Paul or would you be like one of the people he describes as "rooted to the spot"?

American Speakout agreeing on priorities

3 A Listen to people deciding on things to take on a life raft. Which items below do they talk about? Why do they decide to take/reject each one?

- blankets
- canned food
- flashlight (with generator)
- lighter
- dried fruit
- plastic raincoat
- first aid kit
- hand mirror
- fishing kit (line, hook)
- sunscreen
- survival manual
- drinking cup

B Look at the key phrases. Listen again and check (✓) the phrases you hear.

> **KEY PHRASES**
>
> It depends on [what/whether] …, doesn't it?
>
> It's important to … isn't it?
>
> It's (not) a top priority to be able to …
>
> What would we do with a … ?
>
> I'd say that … is/are [essential/vital/crucial]
>
> … to keep you [warm/dry/alive],
>
> … to [prevent/keep/protect] you from [the sun/dehydrating/getting …]
>
> [It/That] hadn't occurred to me.
>
> We need to prioritize them.
>
> I can't see the point of [taking, choosing] …

C Work alone and choose six items from the list in Exercise 3A. Make notes on why they are important and why other items are not as important.

D Work in groups and take turns. Try to persuade the other students that your choices are important, then decide on six items as a group.

writeback an escape story

4 A A website has asked readers to write a story about a lucky escape prompted by a string of words. Work in pairs and discuss. What story can you imagine for the word string below?

August	camping	forest	dry	tent	sleep
smoke	fire	trapped	soup	escape	

B Read the story. What happened and how did the man get out of the situation without being hurt?

It was mid-August, and some friends and I went camping in a forest about an hour's drive from where we were living. It had been a very dry summer, and we should have thought about the dangers of fire, but we didn't. We pitched our tents, made a campfire and cooked a nice soup for dinner. After a while, we were all really tired, so we went to sleep.

About an hour later, I woke up to the smell of smoke. I realized right away that there was a fire and that it was right in front of the tent—in fact, some dry leaves next to the campfire had caught fire, and the front of the tent was starting to burn. I was trapped inside.

Luckily, one of my friends who was in another tent woke up, too, and he poured the leftover soup on the burning tent. That made it possible for me to escape, and I crawled out as fast as I could. We put out the campfire, but I couldn't go back to sleep. I think I was in shock—it was a very lucky escape.

C Choose another word string. Write your story (150–250 words) using three paragraphs.

spring	countryside	lost	dark	fence
garden	dog	sandwich	run	jump	escape

sea	cool	friends	swim	snorkel	hours
tired	cold	stiff	drowning	save	escape

D Read other students' stories. Which one do you think was the most unusual escape?

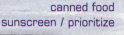

canned food
sunscreen / prioritize

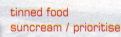

tinned food
suncream / prioritise

V CRIME

1 A Make a list of as many crimes as you can remember.

B Work in pairs and think of:

1 two crimes that involve damage to property.

2 three crimes that involve people and can happen on the street.

3 three crimes that involve technical expertise on computers or other machines.

4 a crime involving money that could be committed by a company.

5 a crime that involves theft but not usually in a street.

C Work in pairs and discuss. Which crimes are most often in the news in your town/city/country?

G -ING FORM AND INFINITIVE

2 A Underline the correct alternatives in the article.

→ OK, you've just been mugged. Your first impulse may be to go on ¹*doing/ to do* whatever you were doing, but don't. First, stop ²*checking/to check* that you're fine. Some victims who have been struck actually forget ³*being/to be* hit and only discover injuries later. Try ⁴*finding/to find* a safe place, maybe a café with people (you may need to borrow a phone). You're probably in shock—give yourself time to stop ⁵*shaking/to shake* and take slow, deep breaths to calm yourself. If this doesn't work, try ⁶*drinking/to drink* some cool water—avoid coffee. Remember ⁷*calling/to call* someone you know and tell them where you are and what happened. If you remember ⁸*seeing/to see* what the mugger looked like, write down the details. If you forget ⁹*doing/ to do* this, you may find that you can't recall much detail later when you talk to the police, and you'll regret not ¹⁰*doing/to do* this.

B Work in pairs and discuss. Which ideas do you agree with?

V SYNONYMS

3 A Rewrite the sentences with a synonym for the words/phrases in bold.

1 Does listening to music when you study **divert your attention**?

2 Can you **snatch** fifteen minutes' sleep in the middle of the day?

3 Would you find it easier **to pretend to be** someone older or younger?

4 If you exaggerate your Internet profile, are you **fooling** people unacceptably?

5 Have you ever **been taken in by** a lie someone told you?

6 Imagine you could **swap** identities with someone for just one day. Who would it be?

B Work in pairs and take turns. Ask and answer the questions.

G PAST MODALS OF DEDUCTION

4 A Work in pairs and read the situations. For each one, rewrite the options using a modal of deduction.

1 A man checked his mailbox every day, but it was always empty. Meanwhile his friends sent him dozens of letters a week.

a) I'm sure the man moved recently. *The man must have moved recently.*

b) Maybe his friends sent mail to the old address.

c) I'm certain the mailman didn't deliver the letters.

2 A pianist performed a concert in a concert hall. She played perfectly, but, at the end, no one clapped.

a) She was probably practicing in an empty concert hall.

b) I'm certain she was deaf.

c) They definitely didn't like the music.

B Look at the extra information below and make a final guess to explain each situation. Then turn to page 162 and check your ideas.

1 The friends wrote the correct address on the letters. The mailmain always put the letters in the mailbox. There wasn't a hole in the bottom of the mailbox.

2 The concert hall was full. No one had hearing problems—everyone heard the performance and liked it.

F REPORTING AN INCIDENT

5 A Complete the sentences with the correct form of a word in the box. One of the words is not used.

> ~~occur~~   if   go   not catch
> remind   become   like   cross
> realize   happen (x2)

1 It *occurred* to me that he/she shouldn't have …

2 He/She _____ me of …

3 It was only later that I _____ …

4 My mind _____ blank.

5 Before I realized what had _____, she/he'd …

6 I _____ _____ the license plate.

7 It all _____ so fast.

8 It _____ my mind that …

9 He/She looked as _____ …

10 He/She seemed _____ …

B Work in pairs. Choose one of the following incidents to report to the police and decide which sentences from Exercise 5A you could use.

• someone shoplifting in a department store

• someone looking at confidential information on someone else's computer

• someone hanging around an ATM with two friends sitting in a car nearby

C Work in pairs and take turns. Role-play the phone call. Student A: you are the police officer. Student B: you have seen the incident.

mailbox / mailman   post box / postman

10 culture

MOVING EXPERIENCES   p116

POPULAR CULTURE   p119

ON YOUR LEFT ...   p122

THE PEOPLE'S PALACE   p124

What area of the arts do you enjoy?

INTERVIEWS

VOCABULARY
ADJECTIVES TO DESCRIBE MOVIES

1 A Work in pairs and discuss. Do you like the types of movies shown in the pictures? What types of movies do you like?

B Work in pairs and check what you know. Cover Exercise 1C and complete the descriptions with a suitable adjective.

1 The documentary really made me think and raised lots of questions. It was …

2 I got lost sometimes—you had to pay attention to keep up with the plot and the action because it was so …

3 The relationship between the two people was sensitively handled and almost made me cry. It was very …

4 Some scenes were scary and made my skin crawl. It was …

5 I was on the edge of my seat and couldn't look away for a single moment. It was really …

6 The acting and direction were all exceptional; it'll win all the awards this year. It was absolutely …

7 I wouldn't be surprised if people start protests against this documentary. It's extremely …

8 There was a lot of violence and blood. For me, it was just too …

9 We couldn't stop laughing; it was …

C Complete sentences 1–9 above with the words/ phrases a)–j). One item has two answers.

a) fast-paced
b) touching
c) gripping
d) gory
e) hysterical
f) creepy
g) controversial
h) full of suspense
i) outstanding
j) thought-provoking

D Check what you remember. Which adjectives in the box are synonyms or near-synonyms for the adjectives in Exercise 1C?

> hilarious   moving   offensive   superb   dramatic
> stunning   poignant   intense

2 A Work in groups. List the names of ten to fifteen movies you all know.

B Take turns. Student A: describe one of the movies using at least three of the adjectives from Exercise 1C. The other students: ask a *yes/no* question each and *then* guess the movie.

A: It's fast-paced; the special effects are fantastic; and some of it is gory.

B: Is it a thriller?

A: Yes.

C: Does it star … ?

LISTENING

3 A Listen to someone talk about a movie he never gets bored with watching. What is the movie, and what is the main reason he likes it?

B Listen again and make notes on the following:

1 why it's family-friendly

2 a memorable thing about the bad guy

3 where the movie got its title

4 what the woman thinks about the movie

5 examples of gripping moments

6 something unusual about the stunts

7 something the two people say about the heroine

8 the woman's preference in movies

C Work in pairs and discuss. If you haven't seen the movie, would you like to watch it based on this description? Is it true that there aren't many action movies which include comedy?

4 A Work alone. Choose a movie you never get bored with and make notes about:

• the actors.
• the plot.
• the setting.
• why you like it.

B Work in pairs. Tell each other about your movie.

C Work with other students. Take turns telling each other about your choice. Which movie you heard about would you most like to see?

> Going to the movies is a popular freetime activity, but, with the rise of online streaming websites, many young people prefer to watch movies on their laptops. Netflix, a popular streaming site, has over 33 million users worldwide.

GRAMMAR

RELATIVE CLAUSES

5 A Check what you know. Complete the online forum messages with *who, whom,* that, which, *whose, where* or *when*.

What movie do you never get bored with?

The *Shawshank Redemption* is a prison movie [1]_____ goes beyond the violence seen in such movies. The story centers on the life-changing relationship between a new prisoner, Andy (Tim Robbins), [2]_____ is imprisoned for murder, and Red (Morgan Freeman), a long-time prisoner [3]_____ he makes friends with. You really care about these two characters, [4]_____ unlikely friendship blossoms over the course of the movie. I must have seen it twenty times, and it's the one movie [5]_____ I never get bored with, especially Robbins' and Freeman's performances, for [6]_____, surprisingly, neither won a major award.

My all-time favorite is *Groundhog Day*, in [7]_____ Bill Murray relives one day over and over again. He plays Phil, a TV weatherman visiting a small U.S. town, [8]_____ he reports on a local annual festival. Phil detests the assignment and the local people, [9]_____ makes his situation even worse when he gets stuck with both. The story is endlessly inventive, by turns hilarious and poignant. It is especially touching in the moment [10]_____ Phil realizes he loves Rita (Andie Macdowell) but can't win her, [11]_____ is a turning point in his transformation into a decent human being. He actually ends up loving the town [12]_____ inhabitants he initially despised. A classic!

B Complete the rules. Use the forum messages in Exercise 5A to help.

1 Defining relative clauses give *essential/extra information* about a person, thing, place or time. Non-defining relative clauses give *essential/extra information*.

2 The relative pronoun *that* can replace *who* or *whom* in *defining/non-defining* clauses only.

3 The relative pronoun can be omitted when it is the *subject/object* of the verb in the relative clause.

4 Prepositions can come (a) at the *beginning/ end* of a clause or (b) *before/after* the relative pronoun. *(a)/(b)* is more formal.

5 *What/Which* introducing a relative clause can be used to refer to the whole of a previous clause.

6 Commas are used before and after *defining/ non-defining clauses*.

6 A Complete the forum message with commas.

It's a movie that appeals to the teenage market and centers on the relationship between Bella who has just arrived in town and her mysterious classmate Edward whose family seems to have a strange secret. When Bella discovers Edward's true identity which happens about a third of the way through the movie she has a big decision to make, a decision that will change her entire life.

B INTONATION: relative clauses Listen to the intonation in the non-defining clauses. Are they higher or lower than the rest of the sentence?

C Listen again and say the recording at the same time, copying the intonation.

▶ page 146 LANGUAGE**BANK**

7 Combine the extracts from reviews using a relative clause.

1 The main role is played by Chiwetel Ejiofor. His portrayal of Solomon Northup earned him several awards.

2 Megastar Chris Hemsworth gives an emotional performance in his latest movie. His career got its biggest boost from his role in *Thor*.

3 *Invictus* is a story about leadership and forgiveness at a critical period. Nelson Mandela had just become president of South Africa.

4 The movie *Star Trek* was based on a popular TV series. William Shatner played the role of Captain Kirk in the series.

5 The movie was Daniel Craig's third outing as James Bond. It was directed by Sam Mendes.

6 Adrian Brody shot to fame after starring in *The Pianist*. He won the Best Actor Oscar for this.

7 *Lost in Translation* takes place in a Tokyo hotel. The two main characters meet and form an unusual bond there.

8 *The Hurt Locker* is a war movie directed by Kathryn Bigelow. The choice of Jordan as the filming location was important for her.

SPEAKING

8 A Complete the sentences below so that they are true for you.

I loathe movies where …

I like the work of the director … , whose …

My favorite actress is … , who …

My favorite actor is … , who …

The movie I most liked recently is …

I like it in movies when …

B Work in pairs and take turns. Talk about your ideas and ask follow-up questions. Find out what you have in common.

MIDNIGHT IN PARIS

Midnight in Paris is set in Paris in the present and in different periods in the past. It stars Owen Wilson as Gil, a Hollywood screenwriter, and Rachel McAdams as Inez, his beautiful fiancée.

As the movie opens, Gil is on holiday in Paris with Inez and her wealthy parents. He is supposed to be in love with his girlfriend, but his love affair really seems to be with Paris in the springtime. One evening, while wandering around the city, he gets lost, and, as the clock strikes midnight, an old Peugeot car pulls up. Inside the car are a group of party-goers who are dressed in 1920s clothes and who invite him to join them. They go to a party where Gil realizes he has been transported to the 1920s, a period which he loves. We see him meeting some of his intellectual and artistic heroes from that time and falling in love with Adriana, Picasso's mistress. Meanwhile, in the present, Gil's bride-to-be and her parents become more and more annoyed and suspicious about his nightly disappearances. Eventually Gil realizes Inez is not right for him and breaks up with her. He decides to stay and live in his beloved Paris.

Skillfully directed by Woody Allen, the movie cuts between the glitter of Paris in the twenties and the present-day city. The script is alternately gripping, shocking and hilarious, and the camerawork is stunning. As Gil, Owen Wilson is appealing in his enthusiasm and love of Paris in the past. However, for me, it is the character of Adriana, convincingly acted by Marion Cotillard, who is the most fascinating of all.

With its charm, sparkling wit and engaging leaps forward and backward in time, *Midnight in Paris* is a light, delightful movie that I'd thoroughly recommend.

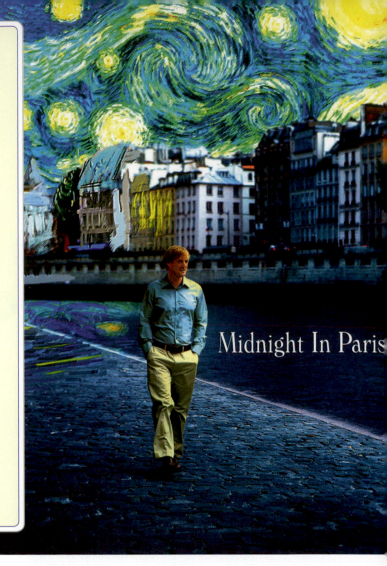

Midnight In Paris

WRITING

A REVIEW; LEARN TO USE ADVERB + PAST PARTICIPLE COMBINATIONS

9 A Work in pairs and discuss the questions.

1 Where do you usually read movie reviews (e.g., on the Internet, in magazines)?

2 What is the <u>main</u> purpose of a movie review?
   • to make people want to see the movie
   • to help people decide if they want to see a movie
   • to give factual information about the movie

3 Which of the topics in the box do you usually find in a movie review?

> plot summary   description of the movie's ending
> actors' names   recommendation
> ticket prices   setting of the movie
> reviewer's opinion of different elements

B Read the movie review above. Would you like to see the movie? Why/Why not?

C Read the review again and write the topic of each paragraph. Use the topics in the box to help.

10 A Underline two adverb + past participle combinations in paragraph 3 of the review.

B Write three adverbs from the box next to each participle to complete the phrases. Some can be used more than once.

> convincingly   harshly   skillfully   widely   sensitively
> overwhelmingly   highly   poignantly   heavily

1 _____ / _____ / _____ directed by …
2 _____ / _____ / _____ acted by …
3 _____ / _____ / _____ praised by …
4 _____ / _____ / _____ criticized by …

11 A Make notes about a movie you have seen recently or a movie you never get bored with. Use the topic areas from Exercise 9C.

B Write a first draft of your review (120–180 words). Use adjectives and at least two adverb + past participle combinations.

C Exchange with another student and read each other's review. Is it interesting and clear? Suggest two or three improvements.

D Write a final version of the review.

G participle clauses
P word stress; connected speech
V the arts; two-part phrases

READING

1 A Work in pairs and look at the pictures. What do you think is the most difficult part of each performer's job?

B Work in pairs and discuss these questions from a magazine article. Make notes on your answers.

1 How do actors cry on demand?
2 Do big stars have to audition for movie roles?
3 How do singers keep their voices steady when they're dancing?
4 Why is rock music played so loud at concerts?
5 Who decides whether something is "art" or not?
6 Why do works of art get stolen if they can't be sold without attracting attention?
7 What's the secret to making an audience laugh?
8 How does a comedian deal with hecklers?

C Work in pairs. Student A: turn to page 163. Student B: quickly read the text on this page. Which four questions above does it answer?

D Read the text again. Write a maximum of five key words for each answer to help you remember the information.

E Work in pairs. Cover the text and look at your notes from Exercise 1D. Tell your partner about the answers.

POPULAR CULTURE Q&A

Want to know the best-kept secrets of popular culture? Read our top questions & answers to find out.

Q:

A: Rock music is characterized by a strong bass line and hard, driving rhythm and percussion parts, which are greatly enhanced by amplification. At some point in the evolution of rock, audiences became almost addicted to the sensations of the music they loved "vibrating" inside them at concerts. The listeners go beyond hearing the music and feel it through their whole body, feel its vibrations, provided it is loud enough. Heavy metal music played softly sounds stupid and can only be played as it was intended to be: very, very loudly.

Q:

A: A big star auditioning for a part is almost unheard of. Actors such as Tom Hanks go straight from movie to movie, so directors and producers have access to a whole portfolio of their work. The closest such actors ever get to anything resembling an audition is when they're invited to chat about the project informally, which gives the director and producer a chance to evaluate the actor without it feeling like a test. The stars don't usually even have to read part of the script. More often, it's actually a matter of the actor choosing whether to work with the director!

Q:

A: Every stand-up comedian knows that making people laugh with prepared material, on stage, is very different from making your friends or co-workers laugh in an informal setting. You need to focus on technique, such as which words to stress, when to pause, how to use facial expressions and body movements, as well as sensing how to work each individual audience. Interestingly, shows with paying audiences are better than freebies. Having paid to be entertained, people are often more ready and willing to laugh.

Q:

A: Criminals steal paintings only when they already have a buyer. Sometimes, a wealthy private collector actually requests a particular piece to be stolen—essentially orders it—for part of their private collection. The collector knows that it can never be shown publicly, but that's not why they want the piece in the first place. Valuable works of art are a favorite commodity for criminal organizations, who will use them in place of cash for making deals with each other. They are also useful for money launderers, since works of art are easier to transport and harder to trace than cash, as well as easily traded on the black market.

characterized characterised

GRAMMAR

PARTICIPLE CLAUSES

2 A Read the article below. In what situations do celebrities use fake names? What is the joke in each chosen name?

Do stars use their real names when traveling?

In short, no. In fact, stars [1]**registered at hotels under their real name** are a rarity—their day can be ruined by paparazzi [2]**trying to take their pictures** and members of the public [3]**taking selfies**. So if you're going to change your name, why not have fun doing it? Names [4]**involving wordplay** are common: Britney Spears uses Ms. Alotta Warmheart among other names, and Brad Pitt and Jennifer Aniston, [5]**married in 2000 but divorced five years later**, used to call themselves Mr. and Mrs. Ross Vegas. And the fun doesn't end there—the name [6]**used by George Clooney** when he was traveling caused him great amusement: Arnold Schwarzenegger. "It was funny; the hotel staff had to call me Mr. Schwarzenegger, when they knew, of course, I wasn't him," said Clooney.

B Work in pairs and look at the participle clauses in bold in the article. Then answer the questions.

1 Which participle clauses in bold replace relative clauses?

2 What is the full relative clause in each case?

3 Which two verb forms can a participle clause begin with?

C Compare the sentences below and underline the participle clauses. Then complete the rule.

1 a) Names that involve wordplay are common.

   b) Names involving wordplay are common.

2 a) The people who worked in the hotel thought the name was funny.

   b) The people working in the hotel thought the name was funny.

3 a) The hotel, which was built in the 1980s and which is often used by movie stars, is famous.

   b) The hotel, built in the 1980s and regularly used by movie stars, is famous.

> **RULES**
>
> 1 When a relative clause has an active verb in the present simple or past simple, the participle clause uses a _____ participle.
>
> 2 When a relative clause has a passive verb in the present simple or past simple, the participle clause uses a _____ participle.

> **American Speak out TIP**
> Using participle clauses can improve the level of your writing and speaking. Try to improve this sentence by using a participle clause: *I couldn't concentrate on the concert because there were so many people who took pictures.*

▶ page 146 **LANGUAGEBANK**

3 A Rewrite the sentences using a participle clause.

1 People who take pictures should ask their subjects' permission first.

2 Movies that are based on books are disappointing.

3 It's great to see rock stars in their sixties who still play concerts.

4 Architecture that was designed in the 1960s is generally pretty ugly and ought to be pulled down.

5 Pictures of people who are posing for the camera don't work as well as spontaneous pictures.

6 Movie and TV stars who appear at the theater attract huge audiences.

7 Jokes that involve racial stereotypes are not funny.

8 Photographers who used software to enhance their pictures were justifiably banned from entering a national competition last month.

B Work in pairs and discuss. Do you agree with the statements in Exercise 3A? Give examples.

VOCABULARY

THE ARTS

4 A Which of the forum comments are generally positive (✓), negative (✗) or mixed (—)?

> ❝ I'd read a lot about this new singer in the music press. She's certainly **creating a stir** with her **groundbreaking** mix of rap and folk. Ever since she got those **rave reviews** in the press, each performance has been a **sell-out**, and it's impossible to get tickets. Everyone says it's the **must-see** performance of the year. Is she really that good? ❞

> ❝ Well, after all the **hype** surrounding her concerts, I went to see her on Friday, expecting something really sensational … but the concert was a real **letdown**! It was a complete **flop** because we couldn't hear her well. ❞

> ❝ Yeah, I was at that gig, and the technical side was pretty bad, but her album is amazing, really innovative. I've never heard anything quite like it before. I just hope she doesn't go **mainstream** and boring like all the other **alternative** artists. ❞

B Work in pairs. What do you think the words and phrases in bold above mean? Use the context, grammar and your knowledge of similar words to help. Then check in a dictionary.

C WORD STRESS Work in pairs and say the words and phrases in bold. Which syllable(s) is/are stressed? Listen to the words in context and check.

D Think of a performance you have seen or heard. Write a forum entry about it using at least four of the words that are new to you.

E Read other students' forum entries. Find a performance you would like to see or hear.

▶ page 157 **VOCABULARYBANK**

well   properly

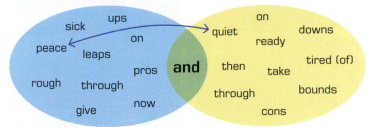

SPEAKING

5 A Choose three of the questions below to answer. Write the name of the thing/person and two or three words to explain why you liked it/him/her.

1 What's the best gig/concert or dance performance you've ever been to?

2 What's the best music album ever made?

3 Who's the funniest comedian you know?

4 What's the most moving, scary or exciting movie you've ever seen?

5 What's the most memorable exhibition you've ever been to?

6 What's the best picture you've ever taken?

7 Who's the painter or other type of artist you most like? What's your favorite work of his/hers?

8 What's the most unforgettable show or play you've ever seen?

B Work in pairs and take turns. Talk about your experiences and feelings.

C Work in groups and take turns. Recommend something you've recently been to/seen/heard.

VOCABULARY *PLUS*

TWO-PART PHRASES

6 A Work in pairs and look at the two-part phrases in sentences 1 and 2. What do you think they mean?

1 There are some basic **dos and don'ts** when taking a good picture.

2 I've worked in the movie business **off and on** for most of my life.

B Check your ideas with the dictionary entries.

> **D** **dos and don'ts** things that you should and should not do: *the dos and don'ts of having a pet*

> **O** **off and on/on and off** for short periods of time but not regularly: *I worked as a secretary off and on for three years.*

from Longman Active Study Dictionary

7 A Match a word from A with one from B to make a two-part phrase.

sick · ups · on · quiet · on · downs · peace · leaps · ready · then · tired (of) · rough · pros · **and** · take · through · bounds · give · through · now · cons

B CONNECTED SPEECH Listen and check. Then listen and repeat, paying attention to the linking, the weak form of *and* /ən/ and the dropping of /d/ in connected speech.

ups‿and downs

8 A Work in pairs. Student A: turn to page 163. Student B: turn to page 161. Read the definitions and then complete five of the sentences below.

1 I hate having music on in the background. I prefer some _____ and _____.

2 I used to go to rock concerts a lot, but nowadays I only go _____ and _____.

3 I'm a reggae fan _____ and _____.

4 I'm _____ and _____ of having to listen to people's favorite music on the train. I wish they'd turn their MP3 players down.

5 Any skill such as playing the piano improves by _____ and _____ if you practice enough.

6 Every relationship has its _____ and _____, so it's not surprising that most bands break up after a few years.

7 I don't like jazz. Some of the pieces go _____ and _____ for far too long.

8 It's OK for my neighbors to play music I don't like. You have to have a bit of _____ and _____. I'm sure they don't like my music!

9 There are _____ and _____ to listening to a live recording as opposed to a studio album.

10 Some of the music videos made by ordinary people on YouTube are a bit _____ and _____, but that's OK.

B Work in pairs and take turns. Help your partner complete the sentences and understand the two-part phrases.

C Change five of the sentences so that they are true for you. Then compare with a partner. How many do you agree on?

▶ page 157 **VOCABULARY BANK**

10.3))) ON YOUR LEFT ...

F giving a tour
P intonation in comments
V dimensions

Greenwich Village, New York, USA

SPEAKING

1 Work in pairs and discuss the questions.

1 Have you ever shown anyone around your town/city?

2 What places of interest in your town/city you would take a visitor to? Why?

FUNCTION

GIVING A TOUR

2 A Work in pairs. Look at the pictures of Greenwich Village and Oxford and discuss. What do you know about each place? Which would you most like to visit?

B Listen to two people showing visitors around Greenwich Village and Oxford. Number the pictures in the order you hear them.

C Listen again and write one fact you hear about each place.

1 the Blue Note Jazz Club
2 the Café Reggio
3 Greenwich Village in general
4 Washington Square Park
5 the Bodleian Library
6 the Oxford colleges
7 the Bridge of Sighs
8 New College
9 the "Schools"
10 Christ Church College

3 A Work in pairs and complete the phrases. Sometimes there is more than one possible answer.

Leading the Way

Let's ¹_____ over to Washington Square Park and then ²_____ back.

Why don't we ³_____ our steps and go back to the Café Reggio?

Giving Facts

It was ⁴_____ on the Arc de Triomphe.

It was built to ⁵_____ the hundredth anniversary of the inauguration of George Washington as president.

In front of us is the Bodleian, ⁶_____ after the ⁷_____—Thomas Bodley.

Commenting on Facts

⁸_____ I'm sure you ⁹_____, Greenwich Village has always been a center of artistic life—very bohemian.

¹⁰_____, the oldest college was actually only founded a hundred or so years earlier!

¹¹_____, the biggest room can seat somewhere in the region of 500 students, although I haven't seen it myself.

We can actually go inside if we're quick. It's well ¹²_____ a visit.

B Compare your answers with the audio script on page 175.

C INTONATION IN COMMENTS Listen to the intonation in the phrases. Then listen again and repeat.

Interestingly, the statue disappeared at the time of his death.

The story goes, he threw it in the lake.

Apparently, it was made of gold.

Surprisingly, no one has ever tried to find it.

▶ page 146 LANGUAGEBANK

E   F

Oxford, England

4 A Complete A's part in the extracts from a tour of Paris.

A: ¹Let's / head / over / the cathedral, Notre Dame.

B: On the island? Do we have time to go inside?

A: ²Yes, / well worth / visit it.

B: … So that's the Arc de Triomphe?

A: ³Yes, / model / a famous Roman arch.

B: And why was it built?

A: ⁴celebrate / one / Napoleon's great victories.

A: ⁵ … So here we are / the Eiffel Tower / named / its designer, Gustave Eiffel.

B: Wow! It's impressive.

A: ⁶Yeah / apparently / can sway two to three inches in the wind!

B Work in pairs and take turns. Practice the conversations using the prompts above.

VOCABULARY

DIMENSIONS

5 Complete the tourist's questions with the noun or verb form of the adjectives in parentheses.

1 What is the _____ of the tower? (high)

2 So the road goes the _____ of the town? (long)

3 When did they _____ the entrance? (wide)

4 What is the _____ of the wall here? (thick)

5 The road _____ here. Why's that? (narrow)

6 What's the _____ of the river and _____ of the water here? (broad, deep)

7 Why don't they _____ the map? It's so small. (large)

8 It's nine o'clock, and it's still light. When do the days _____ here? (short)

LEARN TO
EXPRESS ESTIMATES

6 A Look at the extracts and underline five phrases for expressing estimates (when we don't know the exact number).

1 A: How many colleges are there?

   B: Just under forty. Well, thirty-eight to be exact.

2 A: How "new" is new?

   B: Roughly 1370.

   A: You're kidding!

   B: No, really! Interestingly, the oldest college was actually only founded a hundred or so years earlier!

3 Apparently, the biggest room can seat somewhere in the region of five hundred students.

4 A: How many students are there at the college in total?

   B: To be honest, it depends. In term time, you'd probably get upwards of twenty thousand.

B Which phrases in Exercise 6A could be replaced by 1) *fewer than*, 2) *more than* or 3) *about/around/ approximately*?

C Listen and check (✓) the nearest number.

1 a) 4,080   b) 4,921

2 a) 30   b) 38

3 a) 3,937   b) 4,020

4 a) 444   b) 475

5 a) 6.74   b) 4.10

6 a) 318   b) 371

D Work in pairs and take turns estimating:

• the number of students in your school/employees in your workplace.

• the age of the building you're in.

• the population of your town/city.

• the distance from your home to where you are now.

• the cost of dinner in a good restaurant in your town/city.

• the number of contacts on your cell phone.

• the number of English words you know.

SPEAKING

7 A Work in pairs. Design a one-hour walking or cycling tour of a town/city you know for a visitor. Make notes on:

• four or five places to see.

• a fact or personal opinion about each place.

• some approximate numbers associated with the place (how many people visit it; how much it costs; how old/ long/high, etc. it is).

B Work with a new partner and take turns. Role-play the tour. Student A: lead the way. Student B: ask questions.

DVD PREVIEW

1 A Look at the picture of a new library and discuss the questions in pairs.

1 Which words/phrases in the box would you use to describe the building?

> crazy   makes a bold statement   unique   fresh
> pleasing to the eye   modern   too busy   delicate
> too elaborate   beautiful   amazing   unsightly

2 How is it different from what you expect a library to look like?

3 What facilities would you expect to be included in a 21st-century library?

B Read the program information and look at the pictures. Which of the following do you think you will see in the DVD?

1 The reporter interviews local people, the designer of the building and celebrities.

2 The designer explains why she used rings as part of the design.

3 The local people feel mostly positive about the new library.

▶ The Culture Show: The People's Palace

At a time when many libraries across Britain face budget cuts and closure, Birmingham is opening the biggest public library in Europe. Is this a new breed of super library for the future?

This program explores the cutting-edge building to discover what a 21st-century library looks like, what goes into its design and how local people—the taxpayers—feel about it. Perhaps most importantly, we find out what role the library has in the Internet age.

DVD VIEW

2 A Watch the DVD and check your answers to Exercise 1B.

B Work in pairs and answer the questions. Then watch the DVD again and check.

1 Why and how is Birmingham regenerating its downtown?

2 How does the designer describe the city of Birmingham? What characteristics did she try to reflect in the library's design?

3 Why did she call it a "People's Palace"?

4 What is there inside the library besides shelves of books?

5 What is the "façade bench," and what can you do there?

6 What do people say they like once they're inside the library?

C Watch the DVD again and underline the correct alternative.

1 We started with this idea, that's the *tradition/ heritage* of the proud industrial city, with the steel industry.

2 I think any *funding/investment* of money put into libraries at the moment is fantastic.

3 And in a time of economic *austerity/strictness*, what a bold step to take. Wonderful stuff!

4 There's a lot of people, students, they want to be *independent/individual* but be part of a bigger collective.

5 It's brilliant, yeah, I really like it, it's very *user-friendly/easy-to-use*.

6 I love this in *particular/especially*. I love this outside bit/section with the balcony.

3 Work in pairs and discuss whether you agree/disagree with the statements.

1 Local governments shouldn't spend taxpayer's money on expensive architecture.

2 Libraries still have an important role in the Internet age.

3 For a society to be healthy, it needs public spaces like libraries, parks and theaters.

American Speakout a town project

4 A Listen to three people discussing a new public space or artistic project for their town. Which project does each person, Tim, Nigel and Sarah, like from the list below? Why?

- an outdoor sculpture (modern or traditional)
- a concert space
- a theater workshop space for young people
- a state-of-the-art multiplex cinema
- a botanical garden
- a skateboarding park

B Listen again and check (✓) the key phrases you hear.

> **KEYPHRASES**
>
> I'm really in favor of the …
>
> I think that it would be [beneficial for the community/popular/ …].
>
> The only thing that would concern me though is that …
>
> I'd rather have something that would [appeal to all ages/make a statement/…]
>
> We have to consider [costs/maintenance/ …]
>
> Can you see the [older/younger] generation [using/liking] it?

5 A Work in pairs. You are responsible for choosing an artistic project for your town/city. Choose two items from the list in Exercise 4A. The items must:

- have artistic and/or architectural merit.
- represent the town/city in some way.
- convey a positive image.

B Work with other students. Discuss your ideas and decide on one project.

C Present your decision to the class.

writeback a work of art

6 A Work in pairs. Read about the competition and tell your partner what you would choose and why.

> We want you to write about a favorite work of art or building. It could be a statue or sculpture, a fountain or bridge, a painting or even a favorite room. Send us your description in 150–250 words, and we'll put the five best entries on our website.

B Read the description and check (✓) the topics in the box that the writer mentions.

> setting   when it was made   material   color
> size   who made it   why he/she likes it

My favorite building is in fact a bridge, the Millau Viaduct in southern France. It's an awe-inspiring structure, as much a work of art as it is a bridge. It towers over the valley that it crosses, but is so graceful that it seems to me more an integral part of the natural environment than the architectural and engineering achievement that it is.

It was designed by a French engineer and a British architect who conceived it as a series of towers, which look like the masts of a ship, from which cables are suspended, the cables that support the road surface that runs 1.5 miles across the valley. The highest tower is the tallest structure in France, taller than the Eiffel Tower, and I think the tallest bridge in the world.

This 21st-century masterpiece is breathtaking to behold, and it gives me a sense of calm every time I look at it. No one should miss it if they are visiting this part of France.

C Write your competition entry. Use the box in Exercise 6B for ideas of what to include.

D Read your classmates' competition entries. Which one makes you most want to visit the place they write about?

V ADJECTIVES

1 A Work in pairs. Make a list of as many adjectives for describing movies as you can remember.

B Complete comments 1–4 with a suitable adjective.

1 The ending was sensitively handled and made me cry! Very _____!

2 The script was basically one joke after another. Absolutely _____!

3 It kept my attention for two hours. Utterly _____!

4 My friends and I are still arguing about it. Pretty _____!

C Work in pairs. Write four review comments similar to the ones above. Use a suitable adjective for describing movies in each review.

G RELATIVE CLAUSES

2 A Underline the correct alternative.

I'd like to find …

1 a person *who/for whom/whose* main interests include **doing sports**.

2 a place *that/which/where* I can **speak English with native speakers**.

3 someone *that/whose/whom* knows **a famous person**.

4 a shop *where/which/that* I can buy **reasonably priced clothes**.

5 a person for *whose/that/whom* **money** is not important.

6 three **interesting places in this town/city** *which/to which/where* I've never been to.

B Change the words in bold in four of the sentences above so that they are about things/people you'd like to find.

C Ask other students questions about your sentences in Exercise 2B.

A: Do you know anyone whose main interests include going to the movies?

B: Yes—me.

A: Right. Who's your favorite actor?

B: At the moment, Christian Bale.

G PARTICIPLE CLAUSES

3 A Complete the quiz with the present or past participles of the verbs in parentheses.

Trivia Quiz

1 It's an arts building _____ (stand) in Sydney Harbor and _____ (make) of white tiles to look like sails.

2 It's a company _____ (start) by Steve Jobs, Steve Wozniak and Ronald Wayne, best _____ (know) for its iPod and iPhone products.

3 It's a game _____ (play) by two players, _____ (involve) a small rubber ball and rackets and _____ (take) place in a four-walled court indoors.

4 He was a great leader, born in Corsica, _____ (crown) Emperor of France in 1804 and _____ (defeat) at Waterloo in 1815.

5 It's a statuette _____ (award) to people in the movie world every year by the American Academy of Motion Picture Arts and Sciences.

6 They're a group of people _____ (live) in cold, snowy parts of the USA and Canada, and _____ (use) blocks of ice to build their houses, _____ (call) igloos.

7 It's a Japanese dish _____ (consist) of raw fish and rice _____ (roll) up in seaweed.

8 It's a play _____ (write) by Shakespeare and _____ (feature) a Danish prince.

B Work in pairs and do the quiz.

C Check your answers on page 163.

V THE ARTS

4 The words in bold are in the wrong sentences. Put them in the correct sentences.

1 The musical was a complete **sell-out** and had to close early.

2 Does the Picasso exhibition deserve all those **hype** reviews?

3 The new sculpture is **alternative**. Everyone's arguing about it.

4 He's famous for his **mainstream** work in photography, never done before.

5 You can't get tickets for the show. It's a complete **rave**.

6 I thought the new album was a real **must-see**, very poor.

7 That new comedian is certainly creating a lot of **flop**. Everyone's talking about him.

8 This Virtual Worlds Exhibition is a **letdown** event. Don't miss it!

9 I don't listen to **ground-breaking** pop music much. It all sounds the same.

10 During **creating a stir** Fashion Week you can see some shockingly original clothes.

F GIVING A TOUR

5 A Complete descriptions 1–3 below with the words in the box. Where are the places?

was	story	worth	it	you
honor	named	rebuilt		

was

1 It built in the 17th century by Shah Jahan in of his wife. As may know, it's made of white marble and is well a visit.

2 It was after its designer and was built in 1889. The goes that many Parisians hated it because it was too modern.

3 Parts of it were many times. Believe or not, millions of Chinese died in its construction.

B Write two sentences about a tourist site you know.

C Read out your sentences. The other students guess the place.

going to the movies going to the cinema
Harbor / rackets / honor Harbour / racquets / honour

IRREGULAR VERBS

Verb	Past Simple	Past Participle
be	was	been
beat	beat	beaten
become	became	become
begin	began	begun
bend	bent	bent
bet	bet	bet
bite	bit	bitten
bleed	bled	bled
blow	blew	blown
break	broke	broken
bring	brought	brought
broadcast	broadcast	broadcast
build	built	built
burn	burned/burnt	burned/burnt
burst	burst	burst
buy	bought	bought
catch	caught	caught
choose	chose	chosen
come	came	come
cost	cost	cost
cut	cut	cut
deal	dealt	dealt
dig	dig	dug
do	did	done
draw	drew	drawn
dream	dreamed/dreamt	dreamed/dreamt
drink	drank	drunk
drive	drove	driven
eat	ate	eaten
fall	fell	fallen
feel	felt	felt
feed	fed	fed
fight	fought	fought
find	found	found
fly	flew	flown
forbid	forbade	forbidden
forget	forgot	forgotten
forgive	forgave	forgiven
freeze	froze	frozen
get	got	got/gotten
give	gave	given
go	went	gone
grow	grew	grown
hang	hung	hung/hanged
have	had	had
hear	heard	heard
hide	hid	hidden
hit	hit	hit
hold	held	held
hurt	hurt	hurt
keep	kept	kept
know	knew	known
lay	laid	laid
lead	led	led
leap	leapt	leapt
lean	leaned/leant	leaned/leant
learn	learned/learnt	learned/learnt

Verb	Past Simple	Past Participle
leave	left	left
lend	lent	lent
let	let	let
lie	lay	lain
light	lit	lit/lighted
lose	lost	lost
make	made	made
mean	meant	meant
meet	met	met
mistake	mistook	mistaken
pay	paid	paid
put	put	put
read	read	read
ride	rode	ridden
ring	rang	rung
rise	rose	risen
run	ran	run
say	said	said
see	saw	seen
sell	sold	sold
send	sent	sent
set	set	set
shake	shook	shaken
shine	shone	shone
shoot	shot	shot
show	showed	shown
shrink	shrank	shrunk
shut	shut	shut
sing	sang	sung
sink	sank	sunk
sit	sat	sat
sleep	slept	slept
slide	slid	slid
smell	smelled	smelled
speak	spoke	spoken
spell	spelled	spelled
spend	spent	spent
spill	spilled/spilt	spilled/spilt
split	split	split
spread	spread	spread
stand	stood	stood
steal	stole	stolen
stick	stuck	stuck
sting	stung	stung
swim	swam	swum
take	took	taken
teach	taught	taught
tear	tore	torn
tell	told	told
think	thought	thought
throw	threw	thrown
understand	understood	understood
wake	woke	woken
wear	wore	worn
win	won	won
write	wrote	written

GRAMMAR

1.1

Direct and Indirect Questions

Direct Questions

The word order for most questions is: (question word) + auxiliary verb + subject + main verb.

What does "strategy" mean?   Have you finished yet?

Subject questions: When the question word is the subject of the sentence, use the affirmative form of the verb.

What happened next? NOT ~~What did happen next?~~

Prepositions in questions usually come at the end.

What are you working on?   What was Thailand like?

(Here *like* is a preposition, and the question is asking for a description.)

In very formal English, prepositions can come at the beginning.

In which newspaper did you read it?

Short questions, often ending in prepositions, are common in conversation:

A: I'm going out tonight.   B: Where to?/Whom with?

A: I didn't go to the party.   B: How come?/Why not?

A: I hate spicy food.   B: Why's that?/Such as?

A: Can you lend me a paintbrush?   B: Which one?/What for?

Indirect Questions

Use indirect questions to ask questions in a more polite way or for very personal questions. After the opening phrase, use the affirmative form.

*Could you tell me **what time the lesson starts**?*
NOT ~~Could you tell me what time does the lesson start?~~

*Do you mind me asking **why you left** your last job?*
NOT ~~Do you mind me asking why did you leave your last job?~~

In *yes/no* questions, use *if* or *whether* + the affirmative form.

*Do you know **if Mike's married**?*

Other opening phrases include: *Can I ask (you) ...?, Do you have any idea ...?, Would you mind telling me ...?, What/Why/Where/Who do you think?, I was wondering ..., I wonder ..., I'd be interested to know ..., I'd like to know ..., I want to know ...*

Only use a question mark if the introductory phrase contains a question.

*I wonder where Derek is. **How do you think he did that?***

When a question is very personal, start with *Can I ask a personal question?*

1.2

Present Perfect

The perfect in English always links two time periods. The present perfect links the past to the present in the following ways:

1 **Time up to now:** a completed action or experience that happened at some point in the past before now, e.g., *in my life, this year, today.* The exact time it happened is not specified.

We've met before.   Have you seen Jo this week?

unfinished time period

action
× ————————— |
time not specified   now

2 **Recent events:** a completed action which has a present result or is in some other way relevant to the present. The exact time it happened is not specified.

No coffee for me, thanks. I've already had one.

I've lost my phone. Has anyone seen it?

action   result
×————————————→
time not specified   now

3 **Ongoing situations:** an uncompleted state or repeated action that started in the past and continues up to now.

*How long **have you been** on Twitter?*

*I've **swum** every morning since May.*

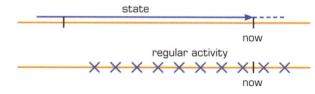

state
now

regular activity
now

Note: The present perfect continuous can often also be used for this meaning. See unit 2.1

Time Phrases to Talk about the Past

Present Perfect	just, already, not yet, ever, recently, lately, since, so far, up to now, until now, over the last year, still not
Past Simple	yesterday, ago, this time last week, on Thursday, on May 12th, last week/month/year/winter, when I was younger, until then
Both	never, always, for, before, in the summer, today, this morning/afternoon (depending on whether the period is finished or not)

1.3

Polite Inquiries

Opening Phrases	
I'd like to I'm calling to	ask/find out about ... inquire about ... talk to someone about ...

Polite Inquiries	
I was wondering/I wonder I'd be grateful/I'd appreciate it	if you could see if there's a place available.
Can/Could you tell me Do you mind me asking	when the manager will be back?
Would there be any chance of Would you mind	giving me a refund?

PRACTICE

1.1

A Write A's questions in full.

A: [1] Where / have / be?

Where have you been?

B: At a meeting.

A: [2] Who / be / with / you ?

B: Just people from the office.

A: [3] What / meeting / like?

B: Oh, you know. Long.

A: [4] you / know / what time / now?

B: Um … is it late?

A: [5] Can / ask / why / you / not / call?

B: My cell was dead.

A: [6] you / have / any idea / how / worried / I / be?

B Put the words in the correct order to make indirect questions.

1 if / you / here / credit / they / know / Do / cards / accept?

2 me / you / model / mind / how / a / you / asking / became / Do?

3 you / coffee / any / at / idea / this / where / time / I / can / get / have / a / Do?

4 you / me / computer / Would / telling / the / available / mind / when / becomes?

5 get / if / married / you're / Can / planning / I / to / ask?

6 was / I / briefcase / that / bought / you / where / wondering.

C Complete the two-word questions.

A: I can't meet you tonight.

B: No? How [1] _____?

A: Because I'm going out.

B: Where [2] _____?

A: To the theater.

B: Who [3] _____?

A: Nobody you know. The tickets were very expensive.

B: How [4] _____?

A: I'm not telling. I'll get home late.

B: What [5] _____?

A: After midnight. You know, you shouldn't ask so many questions.

B: Why [6] _____?

1.2

A Complete the email with the past simple or present perfect of the verbs in parentheses.

To	m.smith24@gmailbox.com

Dear Mom and Dad,

Sorry I [1] _____ (not write) in a while, but things are crazy here. I can't believe it [2] _____ (be) six months ago that I left and that we [3] _____ (not see) each other for that long.

This trip [4] _____ (be) fantastic so far, at least until a few days ago, when things [5] _____ (take) a turn for the worse. We [6] _____ (arrive) in downtown and [7] _____ (check) into the first hotel we [8] _____ (see). Now, you know I [9] _____ (stay) in a lot of one-star hotels in my life, but this one [10] _____ (be) really bad, so we [11] _____ (decide) to go straight out to see the city.

Unfortunately, we [12] _____ (forget) to lock our room, and when we [13] _____ (get) back, our baggage and most of our money was gone. We [14] _____ (call) the police right away, and I [15] _____ (go) back to the police station several times since then, but no one [16] _____ (hand) in any of our things.

Anyway, could you send me $1,000, please?

Thanks and love,

Joanna

B Underline the correct time phrase.

1 I've never played squash *before moving here/before.*

2 No wonder I have a headache! It's two o'clock, and I didn't have a coffee *this morning/this afternoon.*

3 *Up to now/Until I took this course,* I always believed that English was easy.

4 I've known Maria *for/since* ten years now.

5 *So far,/In the first week of the term,* I haven't missed any classes.

6 I had trouble concentrating at work *since/until* I got new glasses.

7 I've never ridden a scooter again *after/since* the accident.

8 I haven't worked *this month,/last month,* so money is tight.

9 I haven't downloaded it *already/yet.*

10 We came back from vacation *this time last week/lately.*

1.3

A Complete the conversation with the words from the box.

~~help~~	be	ago	will	check	out	at	afraid	with	there	chance

A: Yourpick.net. My name's Dave. How can I *help* you?

B: Hi, I'm calling to find about a DVD I ordered. The reference number is 3714.

A: OK. Is a problem?

B: Yes, it hasn't arrived yet, and I ordered it a month. Could you tell me when I can expect it?

A: Bear me a moment. I'm afraid we have no information about the arrival date.

B: And you don't know when it be in?

A: It's coming from the USA, so I'm not. Do you want to cancel?

B: No, but I'd grateful if you could look into it.

A: No problem all.

B: And would there be any of calling me when it arrives?

A: Sure … let me just if we have your phone number …

GRAMMAR

2.1 Present Perfect Simple and Continuous

1 Ongoing Situations

Use either the present perfect simple or the present perfect continuous to talk about situations or repeated actions that started in the past and continue into the present. Often there is no important difference, particularly with verbs such as *work*, *live*, *study*, *do*.

Ella's worked/Ella's been working for the company for a year now.

Use the present perfect continuous to <u>emphasize</u> that an action has continued for a long time or is repeated, often with verbs of duration, such as *wait*, *stay*, *run*, *play*, *sit*, *stand*, *write*, etc.

We've been sitting here for over an hour.
How long have you been waiting?

Use the present perfect simple with state verbs such as *know*, *understand*, *like* to talk about an unfinished situation.

How long have you known Jon?

2 Completed Actions (Recent or in Time up to Now)

Use the present perfect simple with actions which are short and complete, e.g., *drop*, *start*, *finish*, *leave*, *break*, *lose*, etc.

I've cut my finger. NOT ~~I've been cutting my finger.~~

Use the present perfect simple to emphasize a completed action or result. It often answers the questions: *How many?*, *How much?*, *How far?*

He's called me at least four times today.
She's run 200 miles, and she's raised 5,000 dollars so far.

3 Present Evidence

Sometimes the present perfect continuous is used when there is present evidence of a recent longer activity.

They look hot. Yes, they've been running.
NOT ~~Yes, they've run.~~

Sorry about the smell. I've been cooking fish.
NOT ~~I've cooked fish.~~

2.2 The Passive

Form the passive with *be* + past participle. In a passive sentence, the agent (the doer of the action) may or may not be mentioned.

	Active	Passive
Present Simple	The press **follows** him everywhere.	He's **followed** everywhere by the press.
Present Continuous	The police **are monitoring** his emails.	His emails **are being monitored** by the police.
Past Simple	Fire **destroyed** the building.	The building **was destroyed** by fire.
Present Perfect	Someone's **eaten** my sandwich.	My sandwich **has been eaten**.
will	Someone **will tell** you.	You'll **be told**.
Modals	We **can't do** it now.	It **can't be done** now.
-ing Form	I don't like people **criticizing** me.	I don't like **being criticized**.
Infinitive with to	The organizers want people **to give** feedback.	The organizers want **to be given** feedback.

Use the passive:

- to emphasize the main focus of a text or sentence.

  The company has apologized for losing email details of hundreds of its customers. The details were left on a train by a member of staff.

  In the second sentence, the writer uses the passive to keep the focus of the text on the email details and not on the person who left them.

- when the agent is obvious, not important or unknown.

  A man's been arrested on suspicion of murder.

  I hate being watched when I'm practicing Tai Chi.

  I'm being sent a large number of spam emails these days.

- in more formal texts (e.g., academic writing, scientific reports) and certain text types (e.g., some newspaper articles, radio/TV news).

  The issue is discussed later in this paper.

  No survivors have been found in the disaster.

- to create a distance between the agent and the action, for example to avoid responsibility.

  All complaints will be taken seriously.

In formal writing, the following construction is often used:
It is said/believed/reported/thought/understood ... that ...

It is reported that a shockingly large proportion of the world population is out of work.

2.3 Opinions

Use these expressions to express your opinion:

I'm (very much) in favor of/(really) against ...

Personally/Basically, I think/feel/believe that ...

I do think/feel/believe that ...

Agreeing	Partially Agreeing	Disagreeing
That makes sense.	I see your point, but ...	Actually, I think ...
I see what you mean.	I agree to a certain extent, but ...	I'm (still) not convinced.
Good point.	Fair enough, but ...	I'm not so sure.
Exactly/Absolutely/Definitely.	I suppose so.*	I (totally) disagree.
I agree (with you).		

*We use this when we say we agree, but we don't really want to.

PRACTICE

2.1

A Complete the answers with the present perfect simple or continuous form of the verbs in parentheses.

1 Why are you looking so pleased with yourself?

Because I _____ for some new jeans, and I've found a pair I like. (look)

Because I _____ a new pair of jeans. (just buy)

2 You look hot.

Yes, I _____ 15 miles. (run)

Yes, I _____. (run)

3 What's the matter?

We _____ to decide where to go on vacation this year. (try)

We _____ we can't afford a vacation this year. (decide)

4 What's up with Jake?

He _____ his knee. (hurt)

He _____ with Serge again! (fight)

5 I feel sick.

That's because you _____ a whole package of cookies. (eat)

That's because you _____ ice cream all afternoon. (eat)

B Write a question about each sentence. Use the underlined verb in the present perfect simple or continuous form. If both are possible, use the continuous form.

1 I teach biology at the high school.

How long _____ there?

2 I collect antique books.

a) How long _____ them?

b) How many _____?

3 I study English every evening.

How long _____ it?

4 I'm saving up money for college.

a) How long _____?

b) How much _____?

5 I have a house on a Greek island.

How long _____ it?

6 I know Maria well.

How long _____ her?

2.2

A Put the words in the correct order to make sentences.

1 cat's / operated / this / My / being / on / afternoon

2 be / He'll / later / or / sooner / caught

3 badly / in / fire / was / burned / the / Kim

4 of / middle / the / in / up / woken / being / mind / don't / They / night / the

5 is / the / catches / It / that / bird / worm / said / early / the

6 the / asked / whole / I've / give / been / to / speech / to / school / a

7 at / by / She's / be / desk / day / to / her / 9 a.m. / expected / every

8 monitored / sometimes / emails / supervisor / by / their / are / Employees'

9 hurt / you / care / Someone / get / if / could / take / don't

10 crash / nobody / It / has / is / survived / believed / the / that

B Complete the article with the correct active or passive form of the verbs in parentheses.

Google Street View Helps Find Missing Child

Google Street View [1] *has been used* (use) to help find a kidnapped child in rural Georgia. Ten-year-old Maria Nadal, from Atlanta, Georgia, [2]_____ (find) safely at a motel on Tuesday. She [3]_____ (discover) by Police Officer Ned Beales and Deputy Fire Chief Louis Thomas. They [4]_____ (put) the coordinates from Maria's cell phone into Google Street View and were able to identify one of the buildings as a motel.

A woman [5]_____ (arrest). She [6]_____ (believe) to be Maria's grandmother, and family friends said that the woman had complained about [7]_____ (separate) from the little girl. Legal experts say she [8]_____ (might/give) a warning and a fine rather than go to prison because she is a family member.

2.3

A Complete the conversation with the words from the box.

~~in~~ to so point still sure enough it think

in

A: I'm / favor of the idea of compulsory school uniforms.

B: Are you? I'm really against.

A: Well, personally, I with uniforms everyone's the same, rich or poor.

B: I see your, but they can be very expensive—especially as children get bigger.

A: I'm not so. Kids' clothes are expensive anyway.

B: Fair, but having uniforms stops children expressing their personality.

A: I agree a certain extent, but I do think uniforms provide a sense of belonging.

B: I suppose. But, actually, I don't think kids really feel any less lonely just because they have a uniform on.

A: Maybe not, but I'm not convinced.

cookies   biscuits

GRAMMAR

3.1 Narrative Tenses

Use the **past simple** for completed actions in the past that tell the main events in a story.

*When I **arrived**, my friends **left**.*

Use the **past perfect simple** (*had* + past participle) to link the past to a point further back in the past. It is used to talk about completed actions/events that happened

- before another action/event/the story began.

  *My friends **had left** by the time I arrived.*

  Or: *When I arrived at the restaurant, my friends **had left**.*

  Here we say the events (*left*, *arrived*) in a different order from which they occurred.

  friends left   I arrived

  now

- with "thinking" verbs such as *realize*, *remember*, *forget*, *think*, *find out*, *discover* and also with *because*.

  *I suddenly **remembered** I **hadn't called** Sue. I felt terrible **because** I'd **promised** to call her.*

Use the **past continuous** (*was/were* + verb + *-ing*):

To describe an action in progress

- at a specified time or point in the story.
- when another shorter action or event happened (usually in the past simple).

  *He **was sleeping** when the plane landed.*

plane landed

now

sleeping

- to set the scene of the story or a section of the story.

  *I **was walking** along the street when I noticed the man.*

Use the **past perfect continuous** (*had* + *been* + verb + *-ing*) to talk about longer actions or situations which started

- before the story began and continued to the beginning of a story. The length of the action is often mentioned with *for* or *since*.
- before a point or an action in the story and continued up to that action.

  *She **had been living there for a week** before they met.*

they met

living   now

- before a point where there is evidence of a recent activity.

  *David looked very tired because **he'd been working** all night*

3.2 I wish, If only

Wishes about the Present

- Use *wish* + past subjunctive for things you want to change, but it is impossible or not likely.

  *I wish I **had** more time.* (But I don't have more time.)
  *I wish you **were** here.* (But you aren't here.)

- Use *wish* + *could* to talk about possibilities and abilities you want to change.

  *I wish I **could swim**.* (But I can't.)

- Use *wish* + person/thing + *would* to talk about things you want to change because they annoy you. Don't use this to talk about yourself.

  *I wish you'**d listen** to me!*
  *I wish Pat **wouldn't text** all the time.* NOT ~~I wish I would speak English better.~~

Notes:
In formal English, use *I wish* + **were**.   *I wish I **were** taller.*
In spoken English it is increasingly common to use *I wish* + **was**.
*I wish I **was** there.*

Regrets about the Past

Use *wish* + past perfect subjunctive to talk about things that happened or didn't happen in the past and that you regret now.

*I wish I'**d stayed** at home.*
*They wish they **hadn't come**.*
*I wish I'**d never met** him.*

If only

Use *If only* instead of *wish* to talk about the present or past. It can show more emotion than *I wish* although this depends on intonation.

*If only we **lived** nearer my parents.*
*If only I **could** afford a vacation.*
*If only the car **would** start.*
*If only I'**d listened** to my teacher.*

3.3 Expressing Likes and Dislikes

Expressing Likes	Expressing Dislikes
I'm a big fan of ...	I'm not a big fan of/not that eager about ...
I'm very/really/eager about ...	I don't like ... that much.
What I like/love about it is ...	I can't get into ...
The thing I like about it is that ...	I can't stand ...
	What I don't like/hate about it is ...
	The thing I don't like/hate about it is ...

Some of these expressions use special structures to put extra emphasis on the main point:

What I + verb (*about it*) + *be* (*that*) + key information

***What I don't like about it is that** some of the dialogue isn't very natural.*
(compare: *I don't like the unnaturalness of some of the dialogue.*)

The thing I + verb (*about it*) + *be* (*that*) + key information

***The thing I liked most about it was** the plot.*
(compare: *I liked the plot most.*)

PRACTICE

3.1 **A** Complete the sentences using the correct narrative tense.

Last night, I saw Jean at the top of a ladder, climbing into the upstairs window of a house. She was using a ladder to get through the upstairs window because …

1 she _____ (forget) her key.

2 she _____ (rob) the house.

3 she _____ (paint) the downstairs floors all evening and they hadn't dried yet.

4 she _____ (use) the door all her life and she wanted a change.

B Complete the news story by putting the verbs in parentheses in the correct narrative tense. In one case, more than one tense is possible.

Missing Child Found Safe and Sound

A search for a missing child in East Paterson [1]_____ (end) happily last week after five-year-old Ricky Ross was found asleep in his own room. Last Monday, Julie Ross, the boy's mother, [2]_____ (work) in the front yard when she [3]_____ (hear) her son cry out. He [4]_____ (play) in the living room, but, when she [5]_____ (run) to the house, she [6]_____ (see) that the back door was open and there was no sign of her son.

Neighbors [7]_____ (join) in the search, and, when they [8]_____ (search) in the forest behind the house, they [9]_____ (find) a few pieces of children's clothing. There was initial panic, but it was soon clear that the clothing [10]_____ (be) there for years and didn't belong to the boy. Ricky was eventually found by another child who [11]_____ (go) into the boy's room while the search [12]_____ (go) on because she [13]_____ (hear) a noise from the toy box. When she [14]_____ (open) it, there was Ricky safe and sound—he [15]_____ (sleep) in the toy box the whole time, unaware of the panic he had caused.

3.2 **A** Underline the correct alternative in the sentences.

1 It's difficult to work with Harry because he's pretty antisocial. I wish we *liked/ had liked* each other more.

2 We're going to be late for the meal. I wish you *hurried up/'d hurry up*.

3 I have to take buses everywhere. If only I *knew/had known* how to drive.

4 I didn't realize it would be so cold. I wish I *brought/'d brought* my coat with me.

5 We moved to a new apartment last year, but I don't like the area. If only we *didn't live/hadn't lived* here.

6 I never knew your father. I wish I *met/ 'd met* him.

7 I'd like to join a choir, but my voice is awful. If only I *were/would be* good at singing!

8 I'm sorry but it's impossible. I wish I *would/could* help you, but I can't.

B Complete the sentences using the information and the correct form of the verbs in parentheses.

1 We live in the city, and I hate it.
If only we _____ (live) in the country.

2 The bus is late, and my feet are killing me.
I wish the bus _____ (come), and I wish I _____ (wear) these shoes.

3 I think we're lost, and we don't have GPS.
If only we _____ (know) where we were. I wish we _____ (remember) to bring our GPS.

4 The neighbors were playing loud music last night.
I wish they _____ (play) their music so loudly. If only I _____ (sleep) better, I wouldn't feel so tired now.

5 I'm not very advanced because I only started learning English last year.
If only I _____ (start) learning English when I was younger.

6 You bite your nails.
I wish you _____ (bite) your nails.

3.3 **A** Correct the mistake in each sentence.

1 I don't like opera much that.

2 I can't stand on depressing books like that one.

3 The thing I liked about it most it was the surprise ending.

4 Who I love about Lee's movies is that there's always a message.

5 I'm a big fan for historical novels.

6 What I like her acting is that she brings something special to every role.

7 I don't get into classical music.

8 Thing what I hate about graffiti is that it's just ugly.

GRAMMAR

4.1 **Present and Past Habits**

Present Habits

Use the present simple, often with frequency adverbs such as *usually, always, generally, normally, typically,* for regular repeated actions or states.

I usually get along very well with my brother.
NOT ~~I use to get along with my brother.~~

Use *always* + present continuous for a habit which the speaker often finds annoying.

The people next door are always holding late-night parties.

Use *will* + infinitive for regular habits. This use of *will* is not connected to the future.

On Saturdays I'll usually buy croissants, and we'll have them for breakfast.

Past Habits

Use the past simple, often with frequency adverbs, for regular repeated actions or states in the past.

We generally traveled to the campsite by car.

Use *always* + past continuous for annoying habits in the past.

She was always criticizing me.

Use *used to* + infinitive for repeated activities or states in the past which usually don't continue now.

Jon used to smoke, but he doesn't any longer.
It didn't use to be so expensive.
NOT ~~It didn't used to be so expensive.~~

Use *would* + infinitive for repeated activities in the past. Don't use it for states.
Sometimes *would* has the idea of nostalgia. This use of *would* is not connected to conditionals.

We'd sit down together for our meals. Not like families nowadays. NOT ~~We'd be very happy.~~

4.2 **Future Forms**

When talking about the future, the choice of form is often flexible and depends on what the speaker wants to express.

Plans, Intentions and Decisions

Use *be going to* + infinitive to talk about general plans, arrangements and intentions about the future. Use *might/could/may* + infinitive when a plan or intention is not definite.

I'm going to look for a job in New York.
We might go away for the weekend.

Use the present continuous to talk about definite arrangements or plans.

What are you doing today? I'm having lunch with Mitsuko.

The following phrases can also be used for intentions and plans: *planning to/hoping to* + infinitive, *thinking of* + -ing.

Pete's hoping to go to college next year.
Are you thinking of leaving the company?

Use *will* ('ll in spoken English) to talk about decisions made at the moment of speaking. This is often used with *I think*.

I'm tired. I think I'll go to bed now.

Predictions

Use *will/might/could/won't* + infinitive to make predictions based on opinion. Use with verbs such as *think, hope, expect, know, guess, be sure* or adverbs such as *maybe, perhaps.*

I expect Sara will agree.   I'm sure everything will be fine.

Use *will* + *definitely/certainly/possibly/probably* to say how certain you are. Note the word order with *won't.*

Jodie and Al will probably get divorced soon.
You definitely won't get a ticket now.

Use *be likely to* + infinitive for strong possibility and *be due to* + infinitive for something that is expected or scheduled to happen.

She's likely to be tired after the journey.
Meg is due to retire next year.

Use *going to* to make a prediction based on present evidence.

Look at those clouds. It's going to rain.
Lisa's going to have a baby.

Future Facts

Use the present simple to talk about schedules, timetables and itineraries.

The course starts in September.   We leave at 6a.m.

Use *will* + infinitive for future facts.

Your dry-cleaning will be ready tomorrow.
I'll be 28 next year.

4.3 **Describing Procedures**

The Aim of an Activity
The point is to …
The point/goal/aim is for you to …

Emphasize an Important Point
The key/main/most important thing is to …

Different Procedures or Steps
Basically, the way it works is that the first player …
What happens (next) is that you …
The first/next/last thing you do is you …
After you've finished/done that, you …
What you have to do is to …
First,/Next,/After that,/Then,/Finally, you …

PRACTICE

4.1

A Complete the exchanges about present or past habits. Sometimes there is more than one possible answer.

1 **A:** Did you know John before?

B: Yes, we _____ be at school together.

2 **A:** What do you think of your new roommate?

B: She's nice but pretty messy. She _____ leaving stuff around the place.

3 **A:** How often did you see your grandmother when you were young?

B: We _____ see her most weekends.

4 **A:** Did you _____ enjoy being in swimming competitions?

B: Actually, no. I _____ felt relieved as soon as one was over.

5 **A:** Is this a picture of you on vacation when you were young?

B: Yes, we _____ go to Portugal every year.

6 **A:** Do you go to the gym regularly?

B: Every year, I _____ sign up for a year's membership, and then, after a month, I _____ usually stop going.

7 **A:** I was really an awkward child.

B: I remember. You _____ knocking things over, and you _____ turn red when visitors spoke to you.

8 **A:** People who don't work here _____ often park their cars here all day. It's outrageous!

B: Yes, and it's illegal.

B Complete the second sentence so that it means the same as the first. Use the word(s) in parentheses in your answer.

1 I hate the way Mike comes up behind people and looks over their shoulders.

Mike _____ shoulders. (always)

2 What was your address before you moved here?

Where _____ live? (to)

3 I'm really a spontaneous person, and I often start conversations with strangers.

I'm really a spontaneous person and _____ conversations with strangers. (will)

4 Pollution was never a rural problem, only an urban one.

Pollution didn't _____, only an urban one. (be)

5 In the 1960s, the authorities used to keep track of all their citizens' movements.

In the 1960s, _____ all their citizens' movements. (would)

6 Peggy used to borrow money all the time and never pay it back. That was really annoying.

Peggy was _____ back. (borrowing money)

4.2

A Cross out the incorrect option in the conversation.

A: Hey Mike, [1] *are you coming/are you going to come/will you come* on the ski trip this weekend?

B: Of course. I haven't signed up yet, but [2] *I'm likely to do/I'm going to do/I'll do* that now. Where [3] *does the bus leave/is the bus due to leave/is the bus planning to leave* from?

A: It [4] *leaves/might leave/'s leaving* from in front of the office.

B: Great! What are the snow conditions [5] *likely to/going to/hoping to* be like?

A: It's already snowing there now, so [6] *it's being/it's going to be/it'll be* perfect conditions. I'm [7] *hoping/thinking/planning* to try some of the highest runs.

B: Great. [8] *I'll probably see/I'm seeing/I might see* you before then, but, if not, see you on the bus!

B Complete the sentences with an appropriate future form. Sometimes there is more than one possibility.

1 I _____ (stay) at home this evening, but I haven't decided yet. Maybe I _____ (watch) a DVD or something.

2 _____ Sandra _____ (be) there tomorrow? Then I _____ (definitely/go)!

3 The first metro _____ (due/arrive) at 5 a.m., but there is an electrical problem, so it's _____. (likely/delay)

4 Rick _____ (think of/move) abroad. I guess he _____ (be) happier there.

5 The deadline is midnight tonight, so I _____ (probably/not finish) the application in time.

6 I _____ (not see) Ken before the end of the afternoon, but I _____ (definitely/see) him tomorrow.

4.3

A Complete the rules to the game *Cyclops* by putting the underlined words in the correct order.

[1]it works is Basically that the way you have two players and just one die. [2]thing The is they first do roll to see who goes first. [3]Then first the player does what is to roll the die and add up the numbers that they roll. [4]object is The to get a hundred points. [5]point The is to be lucky enough not to roll a one because, if you get a one, you lose all your points for that turn. [6]that is happens What a player gets greedy, thinks he can make a run to a hundred, but then gets a one and loses it all. That's the best part—it's really funny. [7]to is thing key The work in little steps, end your turn after a few rolls and don't get greedy!

GRAMMAR

5.1 Article

Use the indefinite article (a/an):

with singular countable nouns when it is not clear which thing or person is being talked about.	*We got an email from Carla. She's renting an apartment in Berlin with a friend.*
the first time something is mentioned.	*There's a problem.*
in phrases of quantity or frequency.	*2 dollars a pound, 5 days a week, 70 miles an hour*

Use no article:

with plurals and uncountable nouns to talk about things in general.	*Children need at least eight hours' sleep.*
for continents, countries, towns, roads, stations, mountains and lakes.	*Asia, Spain, Moscow, Kings Cross Station, Everest, Lake Garda*

Use the definite article (the):

when it's clear to the listener/reader what is being talked about.	*Lia had the children with her.* (= her children) *I liked the speech you made.*
when something is unique; superlatives.	*The first man on the moon. It's the fastest car.*
when something has been mentioned before.	*There's a problem, and the problem is money.*
for oceans, rivers, organisations, deserts, mountain ranges, decades.	*The Pacific, the Danube, the UN, the Alps, the Sahara, the 1990s*
in fixed lexical phrases.	*What's the matter? The bigger the better.*
with an adjective or a singular countable noun for things in general.	*The city is divided between the rich and the poor. The tiger could soon be extinct.*

Note: a singular countable noun can never stand alone; it must go with *a, an, each, every, this, that, his, her, the,* etc.

5.2 Real and Hypothetical Conditionals

real conditionals

	Conditional Clause	Result Clause
Real (Zero) Conditional	*if* + present simple	present simple
Real (First) Conditional	*if* + present simple	*will/going to/can/ could/may/might/ should* + infinitive

Use the real (zero) conditional to talk about a real situation that is always or generally true with a result that always happens.

If you pay by debit card, you get a 5 percent discount.

Use the real (first) conditional to talk about a real possibility in the present or future. In the main clause, use *may/might/can/could* instead of *will* for an uncertain result, and use *should* for advice.

If you put in the wrong PIN number, the machine will take your card.
If your card gets stuck, you should call the number on the machine.

Hypothetical/Unreal Conditionals

	Conditional Clause	Result Clause
Hypothetical (Second) Conditional	*if* + past subjunctive	*would/could/might/ should* + infinitive

Use the hypothetical (second) conditional to talk about a hypothetical or unreal situation in the present or future. In the main clause, use *might/could* for an uncertain result. With *be*, use *were* or (informally) *was*.

If Valerie practiced more, she could be really good.
If I were you, I'd leave now.

Alternatives to *if*

- Use *providing/provided (that), on condition that* and, less formally, *as long as*, to mean *if* and *only if*, often with real conditions, where the speaker or writer has real reservations.

  I'll get into college provided I pass the entrance exam.

- Use *unless* to mean *if not*.

  I'll arrive at 10 a.m., unless the train is late.

- Use *suppose/supposing, imagine* and, less formally, *let's say* instead of *if* when something is unlikely.

  Suppose you won the lottery, what would you do?

5.3 Suggesting Ideas

Proposing/Suggesting Ideas		
How do you feel about What about Would you consider	this idea? trying something new?	
How does the idea of	making a movie	strike you? grab you?
It'd be great if we could Suppose we	get a celebrity.	

Reacting to or Commenting on Ideas	
+	That's a great/fantastic/excellent/idea. I think we should go for X./I'd go for X. Let's go with that/the health angle.
Unsure	I can't make up my mind. I'm torn between X and Y.
–	That could be a problem. It wouldn't be my first choice. It wouldn't work/It doesn't grab me. (inf) I think we're on the wrong track here.

PRACTICE

5.1

A Complete the text with *a/an*, *the* **or no article (–).**

| Article | Talk |

The Thomas Edisons of Food

When people think of [1]_____ inventors, they might think of Thomas Edison and [2]_____ light bulb or Gutenburg and [3]_____ printing press, but do you know who invented some of the food you eat?

- George Crum was [4]_____ head chef at [5]_____ resort in Saratoga Springs, New York. One day, [6]_____ customer complained that the French fries were too thick, so Crum sliced [7]_____ potato paper-thin and fried it, just to make [8]_____ customer happy. And so, [9]_____ potato chips were born.
- Sausages of all sorts have been common in Europe for centuries, but [10]_____ hot dogs were first sold as sausages in buns by German immigrants on the streets of [11]_____ New York City in [12]_____ mid-19th century.
- Mayonnaise was probably invented by [13]_____ French chef in [14]_____ mid-18th century and was first sold in glass bottles in [15]_____ USA in 1912.
- Popcorn was invented by Native Americans, but it's not clear by which group or where [16]_____ snack food first appeared. Early American settlers ate [17]_____ popcorn with milk for [18]_____ breakfast! So, the next time you're sitting in [19]_____ movie theater, munching on popcorn and potato chips, remember [20]_____ people who first discovered these treats. Now, who were they again … ?

5.2

A Complete the sentences with the appropriate form of the verbs in parentheses.

1 If you give me your phone number, I _____ Pete to call you back. (ask)

2 Would you be interested if we _____ you a free trial? (offer)

3 If it _____, you should wear a waterproof jacket. (rain)

4 If I arrived a day early, it _____ me the chance to look around. (give)

5 I'm going to get worried if she _____ soon. (not call)

6 If I _____ good with numbers, I could help you with your homework. (be)

7 I may go home early if Anna _____ at the party. (not be)

8 You _____ a sport if you want to be in great shape like me. (take up)

B Underline the correct alternative in the sentences.

1 I'll tell you *provided/supposing* you promise to keep it a secret.

2 We won't go *imagine/unless* they pay our expenses.

3 *Supposing/Provided that* you lost your job tomorrow, what would you do then?

4 *If/Providing that* we have enough time, I intend to visit all of my relatives.

5 I'm going to leave *unless/if* you stop being aggressive with me.

6 *Unless/Imagine* we met them in the street; how might you react?

C Complete the sentences so that they mean the same as 1–6 above.

1 I won't tell you unless _____.

2 We won't go if _____.

3 What would you do if you _____?

4 I intend to visit all of my relatives unless _____.

5 I'm going to leave if _____.

6 How might you react if we _____?

5.3

A Complete the conversation with the words from the box.

| ~~think~~ between consider feel go grab sound track awful |

think

A: What do you ⟨ about naming our language school *Tongues4U*?

B: That's a idea!

C: How do you about *Talk2Me*?

A: It doesn't me.

C: Would you *English246*?

B: I think we're on the wrong here. All these numbers.

A: How does *Language Lab*?

B: Hmmm … Not bad.

C: I'm torn *Language Lab* and *Lingo Lab*.

B: Let's with *Language Lab* then.

GRAMMAR

6.1 Modal Verbs and Related Phrases

	Present	Past
Obligation (Strong)	have to go must go make someone go	had to go — made someone go
Obligation (Mild)	should go ought to go am supposed to go	should have gone ought to have gone was supposed to go
Lack of Obligation	don't have to go	didn't have to go
Prohibition (Strong)	must not go can't go am not allowed to go	— couldn't go wasn't allowed to go
Prohibition (Mild)	shouldn't go am not supposed to go	shouldn't have gone wasn't supposed to go
Permission	can go am allowed to go may go let someone go	could go was allowed to go might go let someone go
Ability	can/can't go am/am not able to go manage/ don't manage to go	could/couldn't go was/wasn't able to go managed/ didn't manage to go

Obligation

Must can express that the obligation is internal, not (only) because of a rule.

*I **must** finish this report—I don't want to annoy the boss.*

Use *make someone do something* when someone forces another person to do something.

*My mom **makes** me study for two hours every night.*

Use *be supposed to* especially when the obligation is broken.

*I'm not **supposed** to eat chocolate but ...*

Lack of Obligation/Prohibition

Note the difference between *don't have to* and *must not*:

*You **don't have to** arrive before 5 p.m.* (it's not necessary)

*You **must not** arrive before 5 p.m.* (you're not allowed to)

Permission

Use *let + someone* or *allow someone to* to say that someone gave permission to someone.

*Do you think she'll **let** me take a day off?*

*My company **allows us to** work from home one day a week.*

Ability

For ability on a single occasion in the past, use *was/were able to* or *managed to* (not *could*).

*He **was able to** find his way out of the forest and get help.* NOT *He could find his way ...*

Use *manage to* for something that is/was difficult to do.

*He **managed to** run the race in under three hours.*

6.2 Future Perfect and Continuous

Future Continuous

Use *will + be + -ing* form for:

* something that will be in progress at or around a specific future time.

*I'll **be driving home** when you call, so just leave a message.*

* something that will happen in the normal course of events, not as part of a particular intention or plan.

*I expect I'll **be talking** to Ian tomorrow, so I could ask him then.*

Note: We can use this meaning to introduce requests in a neutral way.

*A: **Will you be passing** the mailbox?*
B: Yes.
A: In that case, could you post this for me?

Future Perfect

Use *will + have +* past participle to talk about something that will finish before a specific time in the future, often with the preposition *by*, meaning *at the latest*.

*I'll **have finished** this report by the end of the week.*

It's possible to use other modals, adverbs and phrases with both forms.

*I **might have finished**/I **definitely won't have finished**/I'd like to have finished by then.*

*This time next week, **I could be relaxing**/I'll probably be relaxing/I'd like to be relaxing on a beach.*

6.3 Persuading

Use the following phrases to persuade someone by giving a strong opinion:

Surely Clearly Anyone can see that	parents need to take more responsibility for their kids' education.

Use negative questions when you want to persuade someone by inviting them to agree with you.

Don't you agree/think (that) Isn't it true/obvious that	texting is harmful for children's writing?
Shouldn't people Doesn't she want to	spend more time at home?

PRACTICE

6.1

A Underline the correct alternatives in the blog.

HOME » TRAVEL

Traveler's Journal—Changing Times

... it was the 1980s, and travel there was very restricted back then. Of course you [1]*had to/must* get a visa to enter the country as well as a permit to travel to most cities. Or at least you [2]*should/were supposed to* get a permit; I didn't always get one, and once, without a permit, I [3]*could/managed to* go to a town that foreigners technically [4]*couldn't/didn't have to* go to. The police called me in and [5]*made/let* me answer questions. I spoke the language a little, so I was [6]*able to/allowed to* communicate with them. Once they were convinced that I wasn't a spy, they [7]*allowed/let* me go, and I was [8]*allowed to/able* stay there as long as I wanted. Of course, it's changed so much now. You still [9]*must/have to* get a visa to enter, but you [10]*must not/don't have to* get a permit to go anywhere within the country. As was always the case, if you [11]*are able/can* speak the language, it's a really enriching experience, and I think everyone [12]*ought to/is supposed to* try to spend at least a few weeks traveling there.

B Rewrite the sentences. Use the word in parentheses so that the meaning stays the same.

1 I fell asleep. It was difficult. (manage)

I_____.

2 We stayed for dinner. There was no choice. (to)

We _____.

3 He gave me permission to listen to my MP3 player. (let)

He _____.

4 It was too dark to see anything. (not able)

He _____.

5 It's a good idea for her to leave before dark. (ought)

She _____.

6 The rule was to pay before going in. We didn't pay at all. (suppose)

We _____.

7 The maximum age to enter this club is eighteen. (not allow)

Adults _____.

8 I had to change my passport picture. (make)

They _____.

6.2

A Complete the sentences with the future perfect or the future continuous form of the verb in parentheses.

1 The movie starts at eight, and it's about two hours long.

At nine, I _____ the movie. (watch)

By eleven, the movie _____. (finish)

2 Her plane lands at 11:45p.m.

At midnight, she _____ for her luggage. (probably/wait)

By the time we wake up tomorrow, she _____ in Madrid. (arrive)

3 The world hotdog-eating champion can eat more than six hotdogs a minute.

In ten minutes from now, he _____ over sixty hotdogs. (eat)

Tonight, in his sleep, he _____ about hotdogs! (dream)

4 Give me a day to think about it.

By this time tomorrow, I _____. (decide)

This time next week, I _____ I had decided differently. (wish)

B Find and correct the mistakes in A's part of the conversations.

Conversation 1

A: [1]Will you seeing Frank today?

B: Yes, do you want me to give him a message?

A: [2]Yes, could you tell him I won't probably have finished the report until tomorrow.

Conversation 2

A: [3]Just think—this time tomorrow, you'll finish all your exams.

B: I know. That's what keeps me going.

A: [4]And you be celebrating with your friends.

Conversation 3

A: [5]Will you use your computer at lunchtime today? I have a problem with mine.

B: No, I'm going out and I won't be back till four if you want to use it till then.

A: [6]I might still using it when you get back. The technicians might not have fixed mine by then.

6.3

A Use the prompts to complete the sentences. Use negative questions where appropriate.

A: [1]Do / agree / people / should / able / start a family when they're teenagers?

Don't you agree that people should be able to start ...

B: What, even at 16 or 17?

A: Yes. [2]Clear / they at the peak of their physical health.

B: [3]But / is / it / obvious / most / 17-year-olds aren't even mature enough to be responsible for themselves?

A: Yeah, [4]but does / depend / the individual? Some 18-year-olds might make good parents.

B: [5]But / sure / they / need / time to sort out their own lives first.

A: [6]But / is / it / fact / that, in some cultures, 18 is a normal age to have a family?

B: Yes, [7]but / anyone / see / that what works in one culture won't necessarily work in every culture.

A: Hmm. Maybe you're right.

GRAMMAR

7.1   ### Quantifiers

	100%	A Large Amount	A Small Amount	0%
Uncountable or Plural Nouns	all, any	a lot of, lots of, plenty of, most	some, hardly any	no, not any
Uncountable Nouns		much, a large amount of, a great deal of	a little, little	
Plural Nouns	both (= all of two)	many, a large number of, quite a few	several, a small number of, a few, few	
Singular Nouns	each, every, any			no, not any, neither (= none of two)

a few/a little = some or a small amount

*There's still **a little** butter left.*

few/little = not many/much or not as many/much as wanted or expected

*Very **few** people came to the meeting.*

any = It doesn't matter which/who

I like <u>any</u> brand(s) of chocolate.

Any is stressed.

Use *both* + plural verb, *neither* + singular verb.

***Both** of us **run** a business, but **neither** of us **is** good with numbers.*

Another + singular nouns and numbers = something is additional to the existing number.

*Could I have **another** piece of cake, please.*
*We have **another** three meetings today.*

Use the pronoun *none* for a short answer.

*How much sugar do we have? **None**.*

7.2   ### Reported Speech

In reported speech, the original verb form often goes back further into the past. Pronouns, time references, etc. also change.

Direct Speech	Reported Speech
present simple/continuous *"I want to be a chef."* *"We're working."*	past simple/continuous *He said he wanted to be a chef.* *She told me they were working.*
past simple/present perfect *"Ben called me last week."* *"I've read your book."*	past perfect *She told me Ben had called her the week before.* *He said he'd read my book.*
will/would/can/could/should *"We'll help you tomorrow."* *"You can stay with me."*	would/could/should *He said they'd help me the next day.* *She said I could stay with her.*

It is not necessary to change the verb form when reporting something that is still true now or was said very recently.

"It's going to rain." Sam's just said it's going to rain.

Reported Questions

Use normal statement word order without *do/does/did* or a question mark.

*"What does Ian think?" She asked me **what Ian thought**.*

NOT ~~She asked me what did Ian think.~~

With *yes/no* questions, use *if* or *whether*.

*"Are you OK?" She asked **if** I was OK.*

Also use *wanted to know*, *inquired* and *wondered*.

*They **wanted to know** what time the train left.*

Reported Requests

Use verb + object + infinitive with *to*.

*"Could you sing?" He asked us **to sing**.*

Time Phrases and Place References

Time phrases and place references usually change.

now → then/at that time

yesterday → the day before/previous day

tomorrow → the following/next day

a week ago → the week before

here → there

7.3   ### Adding Emphasis

Auxiliary Verbs	
add or stress auxiliaries	I **do** hate it when people smoke indoors. It **is** annoying.

Intensifiers	
really, so + any adjective or adverb	It's **so** outrageous. You play **really well**.
absolutely, completely, totally + extreme adjectives	It's **completely** ridiculous.
such (a/an) + (adjective) + noun	It'll be **such an** amazing day. It was **such** terrible weather.

Emphasizing Phrases	
pronoun/noun + *be* + *the one who*	**You're the one who** chose it.
the + adjective + *thing* + *be*	**The best thing was** the music.

Informal Phrases	
There's no way (that) …	**There's no way** Tom stole the money.
What/Who/Where/Why/How on earth … ?	**Why on earth** didn't you say? **Where on earth** did you buy that?

PRACTICE

7.1

A Underline the correct alternative.

What does your ringtone say about you?

Almost everyone now has a cell phone and [1]*a great deal/ a large number/the most* of us have our own ringtone. Is it only so that we can distinguish our own phone from others, or is it because [2]*each/a large number of/both* time our phone rings we want to be able to say, "Listen to that. That's me!"? Maybe [3]*either/both/each* reasons are true. Here is a quick guide to [4]*some/few/a little* typical ringtones and what they say about their users.

If your ringtone is [5]*either/both/neither* a hip hop tune or a current hit, then you are young at heart but not particularly original.

[6]*Any/All/Either* classic rock tune means you're probably over thirty, but you know you're still cool.

[7]*Not much/A few/Very few* people think annoying animal noises are as funny as the phones' owners obviously do. So [8]*no/none/neither* points for maturity there.

You download a new one every month? You must be a teenager, or you have [9]*plenty of/a large number of/ hardly any* time and money.

You never change it? Either you're too lazy, or you don't know how. [10]*Neither/Both/Any* is an acceptable reason!

B Complete sentences 1—10 with a quantifier from the box.

> quite a few   a few   very few   a little   very little
> other   another   any (x2)   either

1 Everyone wanted to get home, so there were _____ questions at the end of the lecture.

2 I'm afraid I've spilled _____ wine on the carpet.

3 _____ of the students (four of us to be exact) have signed your petition.

4 I've watched _____ basketball games, probably twenty or thirty, but I've never seen such an exciting one.

5 Carla couldn't afford a taxi because she had _____ money left.

6 You can click on _____ "save" or "save as" and then give the document a name.

7 Are you having _____ other problems with the photocopier?

8 I like _____ music by Jade. She's great.

9 One car isn't enough. We need _____ car.

10 I don't care what _____ people think.

7.2

A Read the questions then complete the reported speech below.

1 Where have you been all day?

2 What were you watching on TV last night?

3 Have you washed your hands for dinner?

4 Do you have any homework for tomorrow?

5 Are you going to help me with the housework this weekend?

My mother used to ask me questions at the strangest times:

- When I came home from school, she wanted to know [1]_____ *where I ...* _____.
- The morning after we'd spent the evening watching TV together, she asked me [2]_____.
- At 10 in the morning, she used to ask [3]_____.
- In the middle of the summer vacation, she asked [4]_____.
- When she knew I was going on a weekend camping trip with friends, she asked [5]_____.

B Find and correct ten mistakes with reported speech in the story.

WEDNESDAY, FEBRUARY 23

My First (and Most Embarrassing) Job Interview
I was eighteen when I went for my first job interview, at a picture laboratory. The manager asked me take a seat and then asked what's my name. I was so nervous that I told him I don't understand the question. Then he wanted to know do I have any plant experience; I told that I had done some work in my grandmother's garden. He laughed and said that by "plant" he had meant "factory," not trees and flowers. I felt terribly embarrassed and simply told him that I have never worked in a factory. He had my file of pictures, and he asked that I talked about them. I was so nervous that I dropped them all on the floor! Then he asked me if I have any references to give him; I thought he meant movie references, so I ask him, "references to which movie?" I'm hadn't been to movies for months but that I could give give references of the last movie I saw. I was sure that I'd messed up the interview, but then he inquired when I can start! He wanted me that I start the following Monday!

Posted by Online Blog at 8:54PM

7.3

A Make the soap opera script more dramatic by using the words in parentheses. Make any other changes necessary.

A: What's the matter? You look terrible. (on earth)

B: I've just seen Marco with Claudia. I'm furious, I can hardly speak. (so)

A: That's crazy. I'm sure there's a mistake. Why don't you call him? (totally)

B: I'm not going to call him. (there's no way)

A: But Marco's a great guy, and you're good together. (such, so)

B: Well, you can be sure that Claudia's going to regret it. (really)

A: I hope you're not going to do anything stupid. (do)

B: You told me to fight for him. I'm just following your advice. (the one)

GRAMMAR

8.1 Past and Mixed Conditionals

Hypothetical Past Conditional (Third Conditional)

Conditional Clause	Result Clause
If + past perfect	would/might/could + have + past participle
If + past perfect continuous	

Use this to talk about a hypothetical situation and result in the past. The situation cannot be changed.

*If Leon **had known** about the problem, he **would have helped**.*

*If you **hadn't overslept**, we **wouldn't have been** late.*

For a longer action, use the past perfect continuous.

*If I **hadn't been sitting** there, we **wouldn't have met**.*

It is common to use only one clause of the full conditional.

*Why didn't you tell me you wanted some grapes? I **could have bought** you some.*

*I'm surprised Paul didn't tell her what he thought. I **would have said** something.*

*A: **Would you have done** it?   B: Yes, if **I'd noticed** in time.*

Mixed Conditional

Conditional Clause	Result Clause
If + past perfect	would/might/could + infinitive

Use this to talk about a hypothetical condition in the past with a result in the present.

*If she **hadn't missed** her plane, she**'d be** in Mexico now.*

*If **I'd been** successful on the exam, I **might have** a better job now.*

Clause Order

It is possible to change the order of the clauses. Note the non-use of the comma.

*You **would have known** about the meeting if you**'d checked** your emails.*

*You **wouldn't need** a visa to work in Australia if you**'d been born** there.*

8.2 -ing Form and Infinitive

Use an infinitive + to:	Examples
after these verbs: *afford, agree, arrange, decide, expect, hope, intend, learn, manage, need, offer, plan, pretend, promise, refuse, seem, tend, threaten, want.*	*We hope to start the meeting at 9. They promised to be here early.*
after these verbs with an object: *ask, advise, expect, help*, invite, persuade, remind, require, teach, want.*	*Will wants me to go to the party with him.*
after semi-fixed phrases: *be good/ lucky/happy/necessary/the first, have the chance/opportunity/time, somewhere/something/nowhere/ nothing.*	*She was lucky to get the job. There's nowhere to go and nothing to do.*
to express purpose.	*I'm going there to see Tom.*

-ing form	Examples
as a subject or object, i.e., as a noun.	*Doing is better than thinking.*
after prepositions (often part of a fixed phrase): *look forward to, be used to, be accustomed to, be eager about, instead of.*	*I'm not used to getting up early. I'm looking forward to sleeping late this weekend.*
after these verbs: *avoid, come, consider, discuss, deny, enjoy, go, hate, involve, keep, like, love, mind, miss, practice, suggest.*	*Dave came fishing with me. I keep getting headaches. What do you suggest doing?*
after certain phrases: *can't bear/ stand, it's not worth, it's no use, have trouble.*	*We're having trouble finding a hotel.*

Use an infinitive:	Examples
after modal verbs.	*They might be late.*
after *had better, would rather.*	*You'd better take an umbrella—it looks like rain.*
after these verbs with an object: *let, make, help*.*	*Our supervisor let us go early today.*

help can be used either with or without to.   Can you help me **(to) lift this?*

8.3 Handling an Awkward Situation

Preparing the Listener

There's something	I've been meaning to talk to you about. I'd like to talk to you about.

Giving the Message

I hope you don't take this the wrong way, but …
I don't want you to get the wrong idea, but …
It's just that, (you know you borrowed/you said you'd … etc.)

Suggesting a Solution

I have a suggestion/an idea.
I'd feel better if …

Getting the Other Person's Point of View

Do you see where I'm coming from?
How does that sound?
How would you feel about that?
Do you know what I mean?

PRACTICE

8.1

A Choose the correct sentence ending.

1 If the builders had begun the job two weeks ago,
   a) they might have finished it by now.
   b) they might finish it by now.

2 If Chun had started the race better,
   a) she could win the gold medal.
   b) she could have won the gold medal.

3 We wouldn't be lost
   a) if you hadn't given me the wrong directions.
   b) if you gave me the wrong directions.

4 If Marco hadn't ignored my advice,
   a) he wouldn't be in this mess now.
   b) he couldn't have been in this mess now.

5 I would have noticed the hole in the ground
   a) if I hadn't thought about something else.
   b) if I hadn't been thinking about something else.

B Join the sentences using a past or mixed conditional form and the words in parentheses. In some cases both forms are possible.

1 Beth didn't study. She didn't pass the exam. (could)
   If Beth had studied, she could have passed the exam.

2 You didn't invite me to the party. That's why I didn't come. (would)

3 Ludmila lost all her money on the stock market. That's why she's not rich now. (would)

4 Greg wasn't traveling fast. That's probably why he didn't hit the motorcyclist. (might)

5 They stopped the fire. That's probably why it didn't destroy most of the building. (could)

6 The plant died because you didn't water it. (would not)

7 Mei-li was able to afford a new car because she had just won some money. (could not)

8 We were working together in Tokyo, and now we're married. (would not)

8.2

A Find and correct the mistakes in the sentences. Do not change the underlined phrase.

1 <u>It's no use</u> to explain—you never listen anyway.
   It's no use explaining—you never listen anyway.

2 <u>There's no point in</u> go to bed now—we have to get up in an hour.

3 <u>Do you expect</u> that I know all the answers?

4 Listen <u>to your MP3 player</u> during class is rude.

5 My parents never <u>let me</u> to stay out past 8 o'clock.

6 We all <u>look forward to</u> see you in person.

7 <u>You'd better</u> to get ready—the taxi's arriving in ten minutes.

8 The trip was <u>a good opportunity</u> practicing speaking English.

9 <u>They're used to</u> speak English with each other, even though they're both Japanese.

10 <u>I called the station</u> for asking about departure times.

B Use the correct form of the verbs in the box to rewrite the sentences so that they mean the same.

avoid	consider	expect	keep	manage
	remind	teach		

1 Why don't you become a doctor?
   Have _____.

2 I've passed my driving test—after three tries!
   I've _____.

3 I can type without looking. I learned that from my mother.
   My mother _____.

4 We didn't talk to each other all through the party.
   We _____.

5 Jorge thinks that he'll finish the painting by the end of the week.
   Jorge _____.

6 My computer freezes whenever I hit the delete button.
   My computer _____.

7 Don't let me forget to lock the door, Jan.
   Could you _____?

8.3

A Complete the conversation with phrases a)–f). There is one phrase you do not need.

A: Max, ¹_____.

B: Sure, go ahead.

A: Look, ²_____ ...

B: That sounds bad ...

A: ³_____ you know how you always open the window when you come into the office? Well, it's often too cold for me.

B: Oh, right. I find it too stuffy.

A: It's a bit annoying because you don't ever ask us. ⁴_____?

B: Fair enough. Look, I'll make sure I check first. ⁵_____?

A: Good. I'd really appreciate that.

a) How does that sound

b) It's just that,

c) there's something I've been meaning to talk to you about

d) I'm sure we can sort it out

e) Do you see where I'm coming from

f) I don't want you to get the wrong idea, but

GRAMMAR

9.1 *-ing* Form and Infinitive

	+ Infinitive with *to*	+ *-ing* Form
remember forget	for things you plan, want or have the responsibility to do He **remembered to turn off** the lights.	have a memory of an earlier action I'll never **forget visiting** Paris.
try	attempt to do something difficult Angus **tried to change** his ticket, but it was impossible.	experiment to see if something will work **Try** clicking on OK in the box.
stop	stop one action in order to do another (infinitive of purpose) We **stopped to have** some lunch.	finish an action or activity My father **stopped driving** when he was eighty.
go on	for a change of activity She started by defining obesity and **went on to talk** about its causes.	continue Joe **went on working**, although he wasn't well.
regret	be sorry about something you are about to say BA **regrets to announce** a delay of flight BA5276.	be sorry about something you did before We **regretted going** to the party. It was awful.

Verbs Followed by the *-ing* Form or Infinitive with *to* with No Difference in Meaning

These include: *like, love, hate, prefer, can't stand, can't bear, start, begin.*

I hate **writing/to write** by hand.
I much **prefer using/to use** a computer.

In American English, the infinitive with *to* is often preferred. In British English, this is often used to talk about choices and habits.

I **like to go** to the dentist twice a year.

I **hate to interrupt**, but we have to go.

If the verb after *prefer* is in the negative, use the infinitive with *to*.

I **prefer not to write** by hand.

When we use the verbs *begin, continue* and *start* in continuous forms, we usually use the infinitive with *to*.

They're **beginning to annoy** me.
NOT ~~They're beginning annoying me.~~

9.2 Past Modal of Deduction

Use modal verb + *have* + past participle to make deductions or guesses about past actions or states.

You **could have left** it in the café.

Use modal verb + *have* + *been* + *-ing* form to make deductions about continuous actions or states.

She **must have been feeling** ill.

Use modal verb + *have* + *been* + past participle for deductions using the passive.

It **can't have been** stolen from your bag.

must have	you are almost certain that something is true, based on the evidence	I **must have deleted** the email. I can't find it anywhere.
might/ could/ may have	you think it is possible that something is true, based on the evidence	The plane **could have been delayed** by the weather. There's a bad storm at sea.
couldn't/ can't have	you are almost certain something is not true or is impossible, based on the evidence	It **can't have been** the waitress. She wasn't in the room when the bag was stolen.

Note: *have* + past participle (the perfect infinitive) is also used with other modals: *should have (been)* and *would have (been)*.

9.3 Reporting an Incident

Referring to Time	
Before/As soon as/When	I realized what had happened/ was happening ...
It was only (a minute/ much) later	(that) I realized/ remembered ...
It all happened	so quickly/fast/slowly.

Other Phrases for Reporting	
It never occurred to me It didn't cross my mind	(that) he was a thief.
My mind/I	went blank.
I didn't catch	the car's license plate. what he said.

Describing Impressions of a Person or Thing	
He reminded me of	Tom Cruise.
He looked/seemed	as if he were a student. like a student. about 30/very strong.

PRACTICE

9.1

A Match the sentence halves.

1 I tried drinking the medicine,   *b*
2 I tried to drink the medicine,
3 He stopped to smoke
4 He stopped smoking
5 Julia remembers to text me
6 Julia remembers texting me,
7 Xavier went on to perform
8 Xavier went on performing,
9 We regret saying
10 We regret to say

a) but I couldn't—it was too disgusting.
b) but it didn't help.
a) a cigarette before continuing.
b) because he wanted to get in shape.
a) whenever she needs a lift from the station.
b) but I didn't get any messages from her.
a) even though audiences became smaller and smaller.
b) in all of the best opera houses in the world.
a) that the car won't be ready till Monday.
b) that the Games would be a failure.

B Underline the correct alternative. Sometimes both are possible.

Most people prefer not [1]*getting/to get* involved in a crime investigation, according to Detective Jaime Lopez. "I'll give you an example," said Lopez. "Last week, we were just starting [2]*investigating/to investigate* a car theft that had happened in broad daylight downtown, and we realized that our biggest challenge might be to find someone who remembered [3]*seeing/to see* anything at all. We estimate that twenty or thirty people witnessed the crime, but no one tried [4]*intervening/to intervene*, and most people went on [5]*doing/to do* what they were doing. Interestingly, one tourist stopped [6]*taking/to take* pictures of the theft in process but then continued sightseeing. He only came forward three days after the incident. 'Sorry, I forgot [7]*telling/to tell* you that I have some pictures of the crime,' he said, but he didn't seem genuinely to regret [8]*not coming forward/to not come forward* earlier. We tried [9]*identifying/to identify* the thief from the tourist's photograph, but it wasn't clear enough." We asked Lopez how he can bear [10]*doing/to do* such a frustrating job. "I like [11]*helping/to help* people. I love this city. I never stop [12]*being/to be* glad I live here."

9.2

A Rewrite the underlined sentence with *must/might/ may/could/can't/couldn't have*.

1 <u>Perhaps Jenna called while we were out.</u> Let me check on the answer machine.
   Jenna might have called while we were out.
2 Knock louder. You know he's a bit deaf. <u>I'm sure he didn't hear you.</u>
3 I locked the door. I'm certain. <u>Maybe the thieves got in through the window.</u>
4 I can't find the final version of the report in my computer. <u>I realized it was impossible that I saved the document.</u>
5 Ooh, that was a bad knock to your head. <u>I'm certain it hurt a lot.</u>
6 I don't know why Wanda was late for the meeting. <u>Maybe her plane was delayed.</u>
7 <u>I'm sure I've made a mistake.</u> The date looks wrong.
8 Paola should have won the race. <u>It's impossible that she was trying hard enough.</u>

B Complete the conversations with the correct form of a verb from the box and a modal of deduction

look   tell   think   cost   work   switch off

1 A: Look at her necklace. Are those real diamonds?
   B: Yes. It _____ a fortune!
2 A: I tried phoning Mike four times, but he didn't answer.
   B: He _____ his phone, or maybe he left it at home.
3 A: Why was Danielle in the office at midnight?
   B: She _____ late. She had a big meeting the next day.
4 A: I'm sure Len told me you were a doctor.
   B: He _____ of my sister, Rachel, or maybe he confused me with someone else.
5 A: I've lost my boarding pass. It's not in my bag!
   B: You _____ properly. I saw you put it there just now.
6 A: Do you think Yves knows he didn't get the promotion?
   B: I suppose he _____ by the boss, but I doubt it.

9.3

A Correct each of B's sentences by adding a word from the box.

looked   realized   crossed   occurred   if   strange

A: Why didn't you call us when you first saw the man behaving strangely?
B: [1]It never my mind until I saw the picture on *Crimebeat* on TV.
A: And when you saw *Crimebeat* ... ?
B: [2]It to me then that I should contact you.
A: We appreciate that. Tell me what happened.

B: [3]I saw him near the factory. He looked as he were taking pictures of the building.
A: Do you remember anything else?
B: [4]When he saw me, he left quickly, and he guilty.
A: Why didn't you call someone right away?
B: [5]It was only later that I that there was something strange about how he left.
A: Maybe he'd finished?
B: [6]I don't know. It just seemed pretty, but then I didn't think any more about it till I saw the program.

answer machine / boarding pass   answerphone / boarding card

GRAMMAR

Relative Clauses

Defining Relative Clauses

- give essential information about a noun.

  *That guy is the actor **who is going to play the president**.*

  Don't use commas before or after the clause.

- can omit the relative pronoun/adverb when it is the object of the relative clause.

  Ken's just seen a woman (whom) he went to college with.

  He is the subject of the relative clause, *who* is the object, so we can omit *who*.

Pronouns and Adverbs in Relative Clauses

Use the relative pronouns *who/whom* (people), *which/that* (things), *whose* (possession) and the relative adverbs *when* (time) and *where* (place).

*I remember the time **when** you were just a little girl.*

Whose can be used to refer to cities, countries and other nouns which suggest a group of people. It is rarely used with things.

*It's a city **whose** inhabitants always seem to be upbeat.*

Omit words which have been replaced by the relative pronoun.

NOT *She's someone **whom** I know ~~her~~ well.*

Non-defining Relative Clauses

- give additional, non-essential information.

  *That's Sam, **who is going to play the president**.*

- use commas to separate this clause from the rest of the sentence.

- cannot use *that* instead of *who* or *which*.

  *The movie, **which** won the Oscar last year, was made in India.*
  NOT ~~The movie, that won the Oscar last year, was made in India.~~

- cannot omit the relative pronouns/adverbs.

  *Gwen, **whom** I'm going to see later, is my fiancé.*
  NOT ~~Gwen, I'm going to see later, is my fiancé.~~

- can use *which* to refer to the whole of a previous clause.

  *The plane was delayed, **which** meant we were late.*

Prepositions in Relative Clauses

In informal spoken and written English, prepositions usually come at the end of the relative clause.

*This is the book **which** she's famous **for**.*

In formal and in written English, prepositions often come before the relative pronoun. Use *whom* for people.

*He is someone **with whom** I can work.*

Where can be replaced by *which … in*, or, in more formal English *in which*.

*The room **where** she slept/**which** she slept in/**in which** she slept is over there.*

Participle Clauses

- Use participle clauses (clauses that start with a present participle or a past participle) to vary your style or to include more information in a sentence.

- Use them as a shorter alternative to relative clauses. In this use, they are also known as "reduced relative clauses." Form the participle clause by omitting the relative pronoun and any auxiliary verbs.

- Clauses beginning with a past participle have a passive meaning.

  *The children **caught in the rainstorm** came home soaked.*
  = The children who were caught …

  *The movie, **directed by Miyakazi**, won an award for animation.*
  = which was directed by Miyakazi …

- Clauses beginning with a present participle have an active meaning.

  *The team **playing in red** is Chile.*
  = The team that is playing in red …

  *Do you know the man **standing in the corner**?*
  = the man who is standing …

- Clauses beginning with a present participle replace continuous and simple verbs in different tenses.

  *Give me a number **beginning** with three.*
  = Give me a number that begins with three.

  *Anyone **cheating** on the exam failed.*
  = Anyone who cheated on the exam failed.

  *The bus **leaving** tomorrow will stop at Lima.*
  = The bus that is leaving/leaves tomorrow …

Giving a Tour

Commenting on Facts
As you may know,/As I'm sure you know, …   The story goes that …   Apparently,/Supposedly,/Interestingly, …   Surprisingly,/Strangely,/Believe it or not, …   It's well worth (going/seeing/a visit)

Leading the Way		
Let's/We could	head over to	the park.
Should we Why don't we	head back to retrace our steps to	the café?

Giving Facts		
It was	built	to celebrate … to commemorate … in honor of …
	founded by/ named after	(Thomas Bodley).
	modeled on/ modeled after	(the Arc de Triomphe).
	burned down destroyed rebuilt restored	in the 15th century. in the 1990s.

PRACTICE

10.1

A Combine the sentences using a relative clause. Omit the relative pronoun where possible. Sometimes there is more than one answer.

1 The man is marrying Suzanne. He's very lucky.

The man _____.

2 The house burned down yesterday. I used to live in it.

The house _____.

3 Pablo Picasso spent his early childhood in Malaga. His father was also an artist.

Pablo Picasso _____.

4 That was the most important moment of my life. I realized I wanted to be an actor.

The moment _____.

5 The vacation was in Canada. I enjoyed it most.

The vacation _____.

6 Usain Bolt is a global superstar. He was the first man to win six gold Olympic medals in sprinting.

Usain Bolt, _____.

7 I lived with a guy when I was a student. His hobby was fixing motorcycles.

When I was _____.

8 You should make a speech. This is that sort of occasion.

This is _____.

B Add the missing prepositions (*for*, *from*, *in*, *on*, *to* or *with*). There is one extra preposition you do not need.

1 It was the house which I spent my childhood.

2 It was a lesson which I'll always be grateful.

3 She's definitely the woman whom he wants to spend the rest of his life.

4 The movie theater I most often go is the Odeon downtown.

5 Funnily enough, it was the planning which we spent the most time.

6 He was an athlete whom success came as naturally as his speed.

7 He was a friend I could always depend.

8 You're the person whom we always turn when a speech is needed.

10.2

A Complete the sentences with the present or past participle form of the verb in parentheses.

1 A beret is a type of flat hat often _____ on one side of the head. (wear)

2 The large number of people _____ outside meant the doctor would be working late that night. (wait)

3 Items permanently _____ from your inbox can usually be found again if you know where to look. (delete)

4 I knew two people _____ in the fire. (injure)

5 Babies _____ in a bilingual household have more flexible brains. (bring up)

6 The dance _____ place tomorrow is to celebrate the end of the exams. (take)

B Combine the sentences using a participle clause and the correct punctuation. Sometimes there is more than one possibility.

1 The taxi almost drove over a man. He was lying in the street.

2 *Sunflowers* was painted by Van Gogh. It's one of the most popular paintings ever.

3 The army advanced toward the hill. It was led by Napoleon.

4 I don't know the people. They live next door to me.

5 I used to like blockbusters. They involved lots of action.

6 The apartments overlook Central Park. They are the most expensive.

7 Some factories were forced to close during the recession. They still haven't reopened.

8 Many people think that the Taj Mahal is the most beautiful building in the world. It was built in the seventeenth century.

10.3

A Correct eight mistakes in A's part of the conversations.

1 A: So here we are at Margit Island, named from a nun whose father was once king.

B: Wow! It's beautiful.

A: Yeah, interesting at one time it was three islands and only used by people who had land here.

2 A: Supposingly these caves run for miles.

B: What were they for?

A: The story tells that, when there was an invasion, the local people hid in these tunnels.

3 A: That's the Vajdahunyad Castle. It was modeled from a castle in Transylvania.

B: And why was it built?

A: It was built for the city's millennium exhibition in 1896, to memorize the one-thousand-year anniversary of the founding of the state.

4 A: Let's retrace our feet to Castle Hill.

B: Great. We hardly spent any time there this morning.

A: Exactly, and the museum is well worse a visit.

Lesson 1.1 PERSONALITY ADJECTIVES

1 A Match the adjectives in the box with descriptions 1—10.

| cautious   eccentric   flexible   genuine   mean   moody   naive |
| sympathetic   trustworthy   outgoing |

1 My friend always has time for me when I have a problem. She seems to understand and wants to help.

2 Cheung always takes a long time to make up his mind, and he's careful to avoid problems or danger.

3 Joe thought his first job would be easy and people would be nice. He soon learned differently!

4 I really like your fiancé—he seems honest and sincere.

5 Lucia is a great tour guide because she's so friendly and enjoys meeting people.

6 My last teacher wasn't very kind. She often laughed at students when they made mistakes.

7 Noriko is a great addition to the team. She adapts quickly to new situations and doesn't mind change.

8 Karl acts a bit strange sometimes and wears the oddest clothes, but he's a good guy.

9 You can tell Marta a secret, and you know she'll never tell anyone else.

10 Sam's a typical teenager. He always seems to be unhappy, or else he suddenly gets angry for no reason.

B What type of personality do you think the people in pictures A–C have?

Lesson 1.2 WORD BUILDING

2 A Complete the table with the verb forms of the nouns.

Verb	Suffix	Noun
identify	-tion/ -ation	identification appreciation
	-ment	argument development
	-ence	existence defence
	-ure	signature pleasure

B Add the verbs below and their noun forms to the table.

prepare
contribute
fail
donate
react
interfere
prefer
prevent
mix
refer
involve
treat

C Complete the questions with nouns from the table. Sometimes you need to use a plural form.

1 Is your _____ easy to read and has it changed over the years?

2 How do you show your _____ for good service in a hotel?

3 Have you ever taken classes in self-_____, or are you confident you could look after yourself in an emergency?

4 Are you studying English for business or for _____?

5 In a group situation, do you make a lot of _____, or are you fairly quiet until you have something important to say?

6 Do you have a _____ for a particular type of music?

7 Do you carry any _____ with you, such as your passport?

8 Do you enjoy having heated _____ with people, or do you tend to avoid them?

9 Have you ever written a _____ for someone for a job or to go to college?

10 Can you remember a teacher who had a strong influence on your _____ as a person?

D Work in pairs and ask and answer the questions.

A

B

C

D

1 A Match the words in the box to the photos. Which words are not in the pictures?

flood   volcanic eruption   earthquake
homelessness   drought   landslide   drug abuse
domestic violence   debt   obesity

B Match the remaining problems in the box to news items 1–6.

1 A recent report has put the number of overweight adults at one in every three.

2 The amount of money owed by each household in the country has more than doubled in the last ten years.

3 The number of people sleeping on the streets has gone down in recent years.

4 A new rehabilitation center has opened to help people to overcome their addictions.

5 One incident is reported to police every minute, but many women are too frightened to come forward.

6 In schools all over the region, children are taught what to do when they feel the ground begin to shake.

C Write natural disaster (ND), social issue (S) or health issue (H) next to each item. Some can be more than one.

Lesson 2.1 VERBS/NOUNS WITH THE SAME FORM

2 A Underline a word in each question which has the same noun/verb form.

1 What's the worst delay you've ever experienced on a flight?

2 Do you have an exam at the end of the course, or does your teacher test your English every week?

3 Do you ever shout when you're angry, or do you take a deep breath and count to ten?

4 Do you text with your friends more than you call them?

5 When you're cooking, do you weigh everything exactly, or do you just make a guess?

6 Is the best cure for a headache to take a pill or just to relax?

7 Do you think people should get a fine for driving too fast, or should they lose their license?

8 In a restaurant, do you complain if the service is bad? Do you always tip the waiter if it's good?

9 Would you ever lie, or do you always tell the truth?

10 When you compare yourself to other people, are you pretty calm, or are you often in a hurry?

B Work in pairs and discuss the questions.

license   licence

Lesson 3.1
VERBS USED IN STORIES

1 A Match the verbs with the pictures.

1 whisper	4 crawl
2 yawn	5 wander
3 gaze	6 sigh

B Rewrite the sentences from stories. Replace the underlined words with the correct form of a word from Exercise 1A.

1 She would sit and look at photographs of exotic places for hours and simply <u>let out a long breath of sadness</u>, knowing she would never leave her house.

2 His conversation was so dull that, after a while, she <u>opened her mouth wide in boredom</u> and walked away.

3 There was a small space at the bottom of the fence, so he <u>went</u> under <u>on his hands and knees</u>.

4 She <u>said</u> her name <u>softly</u>, as if it were some sort of secret only I should know.

5 He <u>walked</u> through the city <u>with no destination in mind</u>, turning left or right at random.

6 When he reached the river, he <u>looked out</u> at the water without focusing, his mind lost in thought

Lesson 3.2 MULTI-WORD VERBS

2 A Look at the sentences and answer the questions about the multi-word verb *bring up*.

1 We brought up Simon to be polite.

2 We brought Simon up to be polite.

3 We brought him up to be polite.

a) Where can you put a noun object?

b) Where must you put a pronoun object?

B Which is the most useful way or ways for you to record this feature of a multi-word verb?

> 1 To bring up (separable)
> 2 To bring sb. up.
> 3 They **brought me up** to be cautious with money.

C Replace the noun in bold in each sentence with the pronoun in parentheses.

1 Kieron wanted the job, but they turned *him* down ~~Kieron~~. (him)

2 The store had some great clothes, but the loud music bothered **Lena**. (her)

3 Fifty people wanted to be extras in the movie, and the director took on **all fifty people**. (them all)

4 Señor Almeida isn't here at the moment. Can you call **Señor Almeida** back? (him)

5 I finished the essay last night and handed in **the essay** this morning. (it)

6 If I don't know new words, I just look up **the words** in my electronic dictionary. (them)

7 The sound of the doorbell at 2 a.m. woke up **everyone**. (us)

8 Is that a new coat? Anyway, take off **the coat** and hang up **the coat** here. (it, it)

handed in   gave in

Lesson 4.2 UNCOUNTABLE NOUNS

1 A Rewrite the sentences to include an uncountable noun from the box.

> ~~furniture~~   trouble   information
> weather   room   baggage   advice
> news   equipment   research

1 The chairs and desks were relatively inexpensive.

   The furniture was relatively inexpensive.

2 There are a lot of suggestions available to help with debt.

3 Are there any places left in the class?

4 Scientific papers show that obesity has doubled over the last decade.

5 The economic reports from the World Bank are disturbing.

6 Chris has problems hearing clearly.

7 What a terrible day!

8 The sports items are stored in that closet over there.

9 Are there any details available about the free trial?

10 Where are my suitcases?

B Cross out the noun that does NOT collocate with the phrase in the middle of each word web.

information
news   room
a piece of
advice   research

equipment
clothing   advice
an item of
baggage   news

trouble
room   information
a little
transportation   furniture

C Which of the nouns can fit with one or both of the other two phrases?

A piece of clothing …

Lesson 4.3 SPORTS AND ACTIVITIES

2 A Cross out the collocation which is NOT possible.

1 beat / win / tackle / defeat / lose to + an opponent

2 win / lose / play / beat / tie + a game

3 throw / roll / score / pass / bounce + a ball

4 get / shoot / score / miss / let in + a goal

5 do + weight training / judo / chess / yoga

6 play + track and field / baseball / pool / soccer

B Write the correct collocation under the photos A–F

C Which of these sports, games and activities have you tried? Which would you like to try?

3 A Look at the common phrases and idioms in bold which come from some of the sports above. Match each phrase 1–6 with its meaning a)–f).

1 I've told you what I want to do, now **the ball is in your court**.

2 Should we **kick off** today's lesson by looking at our latest blog entries?

3 I think that 70,000 dollars is probably **in the ballpark** for that house.

4 I was very impressed by Jamal. He's really **on the ball**.

5 We need to discuss how to **tackle** the problem quickly.

6 It's **a whole new ballgame** for me, I've never directed a video before.

a) a completely new situation

b) to deal with a problem in a determined way

c) to start something happening

d) a reasonably accurate estimate

e) the next move is yours

f) able to think or understand or react to something very quickly

B Do you have similar expressions in your language?

))) VOCABULARY BANK

Lesson 5.1
COMPOUND ADJECTIVES

1 A Match the beginnings and endings to make compound adjectives for products.

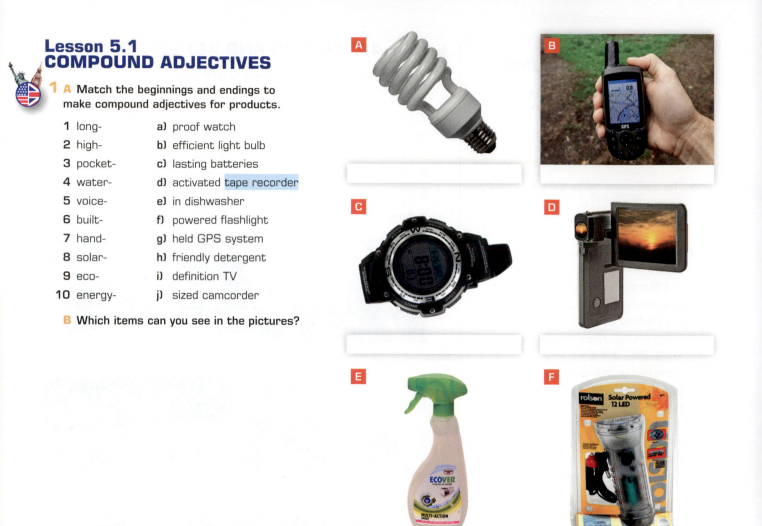

1	long-	**a)**	proof watch
2	high-	**b)**	efficient light bulb
3	pocket-	**c)**	lasting batteries
4	water-	**d)**	activated tape recorder
5	voice-	**e)**	in dishwasher
6	built-	**f)**	powered flashlight
7	hand-	**g)**	held GPS system
8	solar-	**h)**	friendly detergent
9	eco-	**i)**	definition TV
10	energy-	**j)**	sized camcorder

B Which items can you see in the pictures?

Lesson 5.2 ADVERTISING

2 A Complete questions 1–12 with a word from the box.

> commercials   pop-ups   brand   campaigns   logos   influence   slogans   cold calls
> advertise   makes   jingle   trailer

1 Are there too many _____ during TV programs?

2 "Just do it!" and "The world's local bank" are memorable _____. What others do you know?

3 What are the most popular _____ of car in your country? What's your favorite?

4 Which is the most popular sports equipment _____ in your country?

5 Do you think that a _____ for a movie accurately shows what the movie is like?

6 What does an image of an apple with a bite taken out of it mean to you? What other _____ do you know?

7 What type of advertisement would _____ you to try a new food or drink product?

8 Do you ever find yourself singing a particular _____ for a product or a radio station?

9 Can you recall any particularly successful advertising _____?

10 If you wanted to sell a product, where would you _____?

11 How do you feel about website _____? Do they work?

12 What do you say when someone _____ you in the evenings?

B Work in pairs and answer the questions in Exercise 2A.

tape recorder   dictaphone

Lesson 6.1
WORD-BUILDING: PREFIXES

1 A Find a prefix in **A** which means:

1 very small
2 very big
3 many
4 between
5 two
6 across

A

bi   multi
micro   mega
trans   inter

B

lingual   chip
national   media
late   wave   port
task   phone   cycle
scope   val   monthly
city   view   it
-story   byte

B Match a prefix in **A** with at least three endings in **B**.

C Complete the sentences with the correct form of a word formed from a prefix in **A** and an ending in **B**.

1 I left my car in one of those huge _____ parking lots, and now I can't find it.

2 It's a long opera, but there are two _____. We can take a break, and have a coffee then.

3 I've never really been to Hong Kong, only in the airport when I was in _____ on my way to Beijing.

4 The crowd was so noisy, I had to use a _____ to make my voice loud enough.

5 He didn't get the job because he was late for the _____.

6 No, it's too small. You can only see it under a _____.

7 Our newsletter only goes out _____. It's January now, so the next one is in March.

8 People who grow up in a _____ environment end up understanding three or more languages.

parking lots   car parks

Lesson 6.2 TIME IDIOMS

2 A Match the phrases and idioms in bold with pictures A–I.

1 Your food will be here **in no time**.   _D_

2 Sorry, I'll have to **cut this short**.   ____

3 He's **dragging his heels** over the decorating.   ____

4 I was **making up for lost time**—you see I overslept.   ____

5 I've told you **time after time** to take your shoes off!   ____

6 She got home **in the nick of time**.   ____

7 I'm just **killing an hour or two** before my interview.   ____

8 Please **take your time**.   ____

9 The train should be here **any time now**.   ____

B Match meanings a)–i) to the phrases and idioms.

a) to spend time doing something unimportant while you are waiting for something else to happen
b) very soon
c) very quickly
d) to delay doing something
e) to do something without hurrying
f) again and again
g) to stop doing something earlier than you had planned
h) at the last moment before it is too late to do something
i) to do something quickly because you started late or worked too slowly

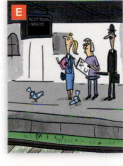

)) VOCABULARY BANK

Lesson 7.1 MULTI-WORD VERBS

1 A Look at the sentence pairs. How are the meanings of the multi-word verbs in bold different?

1 Did your parents **bring** you **up** as a Buddhist?

2 Oh, here's Edith now. Just don't **bring up** anything about her divorce.

3 Anna keeps **putting off** the meeting. I don't think we'll ever get a chance to discuss things.

4 I was **put off** by his behavior.

5 Why did they **turn** Neil **down** for the job?

6 Could you **turn** the stove **down**—the sauce in the pan is going to burn.

7 My car's in the repair shop. It **broke down** on the way to work today.

8 Negotiations between the two corporations have **broken down**, but they may restart next month.

9 The company **took on** ten high-school graduates last month.

10 After Brazil won the semi-finals, they **took on** the favorites, Spain.

11 He **pulled out** without looking and hit another car.

12 Both countries have **pulled out** of the talks, so there won't be any agreement.

B Complete the table with the multi-word verbs from Exercise 1A.

a		hire compete against
b		say no lower the level
c		end one's involvement, or quit drive onto a road from another road
d		make sb. dislike sth. postpone
e		raise start to talk about
f		fail or end unsuccessfully stop working, usually for a machine

Lesson 7.3 PARTS OF A NEWS WEBSITE

2 Match 1–10 to the parts of a news website.

1 breaking news

2 lead story

3 headlines

4 newsfeed

5 forum link

6 weather forecast

7 video link

8 menu bar

9 navigation buttons

10 popup ad

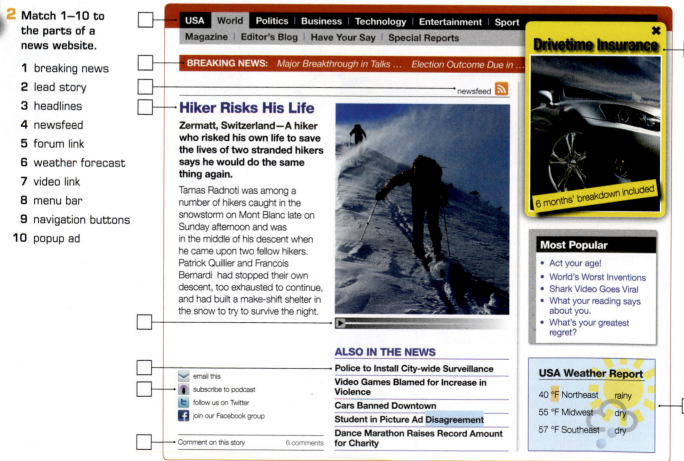

repair shop / high-school graduates
disagreement / °F

garage / school-leavers
row / °C

Lesson 8.1 COMPOUND ADJECTIVES FOR DESCRIBING PEOPLE

1 A Look at the picture and complete the compound adjectives with words from the box.

> brand   broad   brown
> curly   dark   high
> sun   tight

B Which words or phrases can be turned into opposites by using the opposite of the first part?

curly-haired—straight-haired

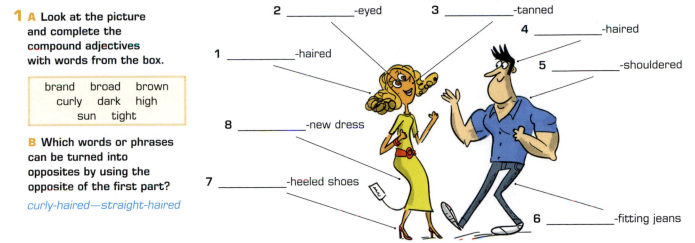

1 _____-haired
2 _____-eyed
3 _____-tanned
4 _____-haired
5 _____-shouldered
6 _____-fitting jeans
7 _____-heeled shoes
8 _____-new dress

Lesson 8.3 BEHAVIOR IDIOMS

2 A Match pictures A–F with the idioms in the box. Two idioms are not in the pictures.

> talk behind sb.'s back   walk all over sb.
> not lift a finger   be always there for sb.
> go out of one's way to do sth.   lock horns with sb.
> (be) a shoulder to cry on   give sb. a helping hand

C Complete the sentences with the correct form of the idioms.

1 She loves to help out. She'll _____ anyone a _____ _____ if they need it.
2 He often sits and watches me clean and doesn't _____ _____ _____ to help.
3 When I'm really upset and need a _____ _____ _____ _____, I always turn to Martin.
4 I don't trust her; she's such a gossip. She's always _____ _____ my _____.
5 He argues about everything. In fact, he'll _____ _____ _____ you on just about any topic.
6 She's the best friend I can imagine. She _____ _____ _____ for me, through good times and bad.
7 He's so kind and generous. He'll always _____ _____ _____ his _____ to help you.
8 Don't just do everything he wants. He's very selfish. Don't let him _____ _____ _____ you.

D Match meanings 1–8 to the idioms in Exercise 2A.

1 be available whenever somebody needs you
2 do something to help, even though it's not convenient for you
3 be in conflict with somebody
4 do something to help somebody
5 give somebody sympathy when they're upset
6 say something (usually bad) about somebody when they're not listening
7 treat someone very badly
8 do absolutely nothing to help

B Which of the idioms in the box do you think are positive, and which are negative?

Lesson 9.1 DEPENDENT PREPOSITIONS

1 Complete the headlines with a dependent preposition.

1 Innocent Man Mistaken _____ Gang Leader

2 Woman Jailed for Hiding Robbers _____ Police

3 Couple Punished _____ Balloon Hoax

4 Mugger Caught after Boasting _____ Crimes in Local Bar

5 Jailed Criminal Prohibited _____ Selling His Story

6 Politician Condemned _____ Involvement in Banking Scandal

7 Murderess Given Strong Sentence for Joking _____ Crime

8 Local Teacher Fired for Participating _____ Protest March

9 College President Conceals Financial Woes _____ Board of Trustees

10 Mother Fined _____ Leaving Baby Unattended in Car

Lesson 9.3 CARS AND ACCIDENTS

2 Match the car parts 1–12 to A–L in the picture.

1 trunk   J
2 hood
3 license plate
4 turn signal
5 door
6 sideview mirror
7 tail light
8 windshield
9 tire
10 windshield wiper
11 sunroof
12 steering wheel

3 Complete the sentences with the verbs and verb phrases in the box in the past simple.

skid   collide with   pull out   overtake   drive the wrong way   swerve   exceed the speed limit   scratch

The car _____ on the ice.

She _____ to avoid hitting the dog.

She increased her speed and _____ the blue car.

He _____. He was going at 60 mph.

She _____ the side of the car by parking too near a wall.

He was driving too fast on a narrow street and _____ another car.

A car _____ in front of him, and he almost crashed into it.

He _____ down the highway.

trunk / hood / license plate / turn signal / door / sideview mirror / windshield / highway

boot / bonnet / number plate / indicator / wing / wing mirror / windscreen / motorway

Lesson 10.2 MUSIC

1 A Match the instruments 1–12 with the pictures.

1 acoustic guitar
2 drums
3 bass guitar
4 violin/fiddle (informal)
5 cello
6 grand piano
7 trumpet
8 trombone
9 flute
10 clarinet
11 saxophone
12 harp

B Can you play any of the instruments above? Which instrument would you most like to learn?

2 Match the phrases and idioms in bold with meanings a)–h).

1 Jim likes to **trumpet** his own achievements.
2 Clara began **fiddling with** her necklace. I could see that she was worried.
3 We need to **drum up** some new business, or we'll have to close down.
4 I'm tired of **playing second fiddle**.
5 Interesting how Larry **changed his tune** after he found out it was his own assistant who stole the money.
6 I know, it looks like an expensive car but I got it **for a song**.
7 The boss wants to see me about my mistakes on the contract. It's time for me to go in and **face the music**.
8 Her name **rings a bell**—maybe I've met her before.

a) take a less important role
b) remind sb. of sth., sound familiar
c) talk positively about oneself
d) touch or play with something in a restless or nervous way
e) get (support or attention) through making a lot of effort
f) accept responsibility for mistakes
g) suddenly take a different perspective
h) very cheaply

Lesson 10.2 TWO-PART PHRASES

3 A Complete the sentences with the words in the box.

| take | death | leave | later | swim | another | miss | nothing |

1 It's only a question of time, and, **sooner or** _____, you'll find a new job.
2 That's the highest salary we can pay you. We can't go higher, so **take it or** _____ it.
3 You've finished the training, and now you have to go out and do the job. It's **sink or** _____.
4 The shop is about twenty miles from here, **give or** _____ a mile.
5 It was **all or** _____—she either had to get in the car with him or lose him forever.
6 This is the biggest choice of my life—it's a **life or** _____ decision.
7 Mark took a **hit or** _____ approach to finding a girlfriend. He simply asked every girl he saw out on a date.
8 I know, we're lost, but, **one way or** _____, we'll find our way back.

B Match meanings a)–h) with the two-part phrases in Exercise 3A.

a) the offer won't change
b) risking everything
c) to within (a small amount)
d) unplanned/disorganized
e) eventually
f) somehow
g) fail or succeed
h) extremely important

Lesson 1.3

6 A Student B: look at Situation 1 below and follow the instructions.

> **Situation 1: (Service Person)**
> You work for the customer service department at an airline. A customer calls for help with a reservation. Use the information below to answer the customer's inquiries.
>
> MA271   Wed. Oct. 19   Dep. Singapore 3:50 p.m.
>
> | | |
> |---|---|
> | Wed Oct. 19 | 2 tourist class seats available |
> | Thu Oct. 20 | 1 business class seat available |
> | Fri Oct. 21 | 1 tourist class seat available |
>
> Change fee: $90
>
> Upgrade to business class: $350

6 B Student B: look at Situation 2 below and follow the instructions.

> **Situation 2: (Customer)**
> You've just received the confirmation below for a hotel reservation you made for some friends. You want to change the arrival date to one day earlier, and you want to upgrade their room if it doesn't cost more than $60. Call the hotel; by the end of the call, you should know (a) which day your friends can arrive and (b) how much the room will cost per night.
>
> | To | h.calderwood8@gmailbox.com |
> |---|---|
>
> **Reservation Confirmation**
>
> **YOUR RESERVATION DETAILS**
>
> | Guest Name | Johns, Mr. and Mrs. |
> |---|---|
> | Arrival Date | July 3rd |
> | Departure Date | July 7th |
> | Standard Double | $250/night |

Lesson 2.1

9 c

The winning proposal was:
Antibiotics—How can we prevent the rise of resistance to antibiotics?

Lesson 2.1

11 A Student B: look at the quiz below. Underline the stress in the words in bold.

> **1** How old was Michael Jackson when he **recorded** his first hit, "I Want You Back"?
> Seven, nine or eleven?
>
> **2** Which of these products is *not* among Italy's top ten **exports**/
> Machinery, pasta or furniture?
>
> **3** How many grams of honey does a worker bee **produce** in its lifetime?
> 2 grams, 250 grams or 1,000 grams (one kilogram)?
>
> **4** In Sweden, what percent of crime **suspects** are men?
> 50%, 80% or 95%?
>
> **5** How long did the shortest war on **record** last?
> 38 minutes, 38 hours or 38 days?

Lesson 3.1

1 c

Performance of a lifetime?

Ending 1
He shouted, "Mommy, I think you are wonderful!" And the crowd burst into a thunderous applause.

Ending 2
He shouted, "Mommy, what's for dinner?" And the crowd burst into a thunderous laughter.

It Pays to Be Honest

Ending 1
She gave him a kiss, saying, "You were right. Pretending I'm pregnant has really helped my tips."

Ending 2
She gave him a kiss, saying "Everything's going to be just fine. I love you, Steve Hunt."

Lesson 7.3

7 B Student A

The top five most dangerous animals;

1 mosquito   **2** Asian cobra   **3** Australian box jellyfish
4 great white shark   **5** African lion

Lesson 4.1

4 B Student A: read Sandra's opinion below. Were your predictions correct?

THE EXPERTS HAVE THEIR SAY:

Sandra McCullough
Psychologist and Parent

What's changed isn't the amount of free time, it's people's ability to do nothing. We think we used to have more free time because, years ago, we didn't use to fill it up with tasks the way we do now. People would sit around and watch TV or read. However, people have been programmed to need new things all the time, and technology has, unfortunately, responded to that need. Watch people on the train, for example, when they have some free time, they'll check social media, read a news site, or play a game on their phone rather than simply relaxing or gazing into space. People say they like spending time with family, but why are they always talking on their cells or checking emails when they're with their "nearest and dearest"? I tell my clients, "Hey, turn off the Internet and enjoy the silence." But most people can't do it. They panic. It's like a drug for them.

Lesson 5.2

6 Student A: work with another student A. Read the first part of this viral video description and discuss the questions.

1 What do you think might happen next?

2 What product do you think it is advertising?

Graffiti Artist (Part 1)
A hooded graffiti artist hangs by a rope to paint a huge mural of a woman's face on the wall of a building. The police come, and the graffiti artist manages to get away. The hood comes off to reveal that the artist is a woman with the same face as the one she's just painted on the wall. She takes out her mirror …

Turn to page 161 and read the ending. Which do you prefer, yours or this one?

Work with Student B. Cover the story and describe the video to your partner. Stop before the ending and ask your partner to guess the ending and product.

Which of the two videos do you think is more effective?

Lesson 6.2

7 C

Key
a) = 3 points
b) = 2 points
c) = 1 point

12–15: You are amazingly optimistic! On the one hand, your positive attitude can make people around you feel good. On the other hand, sometimes people may find your constant cheerfulness slightly irritating.

8–11: You are calm and level-headed and can always see both sides of a situation. This means you don't have great highs and lows but can also mean you miss out on some of the drama of life.

5–7: You're not always easy to be with, usually seeing the negative side of things. However, this can be extremely useful in some situations because you will tend to be more cautious and see what could go wrong with any plans or projects.

4 A Student A

Self-heating Bowl
A metal bowl that heats water or food, has a rechargeable battery in its base and could be used when traveling and for baby food.

Color-changing Ice Cream
Ice cream that changes color based on temperature. For example, it's blue while in the freezer; when you take it out and it's at room temperature, it turns purple; when it starts to melt, it turns pink.

Lesson 6.3

7 B Student A

1 You are going to take part in a radio call-in show, and you are the D.J. Ask Student B to tell you about their situation. Ask for clarification to check you understand. Then invite Student C to give their opinion. Encourage B and C to exchange their points of view.

2 Now change roles. You are a caller. Give your opinion when the D.J. asks you.

3 Now change roles. You are a different caller. Explain your situation to the D.J.:

A well-known social networking site has a minimum age of thirteen. Your daughter is thirteen next week, and she says some of her friends' parents have allowed their children to join. You think she's too young.

Lesson 4.1

4 B Student B: read Gerald's opinion below. Were your predictions correct?

THE EXPERTS HAVE THEIR SAY:

Gerald van Halen
Sociologist and Parent

Nothing has changed except what we mean by "free time activities." Years ago we'd sit with our family in front of the TV all evening and talk; we regarded that as free time spent together. Now if we sit together and check our Facebook pages, is that leisure time? And, if so, is it a good thing? One American study put a whole range of activities in the "leisure" category: watching TV, spending time with friends, playing online games, for example. But there's a huge difference between playing games online and playing a board game with friends or family, and we need to think about which activities are <u>really</u> good for us. When my son's with his friends, they usually watch YouTube clips together, or they'll often play a computer game together. My son's favorite one at the moment is a car racing one, and I think that's OK because they're sharing. It's when they're sitting together but each one is texting or gaming separately, now that worries me.

Lesson 1.3

6 B Student A: look at Situation 2 below and follow the instructions.

Situation 2: Student A (Service Person)

You work for the customer service department at a hotel. A customer calls for help with a reservation. Use the information below to answer the customer's inquiries.

July 3 arrivals

James	2 guests	5 nights
Johns	2 guests	4 nights
Jones	2 guests	3 nights

Rates:	Standard double: $250/night
	Executive suite: $309/night

Room availability information:
July 2: Standard doubles fully reserved.
One executive suite available.

Lesson 5.5

2 B

1 a 2 b 3 b 4 c 5 a

Lesson 5.2

6 Student B: work with another student B. Read the first part of this viral video description and discuss the questions.

1 What do you think might happen next?

2 What product do you think it is advertising?

The Drought (Part 1)
A farmer stands on his porch, looking at his fields. It's dry—there hasn't been rain for months. A young man comes and say "Pa, the corn, it's all gone." The older man stays calm and says "We'll be all right." His other son comes and says, "Pa, the animals. All dead." Again, the man just says, "We'll be all right." He turns and goes to the kitchen …

Turn to page 162 and read the ending. Which ending do you prefer, yours or this one?

Work with Student A. Cover the story and describe the video to your partner. Stop before the ending and ask your partner to guess the ending and product.

Which of the two videos do you think is more effective?

Lesson 6.3

7 B Student B

1 You are going to take part in a radio call-in show, and you are a caller. Explain your situation to the D.J.:

Your son, who is seventeen, has started going out with a young woman who he says is the love of his life. He wants to get a tattoo linking her name and his. You're strongly against the idea.

2 Now change roles. You are the D.J. Ask Student C to tell you about their situation. Ask for clarification to check you understand. Then invite Student A to give their opinion. Encourage A and C to exchange their points of view.

3 Now change roles. You are a different caller. Give your opinion when the D.J. asks you.

Lesson 7.3

7 B Student B

The top five countries with the tallest people:

1 the Netherlands 2 Sweden 3 Denmark
4 Norway 5 Estonia

Lesson 5.2

Student A

> **Graffiti Artist** (Part 2)
>
> She takes out her mirror and puts on lipstick—we can read the brand name. She's gorgeous. Her phone rings, and she answers, saying "I'll be there in five minutes."

Lesson 7.3

7 B Student C

The top five cities for art lovers:

1 Berlin **2** Chicago **3** Florence
4 London **5** New York

Lesson 5.4

4 A Student B

> **Umbrella Light**
>
> An LED light is built into the handle of an umbrella and can be turned on via a button in the handle.
>
> **Self-closing Bag**
>
> A bag of snacks, for example, chips or pretzels, with magnetic strips along the top so that, if you leave it overnight, it will close itself and keep the contents fresher for longer.

Lesson 10.2

8 A Student B

> **T through and through** completely:
> *a typical American through and through*

> **O on and on** used to say that someone continues to do something or that something continues to happen:
> *He talked on and on about his job.*

> **R rough and ready** (= not perfect, but good enough to use)

> **N (every) now and then/now and again** sometimes: *He sees her every now and then at college.*

> **U ups and downs** n [plural] the good and bad things that happen in life, business, etc: *Every marriage has its ups and downs.*

Lesson 9.2

 7 D

Free Gift Wrapping

Preparation:

1 The con artist team goes to a busy shopping mall during the festival season and sets up a tent with a sign saying "Free gift wrapping."

2 An attractive, friendly, female con artist stands behind the counter.

3 The other two con artists are inside the tent, out of sight. They have a scale for weighing things, oranges and packing material.

The Scam:

1 When a customer brings an item for wrapping, the woman passes it into the tent.

2 The two con artists there open the package, remove the item and weigh it, then put the same weight in oranges into the box with packing material and wrap it attractively.

3 They pass it back to the female co-worker, who gives it to the customer. The package feels like the original and won't be opened till later!

Rental Car Scam

Preparation:

1 The con artist team rents an expensive car, changes the license plates and removes any evidence that it's rented.

2 The team places an ad in a newspaper or online offering the car at a very low price.

3 The team finds an empty house, breaks in and puts some toys around the rooms and driveway. This address is given when people answer the ad.

The Scam:

1 An attractive female con artist poses as a young mother and greets customers as they arrive. She explains to the customers why there are no car registration papers. Some of the customers will offer a cash deposit.

2 At the end of the afternoon, the team clears out of the house, returns the car to the car rental company and disappears.

Lesson 9.3

8 A Student B

rents / car registration papers
car rental company

hires / car papers
hire agency

Lesson 9.2

7 A Student A: imagine the following situation happened to you. Add some details about the place, time, the amount of money of the deposit and your feelings. Prepare to tell Student B.

I went to a house to look at a car. I'd seen the ad earlier. There were kids' toys in the driveway by the car. A young woman, the kids' mother I guessed, showed me the car—it was a fantastic bargain, and I wanted to buy it. She couldn't show me the car registration papers because her husband had just taken them to pay the car registration fees. She told me that she had lots of other interested people coming around later, so I gave her a deposit, and she said I could pick up the car at six. At six o'clock, I found eight other people outside the house, no car and no one at home.

B Listen to Student B's situation and discuss his/her questions.

C Tell Student B the situation and discuss these questions.

1 Who was the woman?
2 How did she trick people into thinking she was a mother?
3 Whom did the car belong to?
4 Who were the other eight people?
5 How do you think the scam was done?

D Turn to page 161 to see if your ideas were right.

Lesson 2.1

11 c

Answers to Quiz 1

1 Russia   2 black and white   3 banana
4 the Sahara   5 43%

Answers to Quiz 2

1 nine   2 pasta   3 2 grams   4 80%
5 38 minutes (between Britain and Zanzibar in 1896)

Lesson 7.3

7 B Student D

The top five friendliest countries:

1 Ireland   2 the USA   3 Malawi   4 Fiji   5 Thailand

Lesson 6.3

7 B Student C

1 You are going to take part in a radio call-in show, and you are a caller. Give your opinion when the D.J. asks you.

2 Now change roles. You are a different caller. Explain your situation to the D.J.:

   Your eighteen-year-old son has just passed his driving test. He wants to borrow your car so that he can drive his friends around. He says that his other friends' parents let them borrow their cars. You think he's not ready yet.

3 Now change roles. You are the D.J. Ask Student A to tell you about their situation. Ask for clarification to check you understand. Then invite Student B to give their opinion. Encourage A and B to exchange their points of view.

Lesson 9.3

8 A Student A

Lesson 9.5

4 B

1 The man always checked the mailbox before the postman came. His wife took the letters out when they arrived.

2 A record company was making a recording of the performance and had asked the audience not to applaud so that the recording would be clean.

Lesson 5.2

Student B

The Drought (Part 2)
He turns and goes to the kitchen and opens the fridge. The fridge has lots of food … but there's only one can of cola there—and it's empty. The man says "We're in big trouble."

car registration fees / around   car tax / round

Lesson 10.2

1 c Student A: read the text on this page. Which four questions below does it answer?

1 How do actors cry on demand?

2 Do big stars have to audition for movie roles?

3 How do singers keep their voices steady when they're dancing?

4 Why is rock music played so loud at concerts?

5 Who decides whether something is "art" or not?

6 Why do works of art get stolen if they can't be sold without attracting attention?

7 What's the secret to making an audience laugh?

8 How does a comedian deal with hecklers?

D Read the text again. Write a maximum of five key words for each answer to help you remember the information.

E Work in pairs. Cover the text and look at your notes from Exercise 1D. Tell your partner about the answers.

POPULAR CULTURE

Q&A

Want to know the best-kept secrets of popular culture? Read our top questions & answers to find out.

Q:

A: Singers such as Beyoncé, whose stage show involves her dancing all over the stage, can't always deliver high-quality vocals live because it's physically extremely difficult to control the voice while jumping around. Because of this, many performers rely on a backing track to provide vocals during some songs, and, while they may be singing live, the audience can't actually hear their voice. Some stationary performers use a backing track when they're concerned about difficult parts of the performance, for example, hitting a very high note or even remembering the words to a song.

Q:

A: Every comedian has his or her own strategy for dealing with members of the audience interrupting their performance with rude comments. Strategies range from simply telling the heckler to be quiet ("Shut up!") to humiliating the heckler into silence by insulting them or someone with them such as their girlfriend. Armed with the microphone, the comedian has a great advantage over the heckler. Some comedians, known for their particularly aggressive way of handling hecklers, actually become more famous for this aspect of their act than their scripted sections.

Q:

A: There are certain ways of making it look like you're crying, such as putting glycerine in your eyes, sniffing a freshly cut onion or, on stage, concentrating on a bright point of light. Most actors use more internal techniques that exploit emotional memory. By recalling a time when they were sad or upset, an actor can often get the tears flowing. Or sometimes they'll build an association between an object—a prop they'll be handling during the scene—and that emotion, so that, when they touch the prop, they feel inclined to cry. Interestingly, most actors say it's easier to cry convincingly than to laugh convincingly.

Q:

A: This is an age-old question. The range of works and styles of painting regarded as art at different times is astonishing—from ancient Chinese ink paintings to Leonardo Da Vinci to Jackson Pollock. One argument goes that a painting is art if the painter says it is and gives convincing reasons to support their position. Many artists would reject this idea; they don't care who regards their work as art. We'll probably never agree on who the most beautiful woman or best-looking man is, so we'll just have to enjoy exploring and sharing our notions of art and beauty without a definitive answer.

Lesson 10.2

8 A Student A

G give and take n [U] If there is give and take between two people, each person agrees to do some of the things that the other person wants: *In any relationship there has to be some give and take.*

B be sick and tired of sb/sth to be annoyed and bored with a person or situation: *I'm sick and tired of waiting.*

P peace and quiet When everything is quiet and calm: *All I want is some peace and quiet.*

L leaps and bounds He improved by leaps and bounds (= very much, very quickly).

T the pros and cons (of sth) the advantages and disadvantages of something

Lesson 10.5

3 c

1 Sydney Opera House

2 Apple Inc.

3 squash

4 Napoleon Bonaparte

5 Oscar

6 the Inuit

7 sushi (makizushi)

8 *Hamlet*

Unit 1 Recording S1.1

Conversation 1

A: What would you say?

B: Erm, for me, an important question is "Do you keep to yourself, or do you tend to be around a lot?"

A: Hmm. What are you trying to find out?

B: I suppose I'm looking for a balance because the last thing you want is a person who comes in and goes straight up to their room, and you never see them again till the morning. You know, antisocial. I'm pretty sociable, you know. I like having friends around. I suppose I'm a people person.

A: Yeah.

B: ... but on the other hand, you don't want a roommate who's always there, so you never get any privacy. And especially in the morning. I'm not a morning person—I can't stand people who are all bright and cheerful first thing. You know, when I haven't woken up yet. So, yeah, I'd like someone who is pretty sociable, but not too sociable.

A: Mm, yeah, I agree. I suppose another question is about housework and cleaning.

B: Yes, something like "Who cleans the place where you live now?"

A: How would you answer that question?

B: Who cleans my apartment now? I do.

A: Yeah, me, too.

B: And I'd also ask: "Are you neat?"

A: What answer do you want the person to give?

B: I'd want the answer to be "Oh, yes, extremely." I don't know. I'd hate to live with someone who was really messy all the time, that never washed the dishes, someone that left their stuff just lying all over the place, someone who doesn't do their fair share of the housework. No, that would just drive me crazy. I suppose I'm really neat myself.

A: Yeah, yeah. Um, and what about money?

B: Yeah, it can be a big problem. I had a roommate once, and she used to say, "I know I have to pay the electricity bill, but can I pay it next week?" She promised to pay and then never did. Really unreliable.

A: Oh, yeah. It doesn't matter how nice people are if they have money problems. You need to know they can afford the rent.

B: But I wouldn't ask, "Could you tell me how much you earn?" I think I'd say the rent and the bills have to be paid in advance, so I'd ask "Can you pay three months in advance?" and see what they say.

Conversation 2

A: Ooh that's really difficult to answer ... I would like to think: "handsome, witty, cool."

B: Well, at least you're witty. You're quick, and you make me laugh. And you're good with words.

A: No, but I don't think they'd describe me like that. I dunno. Let me think. Erm.

I suppose they'd say I'm good at coming up with new ideas ... yes ... So I think people would describe me as pretty creative.

B: And the second one?

A: Erm ... well, people know I like doing new things, things that are out of the ordinary.

B: Such as?

A: Oh, well, like last week, I was at the beach with some friends, and it was a beautiful warm evening. And we decided to go for a midnight swim. I mean, we hadn't planned to; it just seemed like a great idea at the time. I like doing new things, different things. So I suppose that means I'm adventurous ... or maybe a better word is spontaneous. Yeah, that's more like it. I get an idea, and I do it, no hesitation, so I'm spontaneous. That's useful in my job, too.

B: Can I ask what you do?

A: I work for a web design company. We design websites for new businesses.

B: Mmm, sounds interesting.

A: Most of the time!

B: So that's two very positive words so far. What's your third one?

A: Well, I think people that know me would say that I'm pretty messy and disorganized. You should see my desk—papers everywhere—and my bedroom! And I'm always losing things. So, yes, my friends would say "creative, spontaneous and disorganized".

B: I'd be interested to know if you agree with them. What words do you think describe you best?

A: Now that's an interesting question. Actually, I'd like to think that I'm fair, you know, nonjudgmental.

B: What do you mean by nonjudgmental?

A: Well, I try not to make up my mind about people until I get to know them, so, yes, nonjudgmental. But I'd stick with "spontaneous" and "disorganized." I think they describe me pretty well. What about you?

B: Erm. Well, people say I'm fun to be with, a good laugh, if you know what I mean. Erm, I'm very practical and down-to-earth.

A: What do you do?

B: I train people in advanced computer software. But don't worry, I'm not a computer geek. I don't sit in front of my computer for hours.

Unit 1 Recording S1.6

A: Hello, English Language College. Can I help you?

B: Yes, I'd like to inquire about a course.

A: OK. Have you seen the information on our website?

B: Well, actually the situation is that I enrolled in a course through your website yesterday, and now I'd like to change.

A: Uh-huh. Could you tell me your name?

B: María Hidalgo.

A: And which course was it?

B: A general English course, pre-advanced.

A: Bear with me a minute. Yes, I have it. What would you like to change to?

B: I've just noticed this morning that you have an advanced course in business English starting next week.

A: That's right.

B: I was wondering if it would be possible for me to change to that group.

A: OK, let me just check. There are still a few places in that group, but you'll have to do a level test.

B: But I've already done an online test for the other course.

A: Mmm, I appreciate that, but for this course you need to do a level test in person.

B: Erm ... Can you tell me why I have to do it in person?

A: It's because it's a specialized course and there's an oral component to the level test.

B: I see. Would there be any chance of doing the level test on the phone?

A: Hold on, let me check ... Sorry to keep you. No, I'm afraid it has to be in person.

B: I see. Do you mind me asking what it involves?

A: There's a written task that you have to do under timed conditions and preparation materials for the oral interview.

B: I see. Sorry to be difficult, it's just that I'm really busy this week and can't make it up to the school for the level test.

A: That's going to be a bit of a problem. I'm not sure what we can do about that.

B: I'd really appreciate your help.

A: Hmm ... You couldn't come in on Thursday evening, could you?

B: No, I'm afraid not. But, I tell you what. I could come in on Saturday to do the level test.

A: The problem is, that's leaving it very late and we might have other applicants.

B: I'd be really grateful if you could hold a place for me till Saturday morning.

A: Can you hold on a minute? I'll just see ... OK, we can do that. We'll provisionally transfer the course fee over as a deposit.

B: That's great. Oh, I have one more question, if I'm not keeping you.

A: No, go ahead.

B: If I don't get into this group, do I lose my course fee?

A: I'm afraid we can't refund the deposit, but you could transfer it to another course.

B: Oh, that's a relief. Would you mind putting that in an email for me?

A: Certainly.

B: Thanks. Could you tell me when the school opens?

A: We're open from nine on Saturday. I won't be here myself, but I'll tell my co-worker to expect you.

B: Thank you very much for your help.

A: You're welcome. Thank you for calling.

Unit 1   Recording S1.8

I'm not the kind of person who likes to be a daredevil or do anything too exciting. But the most incredible thing I think I've ever done was when I went skydiving. So, we went up in a tiny plane. I mean it's so small, so it was pretty scary. And the build-up was just epic.

I was attached to another guy, an expert, by a harness. And I was sitting in front of him in this sort of, it was like a, a tiny tube little plane. And we went higher and higher and higher. And um, the suspense was building up. And then, suddenly, they just open this door, and you're flying through the sky, and you can just see for miles. And it's freezing cold, and the thing I'll remember most is the cold air hitting my teeth, 'cause it was just absolutely freezing. And er, we sort of scuttled out to the edge, and our legs were dangling through the door of the plane. And erm, he just said, I remember him shouting, he said, "Smile!" 'Cause there was a camera guy as well, so you can film it.

And we just, we sort fell forward, and we were just spinning, until he sort of levels you out. It was like I was completely weightless. And it didn't feel like you were falling at all, you were just sort of hovering. And it was still freezing cold on my teeth. And then the parachute, I remember lifting out. And it just sort of pulled me all up—I was like oh! ugh!, like that. And we started spinning around, you know he was doing all these kind of tricks and stuff. And that's when I started feeling sick 'cause it was spinning so fast. But it was just so much fun; it was hilarious, I was laughing, you know, even though I felt sick. It was just the experience of it all and the adrenaline rush.

It was one of the best experiences I've ever had in my life. And it's an activity I'd like to recommend to all my friends because I know they'd absolutely love it, it's hilarious.

Unit 2   Recording S2.1

1
A report out today says that over 800 million people in the world don't have enough to eat. The report, which was published …

2
Twenty people have died in an outbreak of the deadly Ebola virus. The virus, which has resulted in over …

3
If you're traveling downtown today, be careful of pickpockets, especially around the central square. Our reporter Will Nakama is there in …

4
The government has promised that its changes to the income tax will help the poorest people in the country. A spokesperson said …

5
The number of people out of work has risen in the last quarter to seven percent and is now reaching three million. The situation is worst …

6
After four days of smog, only cars with even license plates can enter the city today. It is hoped that this move will improve the air quality after the levels of …

Unit 2   Recording S2.5

A: Have you read this article?
B: Which one?
A: This is really shocking. This, look, look at this about surveillance techniques, on page three.
B: Oh, yeah, yeah, I did have a look.
A: There's gonna be absolutely no privacy for anyone.
B: What you mean like C, the CCTV camera part?
A: Yeah, yeah, yeah, yeah, exactly that.
B: Well I'm glad they're there actually.
A: Why?
B: Well, not long ago, a friend of mine, he was, um, he was robbed at a bus stop, and, um they got the guy because of, um, CCTV. They captured his image, and, um, all the people who did it were arrested.
A: OK …
B: So I think it's, I think it's a good thing in the end.
A: Well, it's good if it's used for that, but don't you feel nervous about the fact that whatever you do, wherever you go, whatever you're doing, someone is watching you and recording what you're doing.
B: But I don't have anything to hide, so it's not really a problem.
A: Anyway, that's not the point though is it? It's an invasion of privacy.
B: Look, I think, statistically, more crimes are solved because of CCTV than not.
A: Right, what about that, that look— this one on page two—CCTV facial recognition, did you see that part there at the bottom?
B: Yeah, I didn't really get that part.
A: Right, so basically, just imagine you're walking down the road, and a camera, a CCTV camera takes your picture, yeah. And then a computer program can then find your name, all your personal information, based on recognizing your face. So where you shop, where you live, what you, what you like, what you buy, who your friends are. And there's nothing you can do about it.
B: That can only be a good thing, 'cause it's gonna catch criminals, isn't it? And, if you have nothing to worry about, then you know it's never really gonna be an issue for you.
A: If it's for that, yeah, I get your point. But …
B: If you haven't done anything wrong.
A: No, no, absolutely, but …
B: The thing that really bothers me though is, um, is the way that marketing, marketing companies can target you, um, because of microchips in, in food packaging and stuff, so people get an idea of, of your shopping habits. I don't want to be sent ads from companies that I don't know.
A: But we're being sent stuff all the time anyway, from companies, that we don't know. I wouldn't mind being sent ads from, you know, uh, companies that I don't know if it's something that I want to buy.
B: Yeah. It's a little confusing really the way I, I feel about the whole thing because, you know, on the one hand, I'm, I'm, I'm pro, uh, using the technology to, you know, catch criminals or whatever. I mean serious criminals. But then, on the other hand, I occasionally er drive, a little bit over the, the speed limit.
A: Right, OK.
B: Occasionally. And you know I, I've been er given quite a few tickets over the years because my license plate gets recognized, and, er, I, er, you know, I think more money should be spent elsewhere to be honest.
A: I get your point, but I do actually think, although I'm really anti the amount of, kind of, you know, filming and, and information they have—when it comes to speeding, I do actually think that's pretty sensible that they, that they can clock what people are doing.

Unit 2   Recording S2.7

Conversation 1

A: Have you seen this? There's a new law about computer games. They want to limit the kind of violent things that can happen in the games, so kids don't see so much.
B: Really? Well, that makes sense. I do think that the violence in those games can make kids more aggressive.
A: Well, according to one article I read, kids are less aggressive if they play these games.
B: How could that be true?
A: Apparently the games give them a chance to use up some of their energy. So they're calmer in real life.
B: That's hard to believe. In my experience, playing those games makes kids more aggressive. So I'm in favor of some kind of control.
A: Hmm. I don't know … I agree to a certain extent, but I think kids can separate real life from computer games. I mean, I don't like computer games, and I hate violence, but actually I think it's more of a problem to put these limits on.
B: I think we'll have to agree to disagree.
A: I suppose so.

Conversation 2

A: Do you ever download music for free?
B: You mean illegally? No, I'm probably one of the few people who doesn't do it. I've always paid for downloads.
A: Why? I mean nobody I know pays.
B: Exactly! And it's just theft, isn't it? I mean, …
A: Oh, I totally disagree.
B: I mean, artists have copyright on their songs, so you're stealing from them. It's as simple as that.

A: But, as far as I know, musicians these days get very little money from CD sales or downloads anyway. So they don't lose out. I mean, they want people to hear their music.

B: Hmm. I'm not so sure about that. If people share the music without paying, how can musicians make any money?

A: Well, the famous ones, they don't need more money, and, for newer groups, file-sharing is the way they get known, so they don't have to spend a fortune, you know, on things like record companies and managers and …

B: Yeah, but …

A: … anyway, nowadays singers and groups make most of their money from concerts.

B: Hmm. I'm still not convinced. Aren't you worried about being caught? For instance, what about that man in the USA? Did you hear about that? Apparently, he got fined about one and a half million dollars for downloading and sharing movies.

A: One and a half million dollars? Ouch!

B: Yeah, so maybe you'd better think again.

A: Hmm. Good point.

Conversation 3

A: Do you think you would ever have cosmetic surgery?

B: Me? No, I don't think so. I'm really against it actually. I think it's …

A: Really, why?

B: Well, basically I think it can be really dangerous—some of the implants you can have, um—

A: Yeah, I see what you mean.

B: Like, Like Mike's girlfriend—she actually had some Botox injections in her forehead.

A: Did she?

B: Yeah, and she couldn't, you know, she couldn't—

A: Couldn't move her face?

B: Yeah, she couldn't smile or frown— her face was just frozen solid.

A: Fair enough, but if someone's very depressed because of the way they look, maybe then they should have some kind of surgery, you know, to help their self-esteem.

B: I think there are other ways to help.

A: And what about if they have a serious health problem? Such as maybe they're extremely overweight.

B: For health reasons maybe, yes, I mean, I see your point, but I still don't like the sound of it. Personally, I think it's too much of a risk. I wouldn't do it myself.

A: I might, if it was to do with my health.

Unit 2 Recording S2.9

D = Denise   J = James

D: Our presentation is about the pros and cons of traditional roles in a family. I'll talk about the pros, and James will talk about the cons. Then you can decide.

J: First, to make it clear what we mean by traditional roles, we're thinking of the man as breadwinner, as the one who earns the money to support the family, while the woman stays at home and takes care of the children. At home, generally speaking, the woman does the housework—the cooking, cleaning, etc.— while the man might do home repairs and take care of the car. Denise?

D: So, on the positive side, the roles are very clearly defined; both the man and woman know who does what, so there's less confusion and fewer conflicts about that. If there are children, there's less pressure on family life, in that, if the woman doesn't work, she has time to manage things such as birthdays, paying bills, taking children to and from the various activities that children do. Also, there's more contact between the mother and children, and that's bound to be good for the health of the whole family. And in reality, a lot of men are better at doing heavier or more mechanical work, such as car repairs. And, let's face it, many women do notice more than men things like how clean or neat a room is, so they're the best person to take care of this. Over to you, James.

J: Thanks, Denise. So, on the negative side, if the man is always the one who works, there can be too little contact between father and child, and that can't be good for the family. Also, in some couples, the woman will be good at tasks traditionally done by the man, and vice-versa. For instance, if the man is a better cook than the woman, or is happier staying at home with the children, while the woman is better at fixing the car and mowing the lawn, then it would be silly for the one who is less good at the task to be the one to do it. Finally, and perhaps most importantly, a lot of women will of course want to work and develop a career, both for their own satisfaction and independence and also to be a role model for their children.

D: Those are just some of the pros and cons. Over to you now to decide which are stronger, the pros or the cons.

Unit 3 Recording S3.2

I = Interviewer   L = Larry Smith

I: In the 1920s, Ernest Hemingway bet ten dollars that he could write a complete story in just six words. He wrote, "For sale: baby shoes, never worn." He won the bet. An American online magazine has now used that to inspire its readers to write their life stories in six words, and they've been overwhelmed by the thousands who took up the challenge. They've published the best in a book, which they've given the title of one of the submissions: *Not Quite What I Was Planning*. I asked the editor, Larry Smith, what made him think of the idea.

L: So, we thought, "Let's ask our readers their six-word life stories, memoirs" and see what happened. We really didn't know what would happen.

I: And what did happen?

L: It was incredible. In a couple of months we got 15,000 entries, and I was just blown away. Funny, poignant— I really believe that everyone has a story, and I was just so inspired by how serious and intense folks took the six-word memoir challenge.

I: OK, but before we look at the examples. It's one thing … because the Hemingway is a story, but it's not a story of a life. That seems to be a bit of a challenge to fit that in six words.

L: Well, it's interesting because some folks clearly tried to tell a whole story of a life in six words, and you can tell; and other times, they're telling a moment in their life, right at this moment, something that they're feeling right now. Or perhaps something that's been a thread throughout their lives.

I: Give us some examples.

L: "Wasn't born a redhead. Fixed that." This woman took life under control. Whether she just always felt that her soul was a redheaded soul or simply at some point in life she was going to make a switch. She could have quit her job. She changed her hair color.

I: But a lot of them are pretty sad, or there's sort of sense of regret or disappointment in a lot of them.

L: I didn't expect that. I thought people would come back with a lot of funny things, some playful things, plays on words … but those are really interesting reality. People really told us, "It's tough out there." "Found true love. Married someone else." "Never should have bought that ring."

Unit 3 Recording S3.4

C = Carl   A = Amy   B = Beth

C: So, Amy, what time's your flight?

A: Oh, it's at one.

C: Right.

A: It's really long as well, about twelve hours.

C: Oh.

A: Listen, I'm gonna need something to read. I reckon, I need a good book. Do you have any ideas?

B: Yeah, actually, yeah, you know *The Hunger Games*, have you ever read that?

A: No, I don't think so.

B: Yeah, no, it's really good, yeah; it sort of describes like this society in the future, you know, about the government taking over and making these kids do a TV show, where they have to basically kill each other.

A: Ooh.

B: Yeah.

A: That sounds a bit violent for me.

B: Yeah, it, yeah, it is, but it raises all sorts of, you know, really interesting questions about society. And the power of TV. Erm, I thought it was really great. I mean I'm a big fan of sci-fi novels anyway. But what I really liked about it was the main character, the girl.

A: Is that the one that's um played by Jennifer Lawrence in the movie?

B: Yes, yeah, yeah, yeah.

A: Right, right.

B: And yeah I really like that character 'cause she's, you know, she's very brave and she's a survivor and she sort of stands for what she believes in, and, yeah, I love her.

A: Yeah, no, it does sound pretty good, but I don't really like sci-fi that much to be honest. So, I don't think that's ...

C: OK, what about ...?

A: What else?

C: Can I suggest something else?

A: Yeah, yeah.

C: What about *The Kite Runner*, have you read that?

A: No, I haven't actually.

C: Oh, it's wonderful.

A: All right.

C: It's just, it's a really moving story about two boys in Afghanistan and ...

A: Oh, yes, yes, yes, and doesn't one of them save someone's life or something?

C: Yes, I mean it goes through the years, and it's so wonderful—it really, I, I loved it. And the thing I love about it is the way it builds the whole story, you know, and, and you get so involved with these characters that you, you just have to know what's gonna happen next.

B: Actually, speaking of getting involved in characters, I really love *Life of Pi*; have you ever read that?

A: I've heard of it, but isn't that a bit weird, it's a bit of weird one, isn't it, about a ...

B: Oh, no, I really enjoyed it.

A: ... boy and a tiger in a boat or something, but ...

B: Yeah it's, it's very, sort of, I think it has a deep and meaningful story behind it, and I really like getting to know him and the fact that he loves these, you know, this tiger, and it is very fantasy.

A: It's not comedy then?

B: No, no.

C: No. I mean, I did start it, but I just I couldn't get into it, I'm afraid.

A: I know, sounds ...

C: I mean, I can't stand books that sort of preach at you. And it felt to me that it was doing that, I

A: Yeah.

C: ... made me uncomfortable.

B: Yes.

A: Sounds a bit serious to me to be honest for a twelve-hour plane journey.

C: I'm not sure we've given any choices that have many laughs ...

B: Yeah.

C: ... to be honest have we?

B: No.

A: I don't know.

C: But actually there's a lot of warmth in *The Kite Runner*, that's what I would say, I mean. It's worth, worth trying, you know, to stick with it.

A: Yeah—do you know what I think, no, I think I might try *The Hunger Games* actually.

B: Yes!

A: ... 'cause I think I've seen the trailer of the movie, and I, yeah, it looks pretty interesting.

Unit 3 Recording S3.7

Fawlty Towers. I absolutely love *Fawlty Towers*; I've seen this hundreds of times, and it's my absolute favorite. It always makes me laugh—in fact, it makes me cry with laughter sometimes ... can't get enough of it. And the main character, Basil Fawlty, played by John Cleese, is absolutely amazing. It's like a lesson in comic acting; the more bad things that happen to this man, the more we laugh. My favorite scene is the scene with Mrs. Richards and Basil Fawlty. And, it's very, very cleverly done. Mrs. Richards wears a hearing aid, and Basil Fawlty hates Mrs. Richards—she's a terrible, grumpy, old, complaining customer whom he really doesn't like. So he comes into the room, and he mimes at her—so he moves his mouth, but he doesn't make any sound—so that Mrs. Richards turns up her hearing aid so that she can hear him.

And then he mimes again, and he moves his mouth again, not making any sound so she can't understand why she can't hear him. So, she turns up her hearing aid again. And then, once he's sure that her hearing aid is on full volume, he shouts at her, "Mrs. Richards!"—of course, which deafens her, and, it's, it's, it's very, very funny, and it's amazing because he gets back at her 'cause she's been awful to him, so, he, you know, he kind of wins in the end but,— Oh, it's just amazing. If you've never seen it, you really should see it. There were very few episodes made. I think there were only, only ever one series, maybe eight episodes ... something like that ... I'm not entirely sure about that, but not very many made and, they're, they're really, really fantastic. Every one is absolutely priceless.

Unit 4 Recording S4.3

Conversation 1

P = Penny   S = Steve   G = George

P: Hi, Steve. Come and sit down.

S: Thanks. Hi, Penny; hi, George. Good to see you.

G: Hi.

P: Are you all packed now?

S: Yeah, all done. It was all a bit of a rush, but I think I'm ready to go. I just hope I haven't forgotten anything.

P: When are you off?

S: The taxi's picking me up at seven tomorrow.

G: Where are you going?

S: France. On vacation, working on a farm there.

G: Work? Not my idea of a vacation!

S: Actually, I don't think it'll be too hard. They said they want me to work in the yard, not in the fields. They have a big yard, and they need someone to look after it.

P: I didn't know you were interested in gardening.

S: I'm not, really, but apparently there might be some building work on the house. They're not sure yet. That's more my type of thing.

G: It still sounds like hard work. I wouldn't call it a vacation.

S: Well, I only have to work five hours a day, and, in exchange, I get free room and board. So it's like a free vacation. Well, almost free.

P: I think it sounds great. Where are you going exactly?

S: It's in the center of the country. Hold on a minute. I have a picture on my phone. Yeah, here, look.

G: Ah, nice location!

P: It looks stunning.

S: Yeah, and this ... is the local town.

G: So it's not all work?

S: No. I get lots of time off. I'm hoping to visit a few places on weekends, and I'm going to Paris one weekend.

P: Yeah, I'm thinking of going over. A weekend in Paris sounds good to me.

G: Actually, looking at those pictures, I'm changing my mind. How did you find out about it?

S: On the Internet—there are lots of sites. The one I looked at was ...

Conversation 2

S = Staff member   H = Husband
W = Wife

S: Yes, sir?

H: Could you tell us what's happening with flight IB3056?

S: Flight IB3056 ...

H: Yes, we've been waiting for over an hour, and we've heard nothing. All it says on the screen is "delayed."

S: Erm, ... I'm afraid the plane has been delayed coming in from Amsterdam, sir. Bear with me a minute. I'll just check the latest information on the computer. Erm ...

W: Thank you.

S: The plane is due to arrive at ... er 10:30 ... at the earliest.

H: But that's over three hours' time!

S: I'm sorry, sir. And it's likely to be later than that.

H: This isn't good enough. We only have a weekend and ...

S: I'm sorry, sir. There's nothing I can do.

W: And is there any way you could get us onto another flight? We're only going for two days, and we've really been looking forward to it. It sounds like we won't get to Seville till the afternoon.

S: I'm sorry, madam. Our 9 o'clock flight to Seville is full.

W: What about another airline? Maybe we could transfer to another flight?

S: I'm really sorry, but that's not possible. It's not our policy except in an emergency.

H: This is an emergency!

W: Bill! Oh, dear. Couldn't the airline at least pay for our breakfast?

S: Well, … here are two vouchers for free coffee, courtesy of the airline.

W: Oh … thank you. Come on Bill, let's go and get some breakfast.

H: I can tell you, this is the last time I use your airline.

W: Come on, Bill.

H: This is the worst experience I've ever had …

Conversation 3

C = Chris   J = Jan

C: Hi, Jan,

J: Oh, hi, Chris. When did you get back?

C: Last night. The plane got in at nine.

J: Welcome home!

C: Thanks.

J: So, how was it?

C: Awesome! I had an absolutely amazing time.

J: And how's your Spanish?

C: *Muy bien, gracias.*

J: Sounds good to me. So tell me all about it.

C: Well, the family was great. Really hospitable. They made me feel at home right away. And incredibly generous. They even invited me out to a restaurant on my last night.

J: Yeah?

C: And María, who did the teaching, was very good, very patient. We spent a lot of time together going for walks along the lake—you know the town is on a big lake …

J: Yeah, I saw your pictures on Facebook—they looked beautiful, absolutely breathtaking.

C: … yeah, and we would chat or just sit around drinking *limonada con soda* and …

J: What's that?

C: Erm, that's freshly squeezed lemons and soda water. It's a typical drink there. But one week was really not enough.

J: So are you hoping to go back?

C: I'd love to. María's invited me, and I might go back next summer, but only if I can afford the flight. But I have a plan. I'm going to look for a new job, with more money.

J: Hey, are you free tomorrow for lunch? Why don't we meet up, and you can tell me more about it?

C: Yeah that would be great. Where should we meet?

Unit 4   Recording S4.5

Conversation 1

A: It's one of these games that involve lying and people trying to figure out if you're lying or not, but it's different and really funny.

B: I like that kind of thing. Are there teams or something?

A: Yeah, there are two teams with three celebs on each team.

B: Er … Three what?

A: Celebs. Celebrities.

B: Oh, right.

A: There's a team captain on each team. Actually, the team captains are well known comedians, and they're on every show.

B: So each team has a comedian and two celebrities?

A: Exactly. The first thing they do is to tell a personal story. So a panelist tells a personal story …

B: Sorry, who tells a story?

A: A panelist. One of the people on one of the teams.

B: Oh, I see.

A: So they tell something about themselves, often something really embarrassing … Now it might be true, or they might be lying. The key thing is to say something that's so unbelievable that it's hard to imagine it's true.

B: And then they vote?

A: Not right away. What happens next is the other team grills the storyteller …

B: Uh, they do what?

A: Grill him. Ask a lot of questions to try and find out if the person's lying.

B: Yeah, you can tell if someone's lying by how fast they answer.

A: Well, the panelists are usually very good at it. It's surprising how hard it is to guess. But, for me, the best thing is the humor, the joking around. It's really entertaining.

B: I'll bet I could figure out if they're lying.

A: Maybe. Anyway, after they've finished, the team that asked the questions decides if it was a lie or not. If they're right, they get a point.

B: What sort of things do they say?

A: Gosh, all sorts of things. One of my favorites was when a female panelist said she'd once kissed one of the other panelists.

B: And was it true?

A: I'm not going to tell you. It's on TV tonight. We can watch, and you can show me how great you are at saying if someone is lying.

B: Oh, great …

Conversation 2

A: Oh, you must have seen it …

B: No, I've never even heard of it. How does it work?

A: Well, it sounds really stupid, but I'll try to describe it. It's basically a race over an obstacle course.

B: Uh … Over a what?

A: An obstacle course. There are lots of things that they have to climb over and balance on …

B: Oh, obstacle, got it.

A: … and if they fall off, they fall into water or mud.

B: Sounds dangerous.

A: It can be.

B: So what are the … obstacles like?

A: Well, there are a lot of different ones. There's the Sweeper.

B: Sweeper, like a broom.

A: Yeah. Basically, the way it works is that twelve of the contestants stand on podiums over water …

B: They stand where?

A: On podiums. These tall columns, or blocks. Like little towers.

B: And is it hard to balance?

A: Well, yes, mainly because of the Sweeper. It's a big arm really, and it turns around and around over the podiums. What you have to do is jump over the arm when it gets to you. Then you have to land on the podium without falling down.

B: And if they get knocked down?

A: They fall into the water. Sometimes really dramatically. That's the thing I like best, those dramatic falls. The last one standing wins the round.

B: Sorry, they win what?

A: The round. That part of the competition.

B: Oh, so there are more obstacles.

A: Oh, yeah. It's not just the Sweeper, there are lots of different types of obstacles: Tippy Tables, Teeter Totters, Dock Maze, Crazy Beams, Doughnuts.

B: Wow. Doughnuts. Crazy. And how do you win?

A: The point is to get around the course in the fastest time. The fastest person is the winner.

B: Sounds like pretty good fun.

A: The studio is amazing. They film it in BA. Imagine, the UK TV crew …

B: They film it where?

A: In BA. Buenos Aires. Argentina.

B: They fly to Argentina to film this?

A: Yeah, it's a big deal.

B: I'd like to see it.

Unit 4   Recording S4.7

A: Excuse me, hello, sorry to bother you, do you have a minute?

B: Ah, yeah, sure.

A: Do you mind if I ask you some questions? I'm just doing a survey on happiness.

B: Right.

A: I'll read out the questions to you, and you can just tell me what you think, if that's OK.

B: Yeah, fine.

A: Great. Um, could you look at this list of five things; so you have, ah, number one car, then two is friendship, three good food, four money and five free time. So which two of these would you find it the most difficult to live without?

B: Which two, the most difficult to live without?

A: Yes.

B: Ah, well, I couldn't live without friendship. I'm, I'm a very social animal. I need, um, family and friends around me, so it can't be that one. Um—oh, no, sorry, that is, to live without … yes …

A: That's one.

B: That is one, so …

A: Then we just need one more.

B: … friendship is definitely one of them. Ah …

A: Yes, number two, OK.

B: Oh, that's difficult. Free time, I don't have any anyway; ah, I could lose the car, I think that wouldn't be a problem. Um, do you know what …
A: How about money?
B: … sad as it is, it's probably money, because money actually …
A: Money, no, most people …
B: … you know leads to happiness in, in indirect ways I think.
A: OK, so I'm gonna put number two and number four for that one. And also, how happy would you say you are, on a scale of one to five, five being very happy?
B: Today or just generally?
A: I think generally.
B: Oh, generally OK, um, oh, ah, three or four, um, three and a half.
A: Ah.
B: Can I have half?
A: No.
B: Oh, OK. Um, well you've made me laugh, I'll have four.
A: Oh, great, I'll put you down for four. And what would you say is missing from your life, so what would make you happier?
B: Ah, probably, ah, working nearer to home?
A: OK.
B: That's, I think you know … just generally the time that would give me …
A: Right.
B: … with family.
A: So maybe it's free time then …
B: Yeah, yeah.
A: … more of that. OK that's great, thank you ever so much for taking part, really do appreciate it.
B: You're welcome.
A: OK, bye-bye.

Unit 5   Recording S5.5

I = Interviewer   J = Jake

I: Jake, you've been in advertising for what, thirty-five years? How have things changed over that time?
J: Well, there have been huge changes in where and how we advertise, but many of the basic principles of marketing are the same, for example, how consumers choose brands.
I: Can you give me an example?
J: Yes, let's imagine a coffee shop downtown somewhere, anywhere, and it sells a thousand cups of coffee a day. Now, if another coffee shop opened next door …
I: … the first owner would be furious.
J: Don't be so sure. How many cups of coffee would each shop sell?
I: I don't know. Five hundred?
J: Logical, but, no. They'd sell at least a thousand cups each.
I: Incredible. Why's that?
J: Choice makes people want things more. With one coffee shop, the question is, "Should I get a coffee or not?" but, with two, the question becomes "Which coffee should I get?"
I: Fascinating. So what else hasn't changed?

J: Pricing is still important. People still like a bargain. But they also like to treat themselves.
I: What do you mean?
J: Well, supposing you wanted to sell a new brand of chocolate and your competitor's price was $2, what price would you set?
I: Mmm, I'd reduce the price. Maybe 1.80?
J: Why?
I: Because consumers want to save money.
J: True, to a certain extent. But experience shows that, if the price is higher, people think your product is better.
I: So $2.50 would be better?
J: Indeed.
I: How about advertising a product? It's all video now, isn't it?
J: Well, not completely, but much more. One thing hasn't changed though, which is the way we respond to color.
I: Oh, you mean like red means danger?
J: Yes, that kind of thing. We have built-in associations for every color. Red is associated with energy, so it's good for energy drinks, cars, sports equipment and things like that. Green suggests safety, so it's often used for medical products. Apparently, yellow and orange stimulate the appetite, so they're used for food ads; blue, on the other hand, supresses the appetite, it's linked more to intellect and precision, so it's used to promote high-tech products.
I: And this … information is used in video ads as well?
J: Sure. If a video ad goes viral, it'll get millions of views. And compared with TV, it's basically free. Your brand name will travel around the world provided the video goes viral.
I: And how can you ensure that?
J: You can't, but there are certain things that can help.
I: Such as?
J: Well about twenty-five percent of viewers will click off the video in the first ten seconds. So you need to grab the viewer in the first five seconds.
I: Uh-huh.
J: And you need to make the video memorable. I'll show you what I mean. I'll describe a video. You tell me the product.
I: OK.
J: Babies on roller skates dancing to hip-hop music.
I: Mineral water.
J: A gorilla playing drums to a famous pop song.
I: Chocolate. OK. I see your point. They were all pretty bizarre.
J: Exactly, and memorable. People will click off unless the video is memorable. And millions of people shared them. And that didn't cost the advertiser anything. It's a great way to enter the market if you're a small business.
I: Yeah, I see. Any other guidelines?

J: Well, make it short. Fifteen to sixty seconds is good.
I: OK.
J: And it matters which day you post it. If you release the video on the weekend, you're dead.
I: But surely that's when people are free?
J: No, the best time is Monday and Tuesday, between eleven and one. Back at work, at their desks, bored.
I: Right. And what about the content?
J: Tell a story. Engage the viewer. For example …

Unit 5   Recording S5.6

M1 = Man 1   M2 = Man 2
W1 = Woman 1   W2 = Woman 2

W1: OK, people, so we're going to look for ways to get people walking more today, and Ben's going to take notes.
M1: Right, OK, I'm just gonna get a pen.
W1: Thank you. At this stage, I think let's just get all our ideas down, and we can discuss them later.
W2: Right, what I think, some sort of branding, we need a sponsor. Like, I don't know, a shoe company, for example.
W1: OK. Next idea.
M1: Well, I think walking is the easiest exercise anyone can do, and …
W1: Benefits of it?
M1: Yeah, the benefits of, of exercise, you know, and losing weight … keeping your heart healthy.
M2: And what about sort of the other side of that, you know, scare people into thinking about what happens if you, if you sit down too much, if you don't, if you're not walking.
W1: Good.
M2: You know health problems and …
M1: Good idea.
M2: I tell you what, what about …
M1: Health.
M2: Could you, you know, I don't know, close public transportation for a day, so everyone has to walk.
W2: That's good.
M1: So that's …
W2: That's really good.
M1: So, what, in a town, in downtown you mean?
M2: Yeah, yeah.
M1: Yeah, that's a good idea.
W2: Hey, we're brainstorming!
M1: OK.
W1: Maybe a video showing just people's feet, so you have walking and talking at the same time.
M1: Yeah—we could maybe, I know, incentivize people by raising money for charity.
All: Yes.
M1: Like distance covered, how many steps or …
W1: Have one more, one more.
M2: Well maybe get some celebrities involved.
W1: That's a great idea as well. Did you get all of that Ben?

M1: Yeah, so we have, we have um sponsorship, health in …

W1: Yes.

M1: … tied with that we have scaring people, you know.

W1: Yes.

M1: We have closing, um, public transportation in the town.

W1: Yeah.

M2: Yeah.

M1: We have a video.

W1: Online, the viral.

M1: Yeah the viral, yeah. And a charity campaign.

W1: Uh-huh.

M2: We're looking with …

M1: And, and, oh, yes, celebrity, I didn't write that down.

W1: Celebrity, yeah, OK, terrific, time's up, and we have some really great ideas. Well done.

Unit 5   Recording S5.7

M1 = Man 1   M2 = Man 2
W1 = Woman 1   W2 = Woman 2

W1: OK, we're gonna look at the list, and we have all the ideas, but we need to cut it down now. So I'm gonna put them up on the screen. And we'll start with the shoe company one, the sponsor, how do you feel about this idea?

M2: Well, actually, that could be a problem. I mean, we want the campaign to be as wide as possible, don't we? So we don't want to link it just with one company, do we?

M1: Yeah, no, that's a good point.

W2: That's true actually.

M1: Yeah, I mean, my idea for example about pursuing the health angle.

M2: Yeah.

M1: I um. I mean, we could get, we could get a TV doctor perhaps to make a program about benefits of walking.

M2: Yeah, yeah.

W1: Nice.

M2: To be honest, it wouldn't be my first choice, I have to say. I mean I, I like it.

W1: If you had the scientific angle to it, it could work.

W2: Yeah, it's a bit obvious maybe. D'you know what I mean; it's kind of …

W1: What, been done?

W2: I think it has actually. I think it's a bit, a bit boring, I think the science thing's a bit boring. And, actually, that's quite a lot of money to …

M1: OK, fair enough.

W2: … to stick something on TV.

W1: All right, so, in that case, would you consider the opposite idea of scaring people into it?

M1: Well, frankly, I don't think that will be effective. You know people have been told about the dangers of lack of exercise for years.

M2: Yeah, it's not a new thing, is it?

W1: All right then. How does the idea of closing public transportation strike you?

W2: I don't think that's realistic, to be honest with you. I don't, I don't think the train and bus companies would go for

that. They'd lose so much money I just, just, I just think …

M1: To put it bluntly it …

W2: disaster OK.

M1: … it wouldn't work.

W1: Because they'd just lose money.

W2: They'd lose too much money.

M2: Actually, I think we're on the wrong track here.

W2: Yeah?

M2: I mean, I think it would be great if we could get celebrities to, sort of, promote walking generally, I think.

M1: That's not a bad idea at all. I think we should go for the feet idea.

W1: With the video of the feet walking.

M1: That's right, yeah.

M2: I mean, I have to say at the moment, I'm torn between the video and the celebrity. You know, I think they're the best two ideas.

W1: All right, so with that in mind, suppose we try combining the two ideas, our favorite ones. So we have the feet video …

W1: But we have it so it's a celebrity.

M2: Famous feet!

All: Yeah, yeah.

M1: Famous feet! That's a good title for it as well.

W1: Oh, and you could …

M2: Yeah, I like it.

M1: Famous feet.

W1: … have it as a competition.

M1: Yeah, terrific!

W1: So to guess whose feet that was, for example.

W2: Yes.

M2: Yeah.

W1: So you have a shot at the feet walking, the person speaking and then you have to guess who it is.

M2: Ah, nice.

M1: Sounds good to me.

W2: Yeah, I like that.

W1: OK, let's go with that.

Unit 5   Recording S5.11

W = Woman   M = Man

W: We would like to introduce to you an idea that will change the way you eat: Yummy Utensils. As you can guess, we're talking about knives, forks and spoons that you can eat.

M: You'll never have to throw plastic knives, forks and spoons in the trash again. At the end of your lunch, after you finish eating, you simply eat your utensils, like this.

W: Yummy Utensils are made of a special vegetable and flour mixture, are strong enough to cut meat and pierce salad, but easy to digest after you chew them.

M: They're tasty, too—a bit like pretzels. Here, would you like to try one?

W: What makes our idea special is that it's not just practical, and it's not a simple gimmick.

M: No, Yummy Utensils are not just practical and fun, they're also

environmentally friendly. Just think of all of the resources that go into making plastic utensils, which are just thrown into the trash and become a permanent part of the waste that we litter the planet with. Yummy Utensils are made from natural ingredients, using the same processes that are used to make bread products and of course create no trash at all. Even if you don't eat your Yummy Utensils and throw them in the trash, they dissolve within days. So there's no damage to the environment.

W: We envision this product being sold in supermarkets, in the same section where you buy picnic supplies. But don't be surprised if they're sold in the snack section—they taste better than some snack foods. And they're certainly better for you.

M: We think that Yummy Utensils will be a hit with families in particular, since they're the biggest consumers of disposable utensils.

W: And kids love having a fork or spoon they can eat. We've done some market testing, and it was amazing how much the children enjoyed them.

M: In the future, we are planning to develop a sweetened version that will make Yummy Utensils the perfect dessert.

W: Thank you for your attention, and we welcome any questions.

Unit 6   Recording S6.3

OK … so … Dear the future me, I hope this letter has found its way to you/me. As I write this, I am sixteen in year eleven; and as I read it, I am twenty. Wow! I will have changed so much. I can only guess what I will be like at twenty. I envision myself at Oxford University, sitting … oh, this is embarrassing … sitting under a tree by the river on the college grounds. I think I'll be wearing something floaty and a bit indie, but I bet, when I get this, it'll be raining. I know, I'm a romantic. I hope that hasn't changed. My plans for myself in the following years are to find a man, someone good-looking, romantic and intelligent who shares my interests. Either way, I hope I'll have someone. I don't remember this … and then I think I'll have three children with long, brown hair and green eyes.

Well, I'll stop now, even though I want to write everything I can down, but I'm running out of time. I hope I'm happy, and I hope this letter makes me feel good about who I was, or am, as I write this. Keep smiling, and while I can't really say bye, but good luck for the future and keep dreaming. Don't change too much, and be happy with who you are—I like who I am now more than any other time. Love, Laura.

Unit 6   Recording S6.4

It all seems really shallow looking back and reading what I thought I'd be doing or hoped I'd be doing. I think my sixteen-year-old self might have been disappointed with where I am, but, because I as my twenty-year-old self have sort of grown up and matured, I'm absolutely ecstatic with where I am, and it doesn't have to be this perfect sitting-by-a-lake kind of image.

Unit 6   Recording S6.6

H = Host   E = Ed   J = Julia
D = Dan   Z = Zara

H: And, up next, it's time for *Just Tell Me I'm Wrong*. Today's topic: how young is too young or, perhaps more accurately, how old is old enough? We've received hundreds of calls, emails and text messages about the right age for a child to do all sorts of things, like have a smartphone. In fact, our first caller asks about just that. His name is Ed. Go ahead, Ed. You're on.
E: Hi. My situation is that my eight-year-old kept asking for a smartphone, and eventually we bought her one a few months ago. Then, last week, I got a bill for over $200! I knew something like this would happen.
H: So basically you think she's too young for a phone?
E: Yeah, yeah, that's right.
H: Surely it's up to the parents to set guidelines.
E: So what you're saying is I should give her some rules?
H: Exactly. Right from the beginning. OK, thanks, Ed. Next caller is Julia. What's your question, Julia?
J: My question is about social networking sites. I don't let my daughter use them. She's only ten, and I'm worried about online bullying.
H: So, in other words, you're worried about kids being mean to other kids.
J: Yeah. You hear so much about it nowadays.
H: That's a very good point. Online bullying is a serious problem ... but isn't it better to talk it over with her? I'm sure they have lessons at school about how to stay safe online. She has to learn some time.
J: So, what you mean is I'm being overprotective?
H: To be honest, yes. And if you try and stop her, she'll only find a way to go onto a social networking site in secret. And if she ends up in a bullying situation and you haven't prepared her, that could be much worse.
J: Oh, dear ... I'm sure you're right, but it's not easy being a parent nowadays.
H: I agree. Thanks for your question, Julia. Let's go to our next caller. Dan, you're on.
D: Hi, my question's also about technology.
H: It seems like that's everyone's main worry. Anyway, go ahead Dan.
D: Well, my son, Seth, he's twelve, and, up till recently, he was a normal twelve-year-old, you know, he used to go out with his friends, play football with me, you know ... we had a great relationship.
H: So, Dan, basically I'm guessing he doesn't want to spend so much time with you now, and you feel ...
D: Oh, no, it's not that. It's just that he spends all his time on the computer now.
H: Surely that's just normal nowadays.
D: It's hard to say. Sometimes, on the weekend, he spends all day in his bedroom on social networking sites or playing video games. I don't think it's right. I mean, for one thing, he never gets any exercise.
H: Don't you think it's just a stage he's going through? I used to spend hours in my bedroom listening to music when I was that age.
D: So what you mean is I should just relax and let him continue with it?
H: Yeah, he'll grow out of it. And you can't force him to go and play football if he doesn't want to.
D: I guess not. Thanks.
H: OK, our next caller is Zara. You're on.
Z: Um, I was wondering how you would deal with a thirteen-year-old wanting to get pierced ears?
H: Thirteen years old? Doesn't she simply want to be like her friends? I imagine a lot of them have pierced ears.
Z: Well ... that's it. I'm not talking about a she.
H: Oh, in other words you're upset because your thirteen-year-old son wants to get his ears pierced.
Z: That's right.
H: Ah ... so it's because he's a boy rather than his age?
Z: I suppose so.
H: Well, does he have friends who have ...

Unit 6   Recording S6.8

W = Woman   M = Man

W: I'm going to speak against the statement: "Employers should give preference to younger applicants when hiring." The first point I'd like to make is that selecting a person for a job on the basis of their age is unfair. It's as bad as choosing someone because of their gender or race or religion. People should be selected for a job because of their abilities and suitability and not because they are a certain age. For example, if a sixty-year-old person is able, physically and mentally, to do a job, they should be judged on the same basis as a thirty-year-old.
M: I would like to speak in favor of the statement. I would like to start off by saying that I fully support equal opportunities for people applying for a job. However, I would like to pick up on the point made by Sarah when she said "if a person is able, physically and mentally, to do a job." I think we need to be realistic here. As people age, this can affect their energy, their ability to react quickly and their memory. In some jobs it may be vital for people to have high levels of energy, for example in a creative industry such as advertising. Or people need to be able to react quickly, for instance, if they're a truck driver, or be able to concentrate for long periods of time if they're an airline pilot. It is simply a fact of life that, as we age, our mental and physical capabilities deteriorate and that, for certain jobs, younger people are better.

Unit 7   Recording S7.2

I = Interviewer   H = Hoaxer

I: Welcome to *Insight*, where the topic for the day is hoaxes, specifically picture hoaxes. It was extremely difficult to get someone who produces hoax pictures, a hoaxer, to agree to appear on the show, and it was only on condition that we promise to keep his identity secret. So, I'd like to welcome my guest to the show.
H: Thank you.
I: For starters, can you explain why you want to remain anonymous?
H: Two reasons, really. I suppose, one is mystery. What I mean is a good hoax picture is more powerful if people don't know where it came from. If people knew I'd produced the picture, the effect would be lost.
I: Fair enough. And the other reason?
H: Well, it's a fact that hoaxers often use photographs taken by someone else, and often without permission, and the original photographer could sue us.
I: So, basically, you're playing it safe then.
H: Yeah, you could put it that way.
I: OK. Now I asked you before the show if you'd ever earned money for your hoax work, and you said that you often work with the police and detectives. What exactly do you do for the police?
H: Well, when a politician, for example, appears in a published photograph in any ... embarrassing situation, say accepting money ... sometimes the police ask me to look at it. Then, if I decide that the photograph is a hoax, they see if they can find out who did it.
I: Right. OK, well, let's look at some photographs that we found on the Internet—some hoaxes; some not. Talk us through the photographs if you would.
H: So, this picture of a bike in a tree looks like a hoax simply because it's such an unusual image. Also, it looks a little like a composite picture ...
I: What's a composite picture?
H: When you combine two or more pictures, that's a composite. In this case, it would be very easy to put a picture of the two halves of the bike over a picture of a tree. In fact, this would be a very easy hoax picture to put together.
I: So, what you're saying is, it isn't real.

H: No, it actually is real. I wasn't sure myself, but I found out it was near Seattle, Washington. So I asked a friend who lives there, and he told me he'd seen it with his own eyes a number of years before. Apparently, there are many different legends about how it got there.

I: Well, I thought that one was definitely a hoax. Let's look at the next one. This one could be real. A man hanging on the landing gear of a jet plane is such an extraordinary sight, maybe that's why it looks a bit fake.

H: Well, even if you'd never seen such a thing, common sense would tell you that a man couldn't survive even the landing. The wind would pull him off.

I: Then it IS a hoax picture.

H: Yes, a classic composite picture. Not badly put together, though.

I: Remarkable. Now this next one could be real, sharks swimming through a flooded suburb. I remember seeing this on the Internet, after one of those big hurricanes.

H: Ha, you've probably seen lots of pictures like this, and maybe this exact one.

I: Why? Why's it funny?

H: I'm ninety-nine percent sure this is a hoax simply because it's a cliché—yet another picture of sharks swimming where they shouldn't be! Look on the Internet and you'll find plenty of hoax pictures of sharks.

I: And that's it? Is there a technical reason why you know it's a hoax?

H: Well, yes. The water next to the fins isn't right. The surface of the water would break differently if there really were sharks there. Look closely.

I: I see. You know, it seems like a lot of work. Why do people do it? It can't be for the money.

H: I dunno. I can only speak for myself, and, to be honest, I'm thrilled when people believe one of my pictures.

I: Because they want to believe it?

H: Well, yes. Maybe we all like to believe something really unusual could be true.

Unit 7   Recording S7.4

Conversation 1

A: Wow!

B: What's that?

A: It's this story. Listen to this. "A woman used a wooden soup ladle to save her husband from attack by a tiger."

B: What? A ladle?

A: Well, her husband was being attacked by a tiger.

B: Where was this?

A: In Malaysia. Apparently, her husband had just gone into the forest. She saw the tiger attack him and grabbed the first thing she could find, which was a wooden soup ladle. And she just charged at the animal yelling at the top of her voice and bashing its head.

B: And it didn't attack her?

A: No. The amazing thing is that the tiger ran off.

B: Wow, there's no way I'd do that!

A: Not even for me?

B: Not even for you! You're the one who's always telling me to stop.

A: Stop what?

B: Stop helping people so much.

A: I didn't mean to stop helping me!

Conversation 2

A: Hey, Mike. Did you buy a lottery ticket?

B: No, why?

A: Well, you want to be careful. It says here that some store clerks are taking the winnings. You know when customers take in a winning ticket and they have to check it in the store …

B: Yeah …

A: Well, these guys have been telling customers that they didn't win, and then they take the winning tickets for themselves.

B: That's so wrong! Suppose it was, like, a big amount?

A: One of the tickets was for $1,000, and the …

B: That's totally outrageous!

A: Yeah. Exactly.

B: So, how did they find it out?

A: The police did some undercover investigations at convenience stores. And … yeah, one of them was for $1,000, and the …

B: Hey, maybe we won something …

A: In your dreams. You don't buy lottery tickets anyway.

B: That's true.

A: But it's weird that the customers didn't notice, isn't it? That's more surprising than the actual theft.

B: Yeah. I do think they should do something about it.

A: Who?

B: The lottery commission.

A: They are doing something about it. They're going to install machines so you can check your own numbers.

B: That is a good idea.

Conversation 3

A: That's extraordinary!

B: What is?

A: This story about the baby in China.

B: What happened?

A: It's about a baby, and apparently it climbed out onto a window ledge on the second floor. Oh, there's a video … And, oh, look, you can see these people underneath just holding out their arms because they know it's going to fall. And there are some people putting cardboard down to try and break the fall. Wow!

B: Let me see. Wow! Look at that man! How on earth did he catch it?

A: "Just human instinct," that's what one man said.

B: What a catch! That's such an amazing thing!

A: It's lucky the men noticed the baby.

B: Yeah, I suppose they saw some movement.

A: Or maybe they heard something.

B: What's that? The woman's bringing something.

A: It's hard to say, but it looks like a cushion.

B: Yeah, it could be a sofa cushion.

A: I guess they thought the baby might fall on it.

B: That must be the luckiest baby alive.

A: Absolutely incredible. Let me see again.

Unit 7   Recording S7.8

M = Man   W = Woman

M: Did you hear this story in the news about this guy who swapped a paper clip for a house?

W: No.

M: It sounds a bit out there, but, apparently, what happened was he started … he was at his desk looking for a job or calling up about jobs …

W: Yeah.

M: … and, um, he saw a paper clip on his desk, and he thought, I wonder what I can do with this paper clip—whether I can swap it for something.

W: Oh.

M: Anyway, so he got onto the Internet, and he made this website—I think it's called the-red-paper-clip dot com.

W: Right.

M: And he put this, this on the Internet, photographs it, puts it on, and sees if anyone wants to swap something with him.

W: And did, did anything happen?

M: Yeah, so first of all, I don't remember all the details, but, as I recall, two Vancouver women, um, took up the first challenge, and they swapped the paper clip with, I think it was a pen shaped like a fish they had found …

W: Random.

M: Yeah—they had found it on a camping trip—yeah random. But he meets up with all these people; he doesn't just send the things. And, so, then from that, I believe, this guy in Seattle wanted the pen and swapped it for a doorknob. And the doorknob was swapped for something to do with camping, …

W: Oh, so he kept trading up each time.

M: Yeah, he kept trading, trading up, so, and then that was swapped for a beer keg, I think. Apparently what happened was all these people were … the same sort of thought patterns as him, and they wanted to sort of meet up, and it was about a social event as well.

W: Ah.

M: Anyway, the next thing he got was a snow globe, and, according to the report, it said a movie director wanted it and said he'd swap it for a part in his movie. And then this town decided they had this house in this town, and that they would swap the house for a part in this movie.

W: No! So he went all the way from the red paper clip to getting a house.

M: … a house. And my impression was that he, he was just crazy at the beginning, but he, he ended up having this—I'm not sure how good the house was but, well, yeah.

W: Well, better than a paper clip.

M: I know basically that's what happened.

W: Wow!

Unit 8   Recording S8.2

<u>M = Man   D = Dominic   H = Heather</u>

M: OK, Dominic and Heather we're going to play a game

D: Oh.

H: Ahem.

M: Its, it's an experiment. Um, what I'm gonna do is—hang on, I'm just gonna get it out of my pocket. I'm going to give you, Dominic, $10.

D: OK, can I keep it?

M: OK—for now. And you have to decide how much you're going to offer Heather.

D: OK.

M: And if Heather accepts, then you divide the money as agreed. You get some, and she gets some.

D: Right.

M: But, if Heather rejects your offer and she doesn't like the way you've split the $10 …

D: Mmm.

M: … then I get the $10 back and neither of you get anything.

H: Um.

D: Ah, OK.

H: OK.

M: Do you understand?

D: Yeah, I think so.

H: Yeah.

M: Are you sure?

H: Yeah.

D: Yeah—so I basically have to choose how much money I'm going to offer Heather.

M: Yeah.

H: And then …

D: And if she's happy with it …

H: I decide if I want it or not.

M: That's right, OK?

H: OK?

D: So …

M: Right there you go.

D: Thank you, that's for me. That's a lot of money, I would really like all of it. Uh, do I just say it now, out loud?

M: Yeah.

D: OK, uh I'm going to offer you $5.

M: Um.

H: All right, I'll accept that.

D: Yeah.

H: Yeah, I will, yeah.

D: Great so we get a five each.

M: You do indeed, and I, and I lose $10.

D: Yeah, that was worth it.

M: OK, so, I mean that's really interesting. Why, why, Dominic, did you decide on that split?

D: Um, I guess, if I offered any less, I didn't think you'd take it.

H: No.

D: So I thought this way.

M: But why, why, why would you?

D: Um, because it's, it's not fair, you know 'cause this isn't any more my money than it is hers really, just 'cause it's a game, you've given it to me.

M: Interesting.

D: Um, it, it was.

M: And why, why did you accept?

H: Um, because I felt that it was equal, you know, an, an equal split, um, I thought it was very kind and yeah generous to give me half.

D: Uh.

M: OK and um, OK then—here's an interesting question. Heather, in your mind what would have …

H: Um …

M: been the lowest amount?

D: Ahem.

H: It act-

M: that you would have accepted?

H: It actually would have been $5 because I think any lower than that and I'd have felt sort of you know.

D: Short-changed.

M: Very interesting.

H: Short-changed, yeah, is the word, yeah.

M: Thanks guys, goodbye.

Unit 8   Recording S8.3

<u>M = Man   D = Dominic   H = Heather</u>

M: OK, guys, uh we're gonna play another game now.

D: Um.

M: It's called the Dictator game. And, uh, I think I'm gonna be very in the hole by the end of the day.

D: More money?

M: Yeah. Another $10 bill.

H: Oh, a ten.

M: And, I'm gonna give it to you again.

D: Thank you.

M: But this time, instead of making an offer which you can, you, Heather, can accept or reject …

H: OK.

M: You have to accept it.

D: Ah.

M: So Dominic …

D: OK.

H: OK.

D: I have the power.

M: It's your decision. You have the power. It's your decision.

D: Um, OK, so I just say it out loud?

M: Yeah.

D: Uh, the offer I'm going to give you this time is $1, and that means $9 will be for me.

M: OK.

H: Well then I accept that 'cause I have no choice.

D: You have no choice.

M: You have no choice. But, but the question here is how do you feel, how do you feel about that?

H: Yeah I feel a bit short-changed, to be honest. I feel a bit cheated really, um.

M: His fairness, from last time has all disappeared.

H: Yeah, mm.

D: Um, I guess I gave you a dollar to still show that I'm, you know, not heartless.

H: Ahem.

D: Uh, you know, so, you know, I want to keep all of it, but, um, I guess with the offer of being able to have more, without the choice.

H: Um.

D: Um, it sort of, it was easier for me, to say, I won't feel so guilty, I don't feel.

H: Yeah tempting, isn't it?

D: Feel a bit guilty now, but, no, I just thought there's no option for her, so I might as well keep more of it.

Unit 8   Recording S8.5

<u>J = Jim   L = Liz</u>

J: Here's your coffee.

L: Thanks, Jim. Oh, I needed that.

J: No problem. Hey, Liz, there's something I've been meaning to talk to you about.

L: Oh, yeah?

J: It's just that … well … you know you borrowed some money from me last week?

L: Oh, right. It was ten dollars, wasn't it? I don't actually have that on me at the moment.

J: It's not that, it's … I hope you don't take this the wrong way, but, um …

L: Right.

J: … it's just that this isn't the first time I've lent you money and er, well you haven't paid it back. I mean, I know it's not a lot, just small amounts each time, but it kind of adds up really quickly … I dunno. Do you know what I mean?

L: Yeah. Sorry. I didn't realize. I know I'm terrible with money. I just forget. Look, I promise I'll give it back, but could you wait a week? Until I get paid?

J: Well, actually, you've said that once before. I don't want you to get the wrong idea, but … it, you know, never happened. And it makes things slightly awkward. It makes me feel just a bit annoyed. Do you see where I'm coming from?

L: Oh. Yeah. I suppose so.

J: Look, I have a suggestion. I'd feel better if we could work out how much is owed, and then you could pay me back a little each week, you know, however much you can afford. How does that sound?

L: Yeah, yeah. That sounds reasonable.

J: OK, great so …

Unit 8   Recording S8.8

OK, here are some things that I think would be useful if you're visiting the States, especially if you're coming here to do business.

So, first of all, with names. When you first meet someone, it's considered good manners to use a title along with their last name, you know like Mr. Smith or Ms. Jones, and so on. But the funny thing is that, in fact, people will in most cases want to use first names, you know be on a first-name basis, like

"Hey, call me 'Bob'" and all that. That might not be comfortable for you but, in fact, if you stick to a more formal Mr. Smith sort of thing, it's not going to be comfortable for them. I also think that, once they know your name, you'll find people use it a lot, so they'll say it periodically in a conversation. If you're not used to it, it can seem strange at first.

Now with meeting people for the first time … It's pretty normal for people to shake hands, or at least guys do. Women usually do, certainly in business, but not always. On the whole, Americans tend to avoid greetings that involve hugging and other close physical contact, except with family members and friends. Having said that, don't be surprised if someone gives you a hug the first time you meet them, either as a hello or a goodbye. You sort of have to keep your eyes open and try to anticipate what they'll do.

When people sit down, like in a meeting, people like to get comfortable, so people cross their legs with one ankle on the other knee. I know this is rude in some countries, but it's normal here. That reminds me, if you're chatting with someone in an office, standing up, they might sit on a desk, which, I know, is a big no-no in places like Japan. Other gestures? Well, if an American wants to show agreement, they'll sometimes give the thumbs up sign or they'll make a circle out of their thumb and index finger. Don't be offended if in your culture this isn't polite. It just means "A-OK" in the States.

Last of all, timing: punctuality is very important for business occasions, and it's unacceptable to be late, and, if you are late, it will be appreciated if you let your contact know if you are going to be late. It's the same for social occasions; you need to arrive on time.

Of course, having said all this, it's important to remember that the United States is huge and there's a lot of variety in what's acceptable in different places. Anyway, I hope this advice helps.

Unit 9   Recording S9.2
Conversation 1
L = Lise   J = Jeff

L: So, what happened was, I was sitting in a café, and this young couple—they looked like tourists—asked me to take a picture of them. And I took their picture, and they thanked me and left, and then I looked at my seat and realized my purse was gone, with my cell, wallet, credit card, keys, everything.
J: No! What did you do?
L: Well, there was a guy at the next table, and he saw I was really upset, and I explained about the bag, and he asked me which bank I was with, and he said he worked for that bank and gave me a phone number and let me use his cell to call them and cancel my credit card.

J: And you believed him?
L: Yeah, I mean, I was in a real panic. I was really grateful for his help. Anyway, I called the number and talked to a woman from "the bank" and gave her my name and address and my account number.
J: She sounded genuine?
L: Yeah, completely. I could hear the sounds of the call center behind her. And she asked me to key in my PIN on the phone and she said they'd cancel my card.
J: Wow. And you did? You punched in your PIN?
L: Yeah, unfortunately.
J: So it was a double scam. They got your bag and your bank account details.
L: I felt so stupid.
J: So who actually took your bag?
L: Well, it can't have been the young couple because I was looking at them all the time I was taking the picture. Their job was just to distract me. So it must have been stolen when I was taking the picture.
J: Was it the guy at the next table, then? The fake banker?
L: I think so. He must have taken my bag when I wasn't looking. Then he could have hidden it in his briefcase or maybe he gave it to another member of the gang.
J: And then he gave you a fake phone number to call the bank.
L: Yeah, and they probably used a recording of a call center so that it sounded like the real bank.

Conversation 2
D = Dan   I = Ingrid

D: I was badly tricked a few years ago when I was working in a jewelry store.
I: You never told me about that. What happened?
D: Well, this woman came in and was looking at necklaces. She was young, attractive, well-dressed, and then a guy came in shortly afterward, and he was just looking around. But then the woman went to pay for a very expensive necklace that she'd picked out, and when she was counting the money out onto the counter, the guy grabbed her, flashed his police I.D. and said he was arresting her for paying with counterfeit money.
I: Fake money! Wow!
D: So he took the cash and the necklace as evidence, wrote down his contact details, and promised me he'd bring the necklace back by the end of the day. I didn't suspect anything. Then he took the woman away, presumably to book her at the police station.
I: And he didn't come back?
D: No, and stupid me, I didn't even begin to suspect anything until it was closing time. So then I phoned the police, and they had no idea what I was talking about. That was it, end of story.
I: How much was the necklace worth?
D: $600. And my boss took it out of my salary. That's why I quit.

I: So the police I.D. was a fake.
D: Must have been. I just didn't check it.
I: And, wait a second, was the woman a real customer?
D: No, the woman must have been working with the guy. She couldn't have been a real customer, or she wouldn't have gone with him …
I: But she might have had fake money.
D: I really don't think so.
I: Talk about an ingenious scam …

Unit 9   Recording S9.5
P = Police Officer   A = Alain

P: Hello, police. Can I help you?
A: Yes, I'd like to report a crime. I've been robbed.
P: I'm very sorry to hear that, sir. OK, I'll need to take a statement.
A: A statement?
P: To write down some details, if that's all right.
A: Yes, sure.
P: Could you give me your name please, sir?
A: Alain Girard.
P: Right. That's Jirard with a J?
A: No, G, and it's Alain spelled A-l-a-i-n.
P: Right, Mr. Girard. Could you tell me exactly when the incident happened?
A: Just now. About an hour ago.
P: Could you be more precise?
A: Excuse me?
P: Could you give me the exact time?
A: I think at 2:50 or 2:55.
P: That's about 2:50 on June the seventh. And where did it happen?
A: Park Avenue.
P: Can you pinpoint the exact location?
A: Pinpoint?
P: Tell me exactly where.
A: Oh. It was near the entrance to the park. Just about 164 feet inside.
P: OK. Could you tell me what happened?
A: I was walking out of the park, and a man was running toward me, and he ran into me hard—
P: He collided with you?
A: Yes, and he said "sorry" and something else, then, before I realized what had happened, he had run off. It was only about thirty seconds later that I realized my wallet was gone and that he must have taken it when he hit me, collided with me.
P: But did it cross your mind that it wasn't just an accident?
A: No, it never occurred to me that he'd done it on purpose.
P: Did you run after him?
A: No, my mind just went blank, and I stood there not knowing what to do.
P: But you were OK? Not hurt?
A: No, just very shocked.
P: OK. Could you tell me exactly what your wallet looked like and what was in it?
A: It's brown leather, and it has my credit card and about 250 dollars and—
P: Hold on a minute, credit card … about 250 dollars, yes?

A: And a picture of my girlfriend.

P: OK. So you saw the man. Can you give me a description?

A: Erm, about twenty, white, pretty tall. And he was wearing a sweater, gray color with a … you know … erm, something you put over your head …

P: A hood? He was wearing a hoodie?

A: Yes, that's the word. So I didn't see his face, not clearly. But he looked as if he were just out jogging, you know; he was wearing some sort of dark pants, for running or for the gym.

P: Tracksuit pants?

A: Yeah. I can't remember anything else, it all happened so quickly.

P: So that's a tall white male, about twenty, wearing a gray hoodie and dark tracksuit pants?

A: That's right.

P: And did he have any other distinguishing marks or features?

A: Sorry?

P: Anything special or different from normal? For example, a scar on his face or anything like that?

A: No, he just seemed like a normal guy, out running. Nothing special. Except …

P: Yes?

A: He reminded me a little of that actor, Vin Diesel. But younger. Do you know who I mean?

P: Vin Diesel, yeah. I'll put it down. And you said he said something to you.

A: Yeah, but I didn't catch what he said. It was too quick.

P: Right, one last question, and then I'll take your contact details. Were there any other people in the vicinity?

A: Vicinity?

P: In the surrounding area—nearby. Any witnesses who saw what had happened?

A: No, there was no one nearby, in the … vicinity.

P: Right, now I just need to take your contact details, Mr. Girard, and I can also give you a phone number to call if …

Unit 9   Recording S9.8

W1 = Woman 1   M = Man
W2 = Woman 2

W1: So, we really need to decide then what it is we get rid of and what is absolutely essential to keep on the life raft. I think that's probably the most important thing, isn't it?

M: I'm sure it's easy to get rid of a few things, isn't it?

W2: Like what?

M: Well, I'm not sure about the lighter. I mean, we can't really start a fire on a raft, can we?

W2: No.

W1: I suppose it depends on what the life raft is made out of, doesn't it?

M: Yeah, but it's not exactly top priority to be able to cook a hot meal, you know, when you really just need to survive.

W1: So no lighter?

M and W2: OK.

W1: OK. So what do you think is important?

W2: I'd say that a blanket is essential.

W1: Interesting choice. What for?

W2: Well, you can use it for a lot of different things. To keep you warm obviously, but you can use a blanket as a towel if you get wet …

W1: If you fall in the water.

W2: … for example. And a blanket can protect you from the sun.

M: That hadn't occurred to me. OK, I'm convinced. So what else?

W1: Well I can't see the point of taking the hand mirror can you?

M: Actually, I can. Because if …

Unit 10   Recording S10.1

A: So, come on, favorite movie of all time.

B: Um, I would have to say, 'cause I love action movies, uh, that it would be *Speed*—have you ever seen that?

A: *Speed*?

B: Yeah, it's with Keanu Reeves and Sandra Bullock.

A: Oh, I like her.

B: She's very good, isn't she? Um, so yeah, I just love any kind of action movie. And I remember watching it when I was really young and watching it with my dad. And it's the sort of, like, a family-friendly action movie, because it's not too violent, it's not too gory but it's just really tense. And I remember just like watching it. We had a cushion, me and my dad, and I was just like, what's gonna happen next? Um, have you seen it?

A: No! I haven't. I, I think I've seen parts of it, like trailers and things but …

B: OK, it's um …

A: No, I knew she was in it.

B: Yeah, so basically, he, uh, there's a bad guy in it. As with every action movie, it has a good villian, and he has no thumb. I remember that, that was like a memorable bit of it, he had no thumb. And so they sort of highjack this … this bus. And it's set so that it can only drive at a certain speed—hence the name. And so it's just basically driving through, through the city, and it can't stop, otherwise there's a bomb, and it's gonna blow it up. Um, so, and there's a, Keanu Reeves, he's, um, he's the good guy, he's uh, a policeman. And he's … he jumps onboard the bus to try and stop this bomb from going off. And, uh, it's just all the different characters on the bus. It's just really …

A: The whole movie is on the bus?

B: Yeah, and, but it's, it's, well not at the beginning, it sort of goes onto the bus. But, uh, it's just I remember it being so tense and gripping, 'cause you just didn't know what was gonna happen. You didn't know.

A: It sounds really uncomfortable to watch, wasn't it?

B: It … it's … I just like that kind of that feeling of like pure suspense 'cause you just have no idea if it's gonna end well or not. And it did end very well. You have to watch it.

A: Well. yeah, as long as there's, you know, a point when you can relax, 'cause I don't like feeling like that the whole way through a movie, anxiety.

B: Yeah, because you know when it's like driving along, and it, 'cause I think it has to stay at fifty miles per hour. And uh, so, uh, if there's, driving along a highway, and it's, there's traffic and stuff, you have to change the route and things, so you just don't know where its gonna go.

A: Oh, OK.

B: And then they get to a bridge that's um, hasn't been finished being built. Uh, so you're not sure how they're gonna get over the bridge and stuff like that. So there's lots of moments where you just think, I have no clue what's gonna happen.

A: Good stunts?

B: Very good, and I heard that he did all his stunts himself, Keanu Reeves.

A: Yes, they always say that.

B: He likes a little action, doesn't he? So, and I think it always helps to have a very good heroine in a movie, and she's, she's beautiful, don't you think?

A: Yes, I love her. I think she's very funny, but, tell me, there's some comedy in there.

B: Um, there's not a huge amount of comedy. Uh, it's one of your traditional sort of American blockbuster action movies. So, yeah, but it's, it's just, it's—there's not many action movies with comedy in them, though, are there?

A: I think that's why I don't watch them.

B: Oh, really?

A: Yeah.

B: What's your sort of, your favorite type of movie?

A: I don't like to feel uncomfortable, so it's just comedy.

B: Watch *Speed*.

A: Mm, mm, OK.

Unit 10   Recording S10.5

Conversation 1

W = Woman   M = Man

W: So here we are in Greenwich Village.

M: It looks very different from the rest of New York.

W: Yeah, the streets are pretty narrow, and the buildings aren't as high.

M: It does look pretty village-like.

W: Yeah, but it's really big. It extends out west that way to the Hudson River, north above Washington Square. We'll go up there in a bit.

M: And you lived here?

W: When I first came to New York, yeah, in an apartment just around the corner, on West Third Street. Actually, you can see the building over there.

M: Near the Blue Note Jazz Club?

W: Yeah.

M: I've heard of the Blue Note.

W: It's pretty famous. There are some great jazz clubs around the neighborhood, and that's one of the best. We can see a show there one night if you want.

M: That'd be great.

W: Now up here on the left is the Café Reggio. It's where I used to hang out and read when I wasn't working.

M: Looks good.

W: Their cappuccino is great. The story goes that the original owner brought cappuccino to America. You can see the original cappuccino machine inside.

M: Cool. We could stop and have a coffee.

W: Maybe a bit later? Let's head over to Washington Square Park and then circle back.

M: OK—lead the way!

…

W: A lot of these clubs we're walking by have a real history. As I'm sure you know, Greenwich Village has always been a center of artistic life—very bohemian. It's always attracted famous writers, dancers and poets. And, in the sixties, it was a big part of the folk music scene: Simon and Garfunkel, Joni Mitchell, Bob Dylan, you know.

M: Before my time! Now what's this?

W: This is Washington Square Park. We'll walk into the park on this side. Can you play chess?

M: A little, yeah.

W: Any of these guys here would be happy to challenge you to a game of chess. They're here all day, every day.

M: Maybe next time—I'm not that good! What's the arch over there? It looks like the Arc de Triomphe in Paris.

W: Well it should, that's the Washington Square arch. It was modeled on the Arc de Triomphe and built in 1889 to celebrate the hundredth anniversary of the inauguration of George Washington as president.

M: Could we sit down a second? I need a break.

W: Why don't we retrace our steps and go back to the Café Reggio?

M: Sounds good. I could really go for a coffee.

Conversation 2

M1 = Man 1   W = Woman
M2 = Man 2

M1: So, this is Radcliffe Square.

W: Wow! Is this right in the center then?

M1: Pretty much.

M2: What's that?

M1: Hold on. Let's just get off our bikes … Right, so that building in front of us is the Bodleian, named after the founder—Thomas Bodley. Believe it or not, despite the fact that it's circular, it's actually a library.

W: Cool!

M1: Yeah, it gets a copy of every book published in the UK.

M2: Who can use it?

M1: Any student at the university. Of course, each college also has its own library—you know the university's divided into colleges, right?

M2: Right. How many colleges are there?

M1: Just under forty. Well, thirty-eight to be exact.

W: So that means thirty-eight libraries?!

M1: Mm, but they're not all as big as the Bodleian. Anyway, we'll need to get back on our bikes for the next bit.

…

M1: Can you hear me if I talk as we cycle along?

M2: Yeah.

W: OK, but don't go too fast. I'm not very steady on this thing!

M1: So, here's the famous Bridge of Sighs, connecting two sides of Hertford College.

M2: I've seen the original.

M1: What, of the bridge? In Italy, you mean?

M2: Yeah, it's in Venice. Beautiful.

M1: OK. We'll go past New College and then onto the High Street.

M2: Is that New College there?

M1: Yep.

W: How "new" is new?

M1: Roughly 1370.

W: You're kidding!

M1: No, really! Interestingly, the oldest college was actually only founded a hundred or so years earlier! Uh-oh, watch out on this corner …

M1: That's the "Schools." It's where the students take their exams. Apparently, the biggest room can seat somewhere in the region of 500 students, although I haven't seen it myself. Anyway, we're turning right here. The street's cobbled, so be careful.

M2: How many students are there at the university in total?

M1: To be honest, it depends. In term time, you'd probably get upwards of 20,000.

M2: Many international students?

M1: Some, but most are from the UK. We'll finish by cycling down this way to Christ Church. We can actually go inside if we're quick. It's well worth a visit.

M2: Christ Church is another college?

M1: Yeah, the biggest and probably the most famous. Have you seen any of the Harry Potter movies?

M2: No …

W: I have!

M1: Oh, well, you'll recognize the Great Hall. It's where they have the feasts in Hogwarts School. You know that part when Harry …

Unit 10   Recording S10.8

S = Sarah   T = Tim   N = Nigel

S: Right, well, we have our shortlist for the new feature that we're going to put downtown. Which one gets your vote, Tim?

T: I'm really in favor of the—the state-of-the-art multiplex movie theater. I think that it would be the most useful and beneficial for the community. I think it will be used a great deal; I think it would bring jobs to the area; and I think it would provide entertainment and activities for young people.

N: The only thing that would concern me though is that that's going to be very, very expensive.

T: Um hm.

S: I mean, I personally would prefer the botanical garden.

T: Oh.

S: Because I think that that will satisfy the needs of many different age groups. I think it would be very good for wheelchairs, for … for blind people, for people with disabilities; there would be areas that would be excellent for young people, and lots of learning opportunities in the education center. And we know from past experience that the older age group certainly enjoy gardens.

T: The only thing that would concern me on that is that you mention youth, but I don't think that you're going to get as many young people involved in a botanical garden. I think if it was interactive then it would be … but just as a thing that was showing, I'm, I'm not so sure.

N: Well, I don't want to harp on about costs again, but we have to consider the maintenance of this botanical garden. There are very high maintenance costs involved.

S: Oh, so, Nigel what, what would you prefer?

N: Well, my vote would go to the theater workshop space for young people. And I know we said we don't want to discriminate against any … we don't want to leave out certain members of our society, but I think we have a problem in this town with kids getting bored, hanging around on street corners. They need something to do, and a theater workshop space is going to get them … it's going to give them a routine, it's going to give them a motivation, and then, when they do their shows, they're bringing along their grandparents, their parents, I feel it's very inclusive.

T: Can you see the older generation wanting it, liking it?

N: I think the older generation want to be sure that kids aren't hanging out on the streets with nothing to do.

S: And could that theater workshop space be used for other things as well?

N: Absolutely.

S: Could it be used for meetings, for other sections of society?

N: … Aerobics … there's going to be a sprung wooden floor, so there'll be dance classes, yoga, pilates, multi-purpose …

Catalogue Publication Data

Authors: Frances Eales, Steve Oakes

American Speakout Upper-Intermediate Student Book with DVD-ROM and MP3 Audio CD

First published

Pearson Educación de México, S.A. de C.V., 2017

ISBN: 978-607-32-4072-7

American Speakout Upper-Intermediate Student Book with DVD-ROM and MP3 Audio CD & MEL Access Code

ISBN MEL: 978-607-32-4053-6

Area: ELT

Format: 21 x 29.7 cm   Page count: 184

Managing Director: Sergio Fonseca ■ **Innovation & Learning Delivery Director:** Alan David Palau ■ **Regional Content Manager - English:** Andrew Starling ■ **Publisher:** A. Leticia Alvarez ■ **Content Support:** Isabel Moreno ■ **Editorial Services Manager:** Asbel Ramírez ■ **Art and Design Coordinator:** Juan Manuel Santamaria ■ **Design Process Supervisor:** Aristeo Redondo ■ **Layout:** Sergio Guzmán ■ **Cover Design:** Ana Elena García ■ **Photo Research:** Beatriz Monsiváis ■ **Photo Credits:** Pearson Asset Library (PAL)

Contact: soporte@pearson.com

This adaptation is published by arrangement with Pearson Education Limited

Pearson Education Limited
Edinburgh Gate
Harlow
Essex CM20 2JE
England
and Associated Companies throughout the world.

© Pearson Education Limited 2015

Used by permission and adapted from
Speakout 2ND EDITION Upper-Intermediate Students' Book
ISBN: 978-1-2921-1601-3
First published, 2015
All Rights Reserved.

First published, 2017

ISBN PRINT BOOK: 978-607-32-4072-7

ISBN PRINT BOOK MEL: 978-607-32-4053-6

Impreso en México. *Printed in Mexico.*

1 2 3 4 5 6 7 8 9 0 - 20 19 18 17

Esta obra se terminó de imprimir en marzo de 2018, en Editorial Impresora Apolo, S.A. de C.V., Centeno 150-6, Col. Granjas Esmeralda, C.P. 09810, México, Ciudad de México.

D.R. © 2017 por Pearson Educación de México, S.A. de C.V.
Avenida Antonio Dovalí Jaime #70
Torre B, Piso 6, Colonia Zedec Ed. Plaza Santa Fe
Delegación Álvaro Obregón, México, Ciudad de México, C. P. 01210

www.PearsonELT.com

Pearson Hispanoamérica

Argentina ■ Belice ■ Bolivia ■ Chile ■ Colombia ■ Costa Rica ■ Cuba ■ República Dominicana ■ Ecuador ■ El Salvador ■ Guatemala ■ Honduras ■ México ■ Nicaragua ■ Panamá ■ Paraguay ■ Perú ■ Uruguay ■ Venezuela

Acknowledgments

The Publisher and authors would like to thank the following people and institutions for their feedback and comments during the development of the material: Australia: Erica Lederman; Hungary: Eszter Timár; Poland: Konrad Dejko; Spain: Pilar Álvarez Polvorinos, Victoria O'Dea; UK: David Byrne, Lilian Del Gaudio Maciel, Niva Gunasegaran

Text acknowledgments

Extract on page 12 adapted from "30 Challenges for 30 Days" by Martijn Schirp, http://www.highexistence. com/30-challenges-for-30-days. Reproduced by kind permission of Martijn Schirp; Extract on page 32 adapted from "You Are Wonderful!", Cultivate Life! magazine, Issue 26 (Phil Evans, http://www.peoplestuff. com.au), http://www.trans4mind. com/cultivate-lifemagazine/issue-026/Regular-Features-page-one.html, copyright © 1997-2014 Trans4mind Ltd. Reproduced with permission; Extracts on page 33 adapted from "What goes around comes around" by Stephen, 18 October 2008, http://academictips.org/blogs/whatgoes-around-comes-around, and "The Falcon & The Branch" submitted by Hemendra Chanchani, 7 March 2014, http://academictips.org/blogs/the-falcon-andthe-branch. Reproduced with permission; Extract on page 35 adapted from Today (feature on 'Life in six words') by host Sarah Montague and guest Larry Smith,28/06/2007,http://www.bbc.co.uk/radio4/today/reports/misc/sixwordlife_20080205.shtml, copyright © BBC Worldwide Limited; Extracts on pages 37, 44, 70, 107, 121, from Longman Active Study Dictionary, 5th edition, Pearson Education Ltd, copyright © Pearson Education Limited, 2010; Extract on page 71 adapted from 'Letters to myself', 22/02/2009, Audio interview on BBC Radio 4 copyright © BBC Worldwide Limited; Extract on page 86 adapted from 'Six topics that keep the tabloids in business', http://www.drewrys.com, copyright © John Drewry; Extract on page 92 adapted from "New York roommates find $40,000 in sofa and return cash to owner", Associated Press, 16/05/2014, copyright © 2105. Reproduced with permission of The Associated Press. All rights reserved; Extract on page 92 adapted from "Unemployed Brooklyn man misses job interview to save 9-month-old boy who was blown into path of oncoming subway train", New York Daily News, 27/06/2012 (Kerry Burke, Joe Kemp and Tracy Connor), copyright © Daily News, L.P. (New York). Used with permission; and Extract on pages 104-105 from "Memories on Trial" by Andy Ridgway, BBC Focus, January 2009, pp.58–61, copyright © Immediate Media Company Bristol Ltd.

Illustration acknowledgments

Fred Blunt: 18, 90, 150, 153, 155; Lyndon Hayes: 161, 162; Eric Smith: 156; Mark Willey: 107; Mariko Yamazaki: 72, 159.

Photo acknowledgments

The Publisher would like to thank the following for their kind permission to reproduce their photographs:

(Key: b-bottom; c-center; l-left; r-right; t-top)

123RF.com: Andrei Shumskiy 7b (icon), Kathawut Rueansai 12, Arcady31 15t, Katre 15tc, Andrei Shumskiy 31b (icon), Andrei Shumskiy 43b (icon), Сергей Тряпицын 43l, Сергей Тряпицын 44cr; Iakov Kalinin 52-53b, Robert Churchill 55cr, Andrei Shumskiy 55b (icon), Robert Churchill 62, Andrei Shumskiy 67b (icon), Andrei Shumskiy 79b (icon), Maska82 91cl, Andrei Shumskiy 91b (icon), Belchonock 92cr, Andrey Kiselev 99cl, Andrei Shumskiy 103b (icon), Andrei Shumskiy 115b (icon), Igor Mojzes 151 (f); **Alamy Images:** Caroline Cortizo 7l, Maximilian Weinzierl 11tr, Mark Harvey 19cl, Blend Images 31l, Glyn Thomas 32tl, Stocksearch 35 (car), Design Pics Inc. 36bl, Art Directors & Trip 38cr, Ben Molyneux 38 (Life of Pi), CBW 38 (The Hunger Games), 38 (The Kite Runner), Redsnapper 39cl, Adam Burton 40-41b, Ross Gilmore 47c, Art Directors & Trip 55r, James Callaghan 58 (d), WENN Ltd 59br, Art Directors & Trip 64-65b, Pacific Press Service 67r, Rafael Ben-Ari 67l, Keystone Pictures USA 69 (5), Marka 69 (1), Pictorial Press Ltd 69 (4), ZUMA Press, Inc. 69 (2); Rafael Ben-Ari 70, PhotoAlto 74l, Pacific Press Service 76-77, Image Source 79r, Dale O'Dell 79cl, Age Fotostock 86-87b, Judith Collins 87cl, Cultura Creative 99tl, Tim Whitby 103cl, Ammentorp Photography 110b, Dorling Kindersley ltd 119b, Ros Drinkwater 121b, Marmaduke St. John 122 (b), Ben Nicholson 123 (e), Adrian Sherratt 149 (a), Art Directors & Trip 152 (f), Newscast 152 (e), Chuck Eckert 158, Glyn Thomas 158c, Alistair Scott 162; **Ardea:** Thomas Marent 16tl; **BBC Photo Library:** Laurence Cendrowicz 31r, Laurence Cendrowicz 40br, Adrian Rogers 80br; Rod Fountain 81b, Guy Levy 81tl, Jeff Overs 88-89b; **BBC Worldwide Ltd:** 28cl, 40cl, 52bl, 64l, 76 88cl, 100cl, 112cl; **Corbis:** Henglein and Steets 8tl, Cardinal 11cr, 167 / Ocean / Alex Treadway 43cl, Dpa / Marius Becker 23t, Monalyn Gracia 43t, Monalyn Gracia 47bc, David Sacks 82, Markus Altmann 91t, Wavebreak Media Ltd 91cr; Ed Bock 98tr; **Digital Vision:** 91r; **DK Images:** Dorling Kindersley 89 (snow globe); **Endemol UK:** 43r, 50-51t; **Exclusivepix:** 83 (a); **Eyewire:** 157 (c), Eyewire 157 (k); **Fotolia.com:** Production Perig 15tr, Rawpixel 15, Trekandphoto 16tr, Timo Darco 26tr, Esebene 31cl, Brian Jackson 36(t), Chones 55t, Winston 55cl, Piotr Adamowicz 56c, Sentello 56r,

Christopher Dodge 57l, Kletr 57cl, artzenter 58 (c), Markus Mainka 58 (b), Mediagram 58l, Photomelon 89 (paperclip), Winston 59l, Pioneer11 60, Diego Cervo 63t, Martincp 63l, Gajus 67cl, Rebius 83 (plane), Sergemi 83 (Man hanging on rope), Savoieleysse 106, albphoto 122 (d), Georgerudy 151 (e), Bergamont 152 (a), Markus Bormann 152 (b), Xuejun li 152 (c); **Getty Images:** Stijn Nieuwendijk, 8cl, Stephen Frink 16-17b, AWL Images / Nigel Pavitt 19l, 20cl, Photodisc / James Lauritz 19t, Alena Yakusheva 19r, Jupiter images 20cr, E+ / Nikada 25c, Imagebroker / Uwe Umstatter 27tr, Alena Yakusheva 28-29b; Archive Photos 35tl, iStock / mamadela 35tc, FilmMagic / Shareif Ziyadat 37tr, Popperfoto 57r, Martha Holmes 58 (a), William Casey 67cr, Cynthia Johnson 69 (3), William Casey 75, Carsten Koall 83 (flooded house), Don Farrall 92bl, Photodisc / Arne Pastoor 94, E+ / Sjharmon 98tc, Stocktrex 103r, Rich Legg 105, Stocktrex 112-113b, Leland Bobbe 115l, Craig Holmes 115r, Daniel Ingold / RF 115cr, Joe Raedle / Staff 115t, Christopher Bierlein 122 (c), Christopher Furlong 124bl, Craig Holmes 124-125, Blend Images / Stewart Cohen / Pam Ostrow 148 (a), Photolibrary / Spencer Grant 149 (b), Ablestock.com 157 (j); **Gulf Images:** 148 (b); **Hartwood Films:** Hartwood Films 81tc; **Imagemore Co., Ltd:** 108, 157 (b), 157 (h), 157 (i); **Nature Picture Library:** Eric Baccega 79l, 80tr; **Pearson Education Ltd:** Steve Shott 27tl; **PhotoDisc:** McDaniel Woolf 126; Tony Gable. C Squared Studios 157 (g); **Rex Features:** Karl Schoendorfer 38-39t; Endemol UK 50tl, 51tl, Kevin Holt / Daily Mail 69 (6), Geoffrey Robinson 79t, 104, Mark Large 121t; **Robert Harding World Imagery:** Jens Lucking 43cr, Jose Azel 47br, Jens Lucking 47tr, Philippe Michel 48-49t; **Shutterstock.com:** Awe Inspiring Images 7t, Sergey Krasnoshchokov 7r, Nejron Photo 7cl, Monkey Business Images 8(t), g-stockstudio 9(t), Pressmaster 9br, Xtock 10(t), Elena Efimova11(t), Nejron Photo 11tl, Vitalii Nesterchuk 11(t), Hvoenok12(t), PHILIPIMAGE 13(t), ScandinavianStock 14(t), Arena Creative 15tl, Awe Selenit 16(t), Inspiring Images 16c, Sergey Krasnoshchokov 16tc, Vitalii Nesterchuk 16cr, Aneese 17(t), amenic181, Lisa F. Young 19b(icon), Mangostock 19cr, Stephen Mcsweeny 20(t), Travel mania 21(t), Sylvie Corriveau 22(t), Szasz-Fabian Jozsef 24(t), Lisa F. Young 24(cr), Jacek Dudzinski 25(t), Hayati Kayhan 26(t), ChameleonsEye 26(t), Halfpoint 29(t), Halfpoint 30(t), Anna Jurkovska 31cr, Igor Bulgarin 32(t), Denis Kornilov 33(t), Toa55 33tr, A_Lesik 34(t), Marie C Fields 34b, Jill Battaglia 35 (money), Alexander Demyanenko 36-37(t), City of Angels 38-39(t), JeniFoto 40-41(t), underworld 44(t), mrmohock 46(t), Philip Bird LRPS CPAGB 47(t), Nito 47tc, Sarawut Onkaew 48(t), Joey Santini 52(t), scyther5 55l, stockphoto-graf 56(t), Primopiano 56l, scyther5 57cr, Syda Productions 59(t), Labrador Photo Video 59tr, NinaMalyna 60(t), Stokkete 61(t), Zoom Team 62(t), Julian Rovagnati 63r, Christina Kohnen 64-65(t), Liligraphie 67t, Olga Danylenko 68(t), Mejini Neskah 69(t), Nadezhda1906 70(t), Olesia Bilkei 71(t), wavebreakmedia 71, igorstevanovic 72-73(t), Kachalkina Veronika 73l, Zvonimir Atletic 73r; Ermess 74(t) amenic 74bc, Creatista 74r, nanhatai 74tc, Marcos Mesa Sam Wordley 75(t), De Visu 76(t), aastock 77(t), Minerva Studio 79cr, Warinezz 80(t), AVN Photo Lab 81(t), MNStudio 82(t), Deborah Kolb 83 (shark fins), Galina Barskaya 84, Chantal de Bruijne 84-85(t), Bloomicon 86(t), jocic 87(t), MaxxiGo 88-89 (t), Christophe Testi 89 (doorknob), Natalia Bratslavsky 91l, 92tr, pathdoc 92(t), stester 93(t), ImageFlow 94(t), nevodka 95(t), StepanPopov 95(tc), hin255 96(t), Ed Samuel (t), Ed Samuel 97(t), Bikeriderlondon 97br, Northallertonman 98(t), NosorogUA 99(t), Rawpixel.com 100-101(t), 100-101b, kornilov007 103cr, Piotr Krzeslak 103l, TFoxFoto 103t, Africa Studio 104(t), alexskopje 106(t), ArtFamily 107(t), Mark1987 108(t), De Visu 109, Barbol 110(t), kornilov007 110(t), Waldemarus 111(t), Romolo Tavani 112(t)-113(t), Christian Bertrand 115cl, Carsten Reisinger 116(t), Syda Productions 117(t), Sarah2 119(t), Goran Djukanovic 119t, Anibal Trejo 120(t), Stockelements 122 (a), S-F 122-123(t), Steve Allen 123 (f), Sabphoto 148 (c), Beboy 149 (d), Iofoto 149 (c), Icsnaps 151 (a), lsantilli 151 (c), Jakkrit Orrasri 151 (d), Tatyana Vyc 151 (b), Fabio Alcini 152 (d), Jakub Cejpek 154bc, Nneirda 154br, Furtseff 157 (f), Italianestro 157 (e), Bombaert Patrick 157 (d), Dario Sabljak 157 (l), Ivonne Wierink 157 (a), Toa55 158br; **SuperStock:** Blend Images 7cr, 31t, Fancy Collection 85; **The Kobal Collection:** 20th Century Fox 116t, Columbia / Tri-Star / Goldman, Louis 116b, Gravier Productions 118; **The Orion Publishing Group Ltd:** Cover Design Orionbooks, Image © Bernd Ott / Gallerystock 38 (Gone Girl).

All other images © Pearson Education